THE BEHAVIORAL AND SOCIAL SCIENCES: OUTLOOK AND NEEDS

A Report by

The Behavioral and Social Sciences Survey Committee
Under the Auspices of
The Committee on Science and Public Policy
National Academy of Sciences
The Committee on Problems and Policy
Social Science Research Council

PRENTICE-HALL, INC.
ENGLEWOOD CLIFFS, NEW JERSEY
1969

September 8, 1969

Dear Drs. Handler and Riecken:

The Committee on Science and Public Policy of the National Academy of Sciences and the Committee on Problems and Policy of the Social Science Research Council take pleasure in transmitting to you, with their joint endorsement, the attached report of the Behavioral and Social Sciences Survey Committee.

The undertaking that produced this report is notable in several respects. It represents the first large-scale effort of the behavioral and social science disciplines to assemble an overall picture of the present state of these fields, and a set of recommendations for public policy that will encourage their rapid and healthy progress over the years ahead. The decision of the sponsoring bodies to cooperate in the study symbolizes the extension of the methods and attitudes of modern science to all the sciences of man, and the growing recognition of the need to apply the knowledge and wisdom of the full range of sciences to the problems of our society.

The main intent of the recommendations of the Committee is not a drastic or dramatic redirection of social science research programs but a continuation and strengthening of trends in growth that have been apparent since before World War II. The historical perspective provided by the report's data and comments shows how far the behavioral and social sciences have come during the past generation, both in their knowledge and in the demands society wishes to place upon them. The report's projections and recommendations show how much still needs to be done—and how a beginning can be made toward doing it—before the behavioral and social sciences will be able to respond adequately to the great need of a modern society to understand human behavior.

The report makes evident the excitement of exploration, the pleasure in discovering pattern in nature, that motivates research in these as in all the sciences. Quite properly, however, in its central concern with public policy, it stresses the application of behavioral and social science, and the measures that should be taken to realize their potential values for society. We would call your attention particularly to the Committee's demonstration that our society is now deficient in careers, parallel to those in engineering, aimed specifically at the application of behavioral and social science, and to its recommendations for expanded university training, across existing disciplinary boundaries, in applied social science. Throughout, the report emphasizes that there is no intrinsic conflict between basic and applied research, but an important complementarity that requires each to thrive if the other is to enjoy healthy growth. What the social and behavioral sciences require is not a redirection of effort from one to the other, but stable and expanding support for both.

The Committee deserves our warm thanks not only for its specific proposals and recommendations, but also for assembling and interpreting a body of new data about the behavioral and social science disciplines that will be an essential ingredient in all discussions about their future. The Committee's work has been a pioneering and successful exercise in cooperation among these disciplines, which we hope foreshadows a growth of such collaboration in the future.

Sincerely,

HARVEY BROOKS, *Chairman*
Committee on Science and Public Policy
National Academy of Sciences

GARDNER LINDZEY, *Chairman*
Committee on Problems and Policy
Social Science Research Council

DR. PHILIP HANDLER, *President*
National Academy of Sciences

DR. HENRY W. RIECKEN, *President*
Social Science Research Council

With this report, the behavioral and social sciences join other major fields of science in publication of comprehensive surveys of their current states and potentials for growth. Previous reports in the same series have been sponsored by the Committee on Science and Public Policy of the National Academy of Sciences. Sponsorship of this report is shared by that committee with the Committee on Problems and Policy of the Social Science Research Council.

The report is the work of the Behavioral and Social Sciences Survey Committee. In addition to assessing the resources and opportunities of the behavioral and social sciences, the Committee has explored possibilities for the application of those resources to the most urgent problems of our society. The Academy and the Council endorse this effort, with the hope that it may prove to be a useful contribution to the work of all those who ultimately must make the most critical decisions relative to those problems.

PHILIP HANDLER
President
National Academy of Sciences

HENRY RIECKEN
President
Social Science Research Council

Washington, D.C.
October 1969

BEHAVIORAL AND SOCIAL SCIENCES SURVEY COMMITTEE: CENTRAL PLANNING COMMITTEE

PREFACE

The Behavioral and Social Sciences Survey Committee was appointed jointly by the National Academy of Sciences and the Social Science Research Council late in 1966 to prepare a report on the present status and future needs of the component disciplines and their joint research activities. This report is one of a series of survey reports concerning major fields of science, describing their current state and future needs.

Despite many topics which are shared in common and a substantial amount of interdisciplinary activity, the basic organization of the behavioral and social sciences is around the separate disciplines. In planning the survey, therefore, panels were created for individual disciplines, and separate panel reports have been prepared, as listed on page xi.

The Central Staff of the Committee has consisted of a chairman, co-chairman, and executive officer, who, with the chairmen and co-chairmen of the panels, have constituted the Central Planning Committee. When "the Committee" is mentioned in the body of the report this committee is meant. The members of the Central Planning Committee have participated throughout in the design of the study. The report was prepared initially by the Central Staff. The Committee reviewed the several versions in detail and the present report and its recommendations represent a consensus.

Pendleton Herring was President of the Social Science Research Council at the time that this survey was initiated. Dr. Riecken was elected President of the Council on January 1, 1969. It was agreed that he should continue as co-chairman of the Survey Committee in spite of his new position.

One of the major tasks undertaken in obtaining data for the report was a questionnaire survey of universities granting the PhD degree in the disciplines represented in the survey. The university survey, conducted early in 1968, included questionnaires to departmental chairmen in the arts and science faculties, to university financial officers in the central administration, to professional schools conducting organized research in the behavioral and social sciences, and to the numerous institutes, laboratories, and centers performing such research within the university but outside the administrative structures of the departments and professional schools. The Bureau of Social Science Research of Washington, D.C., conducted the questionnaire survey under contract. Technical details on the sample and other aspects of the questionnaire survey can be found in Appendix B.

We have also relied greatly upon data gathered by others concerning the behavioral and social sciences outside the university, whether within government or industry. Many government reports, especially those of the National Science Foundation and the National Institutes of Health, proved to be unusually helpful. We have also had a great deal of assistance from individuals within and outside the federal government. Some of those who helped most substantially are listed in Appendix A, but we could not list all those who helped, in one way or another, because the list would have been prohibitively long. Finally, we are grateful for the administrative assistance of the Division of Behavioral Sciences of the National Research Council.

This volume begins with a summary and some of the major recommendations. Although the summary gives in digest form the reasons in support of these recommendations, a fuller discussion of them can be found in the report itself, as well as additional recommendations. The volume concludes with Appendixes, which include details concerning our procedures and some suggestions for a followup of this survey and for surveys of this kind in the future.

This survey has been made possible by funds granted by the National Institutes of Health, the National Institute of Mental Health, the National Science Foundation, and the Russell Sage Foundation. The Committee is warmly grateful to these agencies for their support.

In addition to this report, the following reports were undertaken by panels of scholars working under the auspices of the Survey Committee. The series is to be published by Prentice-Hall, Inc., Englewood Cliffs, N.J. 07632.

Anthropology
Economics
Geography
History as Social Science
Political Science
Psychiatry as a Behavioral Science
Psychology
Sociology
Statistics, Mathematics, and Computation in the
    Behavioral and Social Sciences

Each report has been prepared by the chairman (or chairman and co-chairman) of the panel, with the participation and review by panel members. Each report has also been reviewed by representatives of the Committee on Science and Public Policy, National Academy of Sciences, and the Committee on Problems and Policy, Social Science Research Council.

CONTENTS

SUMMARY AND MAJOR RECOMMENDATIONS

We are living in social crisis. There have been riots in our cities and in our universities. An unwanted war defies efforts to end it. Population expansion threatens to overwhelm our social institutions. Our advanced technology can destroy natural beauty and pollute the environment if we do not control its development and thus its effects. Even while scientific progress in biology and medicine helps to relieve pain and prolong life, it raises new problems relating to organ transplants, drugs that alter behavior, and the voluntary control of genetic inheritance.

At the root of many of these crises are perplexing problems of human behavior and relationships. The behavioral and social sciences, devoted to studying these problems, can help us survive current crises and avoid them in the future, provided that these sciences continue to make contributions of two kinds: first, in increased depth of understanding of human behavior and the institutions of society; and, second, in better ways to use this understanding in devising social policy and the management of our affairs. Recommendations for achieving such growth are the central concern of this survey and this report.

Social problems are most visible during crisis, but they persist even in relatively calm times, for the human needs that underlie them are continuous. Our concerns must include health and access to medical care, raising children to become effective and satisfied adults. We want a society that provides educational services in classrooms, museums, libraries, and the mass media, and that offers abundant opportunity for satisfying and productive work without fear of unemployment. People need pleasant, livable housing, efficient and

1

economical means of transportation, and opportunities for esthetic outlets and the appreciation of nature. The social order must provide safety for citizens and freedom of movement without fear of attack or molestation. It must encourage individuality and cultural diversity, while reducing intergroup tensions; and it must progress toward international understanding and the elimination of war as an instrument of national policy.

These are large issues, involving values and goals as well as means. The job of the social scientist is clear. He can keep track of what is happening, work at understanding the sources of conflict and resistance to change, and try to determine both the intended and unintended consequences of problem-solving actions. Through the development of general scientific principles and the analysis of specific instances, social scientists seek to illuminate the ways in which the society is working.

This survey was undertaken to explain the behavioral and social sciences and to explore some of the ways these sciences could be developed and supported so that their potential usefulness to society can be realized. The survey is directed to two tasks: first, to assess the nature of the behavioral and social science enterprise in terms of its past growth, present size, and anticipated development; and second, to suggest ways in which these sciences might contribute both to basic understanding of human behavior and to effective social planning and policy-making.

The Scope of the Behavioral and Social Sciences

This survey embraces nine behavioral and social science disciplines: anthropology, economics, geography, history, linguistics, political science, psychiatry, psychology, and sociology. It also takes into account the social science aspects of statistics, mathematics, and computation. The survey recognizes the contributions to behavioral and social science by professionals in business, education, law, public health, medicine, and social work, although it does not cover these fields in detail. The importance of collaborative work in solving social problems emphasizes the links between these sciences and engineering, architecture, and the biological and physical sciences.

The behavioral and social sciences have shared in the rapid expansion of knowledge common to all fields of scholarship over the last decade and have attracted an increasing number of trained workers (Figure SR-1). Increasing proportions of bachelor's and master's

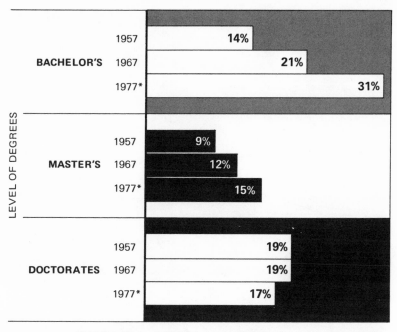

FIGURE SR-1 DEGREE PRODUCTION IN THE BEHAVIORAL AND SOCIAL SCIENCES AS PERCENTAGES OF DEGREE PRODUCTION IN ALL FIELDS.

* Projected.

[Source: Tables 9-1, 9-3, 9-5.]

degrees were granted in these fields between 1957 and 1967, and the trend will probably continue. The relative proportion of doctorates may decline slightly, not because of a slowing down in their production but because of very rapid increases in other fields, notably in engineering. Ironically, despite the increase in the number of degrees granted (Figure SR-2), the social sciences face manpower shortages because of the upsurge of interest in them.

Behavioral and social scientists are more inclined to pursue academic careers than are many other scientists, although a trend toward greater nonacademic employment is apparent. Approximately half of all professional behavioral and social scientists work in universities or four-year colleges. Many others work in other educational settings, such as junior colleges and secondary schools, and in public-school administration. The rest are employed in government, hospitals,

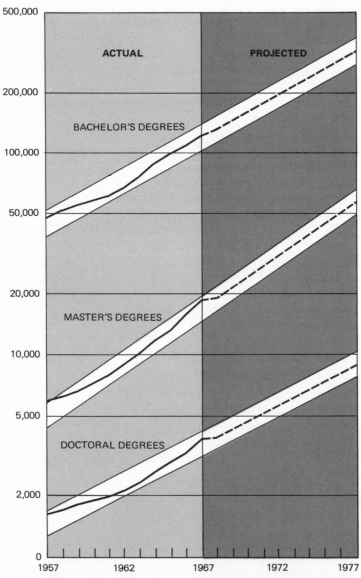

FIGURE SR-2   BEHAVIORAL AND SOCIAL SCIENCE DEGREES ACTUALLY AWARDED, 1957–1967, AND PROJECTED TO 1977 (LOGARITHMIC SCALE).

[Source: Appendix Tables A-11, A-12, A-13.]

research centers, and industry; economists and psychologists find more employment outside universities than do others.

Sciences of Behavior and the Problems of Society

All sciences make some distinctions between basic research, applied research, and the development of products, processes, or services based on research. The history of science shows that the relationship between basic and applied science is complex, with basic research sometimes lagging behind, and sometimes leading applied research. But the scientific method can be applied to problems of a practical nature, whether or not the applications can be derived from the basic science of the time.

The third category of scientific activity—development—is more difficult to define for the behavioral and social sciences. The result of development in the physical sciences or in engineering is usually a tangible product, such as a color television set or a space capsule, and it is relatively simple to determine developmental costs. Although there are some tangible products of behavioral and social science, such as computerized instructional systems, many useful ones are services or processes in the public domain, such as a parole system, a new form of welfare payments, or a form of psychotherapy.

If the usefulness of social-problem-relevant research is to grow, the scale of social science research will have to expand, because many problems can be studied only on a national or international level. As this scale increases, the basic sciences of human behavior should benefit, much as the natural sciences have benefited from increases in the scale of their own research.

The Committee has considered several steps to strengthen the behavioral and social sciences, both as sciences and as contributors to public policy.

One step is to develop improved *social indicators*: measures that reflect the quality of life, particularly in its noneconomic aspects. Some data for constructing social indicators now exist. We have data on educational opportunities, adequacy of housing, infant mortality, and other statistics bearing on health, highway accidents and deaths, violent crimes, civil disorders, reflections of cultural interests (library use, museum and theater attendance), and recreational activities. We now need a major effort to find indicators that can accurately reflect trends for the nation as a whole as well as differences among regional, sex, age, ethnic, and socioeconomic groups. Most social changes are gradual. A sensitive social indicator should tell us whether, in the area to which it pertains, things are getting better or worse, and to what degree.

Social indicators should help us measure the effects of social innovations and changes in social policy as well as assess their unintended by-products. New methods of construction as well as changes in building codes could be reflected in changes in indicators of the quality of housing. Broad programs for increasing highway safety might affect accident indicators and also the consumption of alcohol under certain circumstances.

Indicators that measure our economic state are in use, but they are not precisely analogous to the *social* indicators we are proposing. Economic values can be expressed in dollars, and economic indicators can be aggregated to produce a single economic unit, such as the gross national product (GNP). There is no corresponding unit of value by which to measure the quality of life. This is not an obstacle to the development and use of separate quantitative indicators, each of which measures some aspect of the quality of life, even though it may not be possible to combine them into a single number.

The development of a useful system of social indicators is not simply a matter of measuring many aspects of society. The central problem is to decide which among many measurable attributes most truly represent the fundamental characteristics with which we are concerned. Thus, progress toward valid indicators will depend largely on the understanding we obtain from research into the basic structure and processes of our society. Conceptual and theoretical work at the highest level is necessary if we are to interpret the changes taking place.

To expedite the development and use of a system of social indicators, we offer the following recommendation:

RECOMMENDATION: SOCIAL INDICATORS

The Committee recommends that substantial support, both financial and intellectual, be given to efforts under way to develop a system of social indicators and that legislation to encourage and assist this development be enacted by Congress.

We believe that the resources of the federal government will have to be called upon to develop successful indicators. The estimated annual cost of running an organization to carry on developmental work is $1.5 million. Access by such an organization to data routinely collected by federal agencies would facilitate its work. Because the effort would be in the national interest, we suggest that the task of developing social indicators be undertaken directly by the government; in Chapter 6 we discuss several alternatives for locating an indicator agency within the federal system.

If social indicators are to be useful to society, they will have to be interpreted and then considered in conjunction with the making of social policy. Just as the annual Economic Report of the President interprets economic indicators, an annual social report should eventually be produced that will call attention to the significance of changes in social indicators.

Because of the particular problems involved in developing sound, workable social indicators, we are hesitant to urge an official social report now. We favor, instead, a privately sponsored report during the next few years, perhaps through the initiative of either the National Research Council or the Social Science Research Council, or through a joint effort of the two.

If such an annual social report proves substantial after reasonable experimentation, it might then become a government responsibility like the annual economic and manpower reports now made for the President. This approach is also discussed in Chapter 6, where we offer the following recommendation.

RECOMMENDATION: A PRIVATELY DEVELOPED ANNUAL SOCIAL REPORT

The Committee recommends that behavioral and social scientists outside the government begin to prepare the equivalent of an "Annual Social Report to the Nation," to identify and expedite work toward the solution of problems connected with the eventual preparation of such a report on an official basis. Support for this endeavor should come from private foundations as well as from federal sources.

A natural next step would be to establish a council of social advisers to consider the policy implications of the report. We do not recommend the establishment of such a council until the annual social report shows that social indicators do indeed signal meaningful changes in the quality of life.

For the present, we urge full participation of behavioral and social scientists in the Office of Science and Technology and in the President's Science Advisory Committee, as well as in the numerous advisory bodies attached to administrative agencies and the Office of the President (see Chapter 5).

Behind the development of social indicators and an annual report lie some basic steps: to gather better social data and to store it in usable form, with the necessary safeguards against invasion of privacy. Fortunately, we have the experience of the Decennial Census and the Current Population Survey, without which a great deal of social science, particularly demography, could not have been developed. There are also many sample surveys that deal with employment and other economic factors and statistical reports on agriculture, health, and other aspects of life.

Even in a non-Census year, the federal government spends more than $118 million on statistical programs. Data are scattered through government agencies in many forms, and suggestions for centralizing those data in some form of national data system have been made several times. We see many problems in such plans and therefore recommend that the President appoint a special commission with a full-time professional staff and a broad-based advisory committee to make a detailed study with recommendations. Suggestions should come from data-collection agencies of government, from representatives of the various behavioral and social sciences, from computer specialists, and from the public.

Further specification of the task of the proposed commission is given in Chapter 7. We summarize our position in a recommendation:

RECOMMENDATION: A NATIONAL DATA SYSTEM

> *The Committee recommends that a special commission be established to investigate in detail the procedural and technical problems involved in devising a national data system designed for social scientific purposes; that it recommend solutions for these problems and propose methods for managing a system that will make data maximally useful, while protecting the anonymity of individuals.*

Protecting respondents' anonymity is very important and may prove to be among the most difficult problems to be dealt with. We propose, therefore, that it be faced in advance of the report that the special commission on a national data system may issue, and that some method be found for continuing to monitor the data systems as new methods of data storage and retrieval are created. The benefits of having policy guided by accurate information about the welfare and quality of life of the citizen can be very great, but it would be a sad consequence if, in the process of obtaining this information, the availability of data about individuals became a limitation on their freedom. To this end we offer the following recommendation.

RECOMMENDATION: PROTECTION OF ANONYMITY

The Committee recommends the establishment within an appropriate agency of the federal government, or as an interagency commission, of a high-level continuing body, including nongovernmental members, to investigate the problems of protecting the anonymity of respondents, to prescribe actions to resolve the problems, and to review the dangers that may arise as new techniques of data-matching are developed.

Behavioral and Social Science Research in Universities

In PhD-granting universities, research in the behavioral and social sciences is conducted in departments of colleges of arts and sciences, in professional schools, and in institutes and research centers that exist outside the departments. Research funds are almost equally divided among these three administrative units, although departments employ more behavioral scientists because they have teaching responsibilities as well as research assignments (see Figure SR-3).

Doctorate-granting departments are usually heavily committed to research, whereas professional schools are more variable in the extent to which they foster organized research in the behavioral and social sciences. Many schools of business, education, and medicine have fairly well established traditions of research relating to the behavioral and social sciences. Schools of law and schools of social work, however, give less attention to organized research in these sciences. Neither of these has anything like the behavioral and social science research expenditure per school that is found in schools of business, education, or medicine.

Law schools have not had sufficient access to research funds, their faculties have had little free time for research, and they have not

ALLOCATION OF ORGANIZED RESEARCH FUNDS FISCAL YEAR 1966
$225,556,000

*Multiple-discipline institutes account for 80% of the total institute research expenditures

BEHAVIORAL AND SOCIAL SCIENTISTS
ON UNIVERSITY STAFFS
N = 18,498

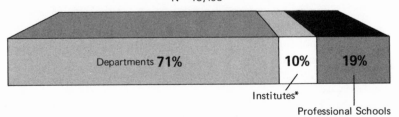

*Multiple-discipline institutes account for 75% of full-time research personnel within all institutes

FIGURE SR-3   DISTRIBUTION OF BEHAVIORAL AND SOCIAL SCIENCE RESEARCH FUNDS AND RESEARCH PERSONNEL AMONG DEPARTMENTS, INSTITUTES, AND PROFESSIONAL SCHOOLS, PHD-GRANTING UNIVERSITIES, FISCAL YEAR 1967.

[Source: Questionnaire Survey.]

developed a pattern of employing research technicians as schools of business, education, and medicine have. A growing number of law schools desire to change this state of affairs and to introduce more social science research; in Chapter 11 we offer a recommendation for inducements to aid them in doing so.

University institutes devoted wholly or in part to behavioral science research have proliferated for a number of reasons, including administrative convenience, exploration of interdisciplinary work, and concentration on research on social problems. Approximately a fourth of the scientists working in institutes and a fifth of the research money are in institutes representing only one discipline. The rest of the personnel and funds are in interdisciplinary institutes. Approximately one fifth of all institutes are oriented toward research contributing to the solution of social problems, as in the many urban institutes that have recently been formed in universities.

Despite the variety of administrative arrangements discussed above, universities are still often handicapped when trying to do fully satisfactory research into social problems.

Disciplinary departments in universities, which grant most of the PhD degrees, are often better suited to basic research than to applied research. Their faculties sometimes cooperate with other departments and institutes on research, but such work usually lacks the continuity and staffing necessary for applied research. Furthermore, disciplinary values tend to favor research oriented toward problems of particular disciplines. Departments try to achieve a balance between specializations in the disciplines, which, while admirable in itself, presents problems in organization of large task forces to study significant social problems.

Institutes usually have limited full-time staffs and rely heavily on part-time workers from the disciplines. Consequently, they have little control over the education of most of their workers. The result is that much of their research leads back to disciplinary interests because that is where professional advancement lies. Moreover, the availability of research funds for institutes is unstable by nature, and the level and character of research fluctuates according to the money available.

Professional schools are concerned with particular kinds of applied research related to their professional foci; thus many general social problems tend to lie outside the sphere of any single school. Professional schools also have the mixed blessing of a close relationship with client systems (such as hospitals, businesses, courts, or legislatures). This linkage is helpful in directing research to significant problems, but it also tends to limit the research to the interests of its clients. Further, research goals must compete with the primary task of training a body of professional workers. Often research suffers.

In view of these limitations, we believe a new university organization should be created for training and research on social problems. To clarify the essential elements of this organization, we have proposed a new school, which we call a Graduate School of Applied Behavioral Science.

RECOMMENDATION: A GRADUATE SCHOOL OF APPLIED BEHAVIORAL SCIENCE

The Committee recommends that universities consider the establishment of broadly based training and research programs in the form of a Graduate School of Applied Behavioral Science (or some local equivalent) under administrative arrangements that lie outside the established disciplines. Such training and research should be multidisciplinary (going beyond the behavioral and social sciences as necessary), and the school should accept responsibility for contributing through its research both to a basic understanding of human relationships and behavior and to the solution of persistent social problems.

Such a recommendation should, of course, be adapted to local situations. However, such a school should be of scientific stature commensurate with that of the best medical and engineering schools. It should have a core faculty with tenure, like any professional school, and it should not be organized along disciplinary lines. Disciplinary departments would, of course, continue outside the new school. If the school develops topical subdivisions (such as urban research centers, or centers studying the development of new nations), these subdivisions should be terminated when they are no longer pertinent.

The new school should have its own PhD program, and it should attempt to educate its students for inventive development relevant to social problems. In other words, the school should do empirical research on significant social problems and train professionals to carry on this kind of research.

Such a school will require considerable planning, and it will face many obstacles. Among these is the problem of developing professional identity for its graduates. Many of them will probably be employed in nonacademic settings, and the university-professorship model of career aspirations will not serve. It may be necessary, therefore, to create a new professional society and new journals devoted to applied behavioral science in order to define a new professional identity.

The word "applied" in the title promises that the school will cover that end of the spectrum, but, of course, it must also be concerned with basic research. A high-level applied school will inevitably work on basic problems of data-collection and analysis, model-building, and simulation. Work on social indicators, even on a local scale, could improve the statistical basis of the indicators and investigate how to combine them or substitute one for another. Beyond such methodological problems, each Graduate School of Applied Behavioral Science should have some specialized areas of research, for the whole of applied behavioral science is too broad to tackle all at once. The problems of the cities, of poverty, of crime, of nation-building, of conservation, of regional governments, of individual growth and development, of early education—any one of a range of problems—could serve among the specialties in one school.

Instructive precedents in a number of universities exhibit many qualities of the proposed new type of school; Chapter 12 discusses these and the proposed school at greater length.

Behavioral and Social Sciences outside the University

Substantial numbers of social scientists work in non-academic settings for federal, state, and local governments, for business and industry, and for nonprofit research organizations. Their functions, however, are not too different from those of their university colleagues.

The federal government estimates an 18.4 percent growth in federal social science employment from 1967 to 1971, and a similar growth is reported by state governments and nonprofit organizations. The percentage growth in federal social science employment is greater than the growth in overall federal employment and total federal scientific employment for the same period. Chapter 13 reports the limited data we have collected.

One indication of the amount of nonacademic research in the behavioral and social sciences is the amount of federal funds for non-academic research performers, both to private research organizations and to the government. Roughly half of the federal funds go to nonuniversity research, and it is divided about equally between the government, on the one hand, and industrial firms and nonprofit institutions on the other (Table SR-1).

The Financing of Research

In 1966–1967, some 3.4 percent of the nation's total research and development expenditure was spent on the behavioral and social sciences—about $803 million. This was more than double

TABLE SR-1 FEDERAL OBLIGATIONS FOR BASIC AND APPLIED RE-
SEARCH IN BEHAVIORAL AND SOCIAL SCIENCES, FY 1967, BY PERFORMER

	Federal Obligations for Basic and Applied Research (millions of dollars)		
	All Fields of Science	Behavioral and Social Sciences	Behavioral and Social Sciences as Percent of Total Obligations
Intramural (within government departments and agencies)	$1,574	$ 77[a]	5
Extramural, Nonuniversity			
Industrial firms	1,437	77[a]	3
Nonprofit institutions	269		
Others	646		
Total, Nonuniversity	$3,925	$154	4
Universities	1,348	143[b]	11
Grand Total	$5,273	$297	6

[a] Estimated from residual funds after removing amounts to universities.
[b] Estimated from the Survey.
Source: *Federal Funds for Research, Development, and Other Scientific Activities: Fiscal Years 1967, 1968, 1969*, NSF 68-27 (Washington, D.C.: National Science Foundation, 1968), Vol. 17, pp. 124, 130.

the amount spent for social science research and development in 1961–1962 (Table SR-2).

Between 1959 and 1968, federal support of behavioral and social science research increased at an average rate of approximately 20 percent a year. Since today's social problems are so urgent, it is important to maintain growth at least close to this level. We distinguish between *normal projected growth* (no increase in the scale of research operations) and *projected new programs* (the addition of new large-scale research). In Chapter 14 we discuss the matter more fully and offer the following recommendation concerning normal research support.

TABLE SR-2   SUPPORT OF RESEARCH AND DEVELOPMENT IN THE BE-
HAVIORAL AND SOCIAL SCIENCES, 1962, 1967, BY SOURCE (IN MILLIONS
OF DOLLARS)

Source of Funds	1961–1962	1966–1967
Federal government		
Basic research	$ 46	$ 132
Applied research	74	159
Development	68	97
	$ 188	$ 388
State governments	5	15
Industry	130	289
Colleges and universities	24	48
Foundations	23	24
Nonprofit institutions	14	39
Total, behavioral and social sciences	$ 384	$ 803
Total, all fields of science	$15,604	$23,686
Behavioral and social sciences as percent of total science	2.5	3.4

Source: Table 1-2 and Table A-8, Appendix.

RECOMMENDATION: RATE OF FEDERAL FUNDING FOR NORMAL RESEARCH SUPPORT

The Committee recommends an annual increase in funds available from the federal government for support of basic and applied research in the behavioral and social sciences of between 12 and 18 percent to sustain the normal growth of the research enterprise over the next decade.

To sustain normal growth in the behavioral and social sciences, the indicated increase in research funds will be needed, and a correspond- ing increase will also be needed for instructional funds, student aid, space, and equipment. Our recommendation also applies to funding for behavioral and social science research outside the universities.

The costs of projected new programs are not included in the normal-growth projections, for they are of a different character from the steady and gradual increase required by the increases in the num- ber of social scientists and the growing sophistication of research techniques. However, the new programs require abrupt increases in funding, with each program having minimum start-up costs. The operating costs of the various new programs, when they are in full swing, are likely to total an additional $100 million annually, as explained in Chapter 14.

The agencies supporting the behavioral and social sciences are chiefly the Department of Health, Education, and Welfare (primarily through the Office of Education, the National Institutes of Health, and the National Institute of Mental Health), the Department of Defense, the Department of Agriculture, and the National Science Foundation. We welcome their continued support and believe that other agencies should expand their use of behavioral and social science research, through both intramural and extramural support. In short, we endorse the principle of pluralistic support for the social sciences.

Proposals to establish a national social science foundation pose some problems concerning the role of the National Science Foundation. The implication that social science is important enough to warrant a special foundation is gratifying, but the issues are complex, and the members of the Committee are somewhat divided in their views. Because the charter of the National Science Foundation has recently been enlarged to permit support of applied research, and explicitly to support the social sciences, we favor giving it the opportunity to exercise its new functions. However, we also suggest that, if the National Science Foundation is unable to exercise its new obligations in social sciences, then a new foundation may be needed. Recommendations bearing on the National Science Foundation appear in Chapter 14.

Private foundations have been a significant source of support to the behavioral and social sciences through the years, frequently playing innovative roles and contributing in a variety of ways to the development of these sciences. The role of the foundations is discussed in Chapter 15.

Worldwide Development of the Social Sciences

Worldwide interest in the social sciences is growing, partly in response to the processes of development and modernization in new nations. Social scientists in other countries seek to strengthen their professional capabilities, and there is considerable American interest in study and research overseas.

Collaboration across national boundaries is especially important in the social sciences. Generalizations based on work in only one country may be too parochial and circumscribed, and some kinds of situations important to an understanding of human behavior cannot be studied satisfactorily in any one nation. In Chapter 16 we offer some suggestions about the relationships among social scientists on an international basis, and we discuss the strengthening of organizations devoted to furthering international social science.

Outlook for the Behavioral and Social Sciences

As the sciences advance and research at their growing edges becomes more demanding of special knowledge and skills, the tendency toward specialization increases. This trend is important for the advancement of the frontiers of science, but it also runs counter to the demand for science to deal with problems of great complexity in an integrated way. While we recognize the legitimacy of specialization within disciplines, we recommend more attention to large-scale research concerning our rising social problems.

Our society cannot delay dealing with its major social problems. We cannot consume our resources and pollute our environment and then hope to replenish and restore them. We cannot permit international relations to deteriorate to the point of resorting to nuclear weapons. Social unrest, a result of rising expectations and frustrated hopes, will eventually reach a point of no return.

The social sciences will provide no easy solutions in the near future, but they are our best hope, in the long run, for understanding our problems in depth and for providing new means of lessening tensions and improving our common life.

1
THE DOMAIN
OF THE
BEHAVIORAL AND
SOCIAL SCIENCES

The behavioral and social sciences deal primarily with the behavior of man in his relation to his fellow men and the environment they share. The recurrent crises of our times—Vietnam, the Middle East, public services in our cities, racial tensions, the problems of new nations, overpopulation, the threats of nuclear war, student revolts, environmental pollution—have given a sense of urgency to social problems and problems in the social control of technology that call for an understanding in depth to obviate the need for hasty ameliorative measures taken in desperation. The achievement of such an understanding is a task that faces social scientists, not as a response to crises, but as a continuing effort to understand human behavior and human institutions and to provide knowledge for those who must plan and make policy to meet human needs.

The range of interests of these sciences is reflected in the variety of disciplines surveyed: anthropology, economics, geography, history, linguistics, political science, psychiatry, psychology, sociology, and aspects of mathematics, statistics, and computation. However, this list is not exhaustive; professional studies in business administration, education, journalism, law, medicine, public health, and social work have also developed important social science research activities. Furthermore, much research that is relevant to understanding modern life requires collaboration among social scientists, physical and life scientists, engineers, and others.

THE CONCERNS OF THE BEHAVIORAL AND SOCIAL SCIENCES

The common problems of man and his institutions permit the various disciplines to be considered members of one family of

19

sciences, here called the behavioral and social sciences. There is, however, a wide range of interests and styles within the disciplines, ranging from the close affiliations of physiological psychologists and physical anthropologists with the biological sciences to the broad interest of political scientists in international affairs and historians in man's past. Many disparate interests are found within fields of study, as well as between the various fields; for example, the range from archeology to problems of developing nations within anthropology or from animal behavior to studies of international conflict within psychology. Because of these widely scattered but interrelated interests we have not attempted to divide the behavioral and social sciences into classes, although the two terms—behavioral and social—suggest that others have attempted to make such distinctions. When this distinction is made, the behavioral aspects of these sciences tend to be identified as those concerned with the individual as the unit of analysis, and the social aspects, as those for which the institution or some other aggregate of persons is the focus of analysis. For this survey, however, the terms "behavioral" and "social" are used interchangeably.

The objectives of behavioral and social scientists are essentially the same as those of other scientists: to establish a body of fact and theory, demonstrable and communicable, that contributes to knowledge and understanding that will permit man to manage his affairs with greater rationality. The individual scholar becomes fascinated with an unknown area that he is prepared to explore; this becomes an exciting intellectual quest, and his contribution moves the body of knowledge ahead, thus serving the purposes of education and the broadening of understanding, whether or not there is any immediate application to human affairs. Others, however, do their investigating in the turmoil of life as it is lived, in the hope that they may develop insights that can be used promptly. The distinctions between basic and applied social science are seldom sharp, and important scientific contributions can be made all along the line, with applied findings serving basic science just as basic science serves applications.

The activities of social scientists are inviting because their problems are so obviously important to man; the fields pose difficulties because the substantive problems of human behavior and human institutions are enormously complex, and the objects of inquiry do not remain unchanged while they are being studied. But methods have been found to make scientific investigations possible, and to arrive at reasonably firm conclusions, subject always to the self-correcting and changing character that all sciences share. The base becomes firmer to bring increasing precision and clarity to activities such as the following:

1. *Explaining* observed social events both in terms of trends from the past and according to the interplay of present social forces.

2. *Anticipating* the consequences of alternative social policies, social actions, or changes in social arrangements. The fact that social prediction will always be contingent upon subsequent events, and hence will always lack complete accuracy, means only that some estimate of the degree of uncertainty must enter into a responsible prediction.

3. *Designing* social instrumentalities for carrying out specified policy decisions. Such designs can be the result of genuine acts of synthesis, based on both data and theory.

4. *Advising* those responsible for formulating policies for achieving agreed-upon social goals, such as improving health, reducing crime, constructive uses of leisure time, and dignified and satisfying conditions of work. Where social goals are in conflict or unclear, recommendations can include procedures for their resolution or clarification.

5. *Comparing* and *evaluating* the outcomes of various courses of action provisionally adopted, including the reappraisal of these outcomes and their unforeseen by-products.

This list of activities calls attention to two complementary needs: (1) to maintain and extend fundamental research in the several disciplines and in their areas of overlap (among themselves and with other disciplines) and (2) to widen the opportunities for behavioral scientists (both those in training and those already established) to become involved in applied research that bears more directly on social problems. In the support of training and research and in the institutions designed to conduct such training and research, careful attention should be given to the respective needs for basic, applied, and policy research, with full awareness that the healthy development of any science requires the interplay of these facets and high levels of talent all along the spectrum from the most basic to the most applied.

It would be a mistake to gloss over the debate within the behavioral and social sciences concerning the proper objectives to be fulfilled and the most appropriate interrelationships among the fields of scholarship. For example, within psychology there are those who feel so strongly about their affiliation with the life sciences that they prefer to think of psychology as part of behavioral biology rather than as a full member of the social sciences, and within history there is a strong affiliation with the humanities, so there is some uneasiness about an identification of all of history with the behavioral and social sciences.

In regard to policy considerations, some social scientists note that the citizen role can become confused with the scientist role, and they fear that too much involvement in policy decisions may weaken the status of their fields as sciences. The issues are genuine ones, and the social scientist is to some extent more vulnerable than other scientists because of the direct pertinence of his work to human behavior and institutions. For example, when a social scientist gives a plausible explanatory account of critical events—how black-power movements arise, or why students obstruct universities—he is likely to be interpreted as endorsing the events that he explains. As a citizen he may either deplore them or delight in them, but as a scientist it is his role to explain them. Thus, these roles may on occasion become confused when the scientist is called upon to advise on policy. In view of the special complexities and unpredictables inherent in the social sciences, it may well appear that the disparities of opinions and convictions among social scientists are more marked than among other scientists.

THE SIZE AND NATURE OF THE BEHAVIORAL AND SOCIAL SCIENCE RESEARCH ENTERPRISE

Although the behavioral and social sciences have been described as academic disciplines, they are not confined to colleges and universities. Both government and industry make major contributions. For example, the U.S. Decennial Census has become a major resource of social science, as have statistical series issued by the Departments of Labor, Commerce, and Health, Education, and Welfare, and other agencies of the federal government. The Department of Agriculture, particularly through its Economic Research Service, has contributed to the analysis of marketing and price fluctuations as well as to the study of communities. The social scientists in the government do more than collect data; there are excellent intramural laboratories, such as those in the National Institute of Mental Health, where they engage in both fundamental and applied behavioral research.

Industry, too, not only uses social scientists but performs research that contributes to social science knowledge. The life-insurance industry, for example, because of its need for life-expectancy tables, has helped to improve on many kinds of statistics, particularly in the health field. Although the social survey had a long prior history, it was the commercial research service groups that later developed opinion surveys, particularly for the analysis of markets, consumer preferences, advertising effectiveness, and election predictions. Methods of occupational research, originated within the U.S. Employment Service during the depression years, have been widely used since that period, not only by state employment agencies, but by industry as well.

In assessing the growth and present status of the total behavioral and social science enterprise it is necessary to recognize that personnel with scientific training in these disciplines are widely scattered throughout the economy.

The behavioral and social sciences have shared in the rapid growth of all fields of scholarship, a growth greatly accelerated through federal funds provided since World War II, and especially in the last decade. A rough idea of this growth, and of the present number of recognized scholars in the various fields, is provided by the memberships in the major scientific and professional associations (Table 1-1). By 1967 there were some 100,000 members of these societies, about 50,000 of whom were on the faculties of four-year colleges and universities. The

TABLE 1-1 MEMBERSHIP GROWTH IN MAJOR BEHAVIORAL AND SOCIAL SCIENCE ASSOCIATIONS, 1947–1967 [a]

Association	Number of Members		
	1947	1957	1967
American Psychological Association	4,661	15,545	25,800
American Economic Association	7,529	12,092	23,305
American Historical Association	4,207	6,300	17,839
American Political Science Association	4,598	6,650	14,685
American Sociological Association	2,218	5,482	11,000
American Anthropological Association	1,692	3,656	6,634
Association of American Geographers	1,350[b]	1,657	4,414
Total	26,255	51,382	103,677

[a] Because of some nonprofessionals in the associations, overlaps in membership, and many professionals who are not members, the numbers are representative only as approximations of the sizes of the professions.
[b] 1948.
Source: Association records.

TABLE 1-2 SUPPORT OF RESEARCH AND DEVELOPMENT IN THE UNITED STATES BY SOURCE AND FIELD OF SCIENCE, 1967 (in millions of dollars)

Source of Funds	Total	Physical, Biological, and Engineering Sciences	Behavioral and Social Sciences	Behavioral and Social Sciences (percent of funds)
Federal government:				
Basic research	$ 2,226	$ 2,094	$132	6%
Applied research	2,811	2,652	159	6
Development	9,439	9,342	97	1
Subtotal	$14,476	$14,088	$388	3%
State governments	77	62	15	19
Industry	8,467	8,178	289	3
Colleges and universities	327	279	48	15
Foundations	77	53	24	31
Other nonprofit institutions	262	223	39	15
Total	$23,686	$22,883	$803	3.4%

Source: See Appendix C for sources of data and methods of estimation.

rest work in government, school systems, hospitals, specialized research centers, and industry. There is no reliable way of knowing, at present, how many professional workers do not belong to the professional societies, but the number is probably substantial.

Although precise data are not available, we have attempted an estimate of the total support for research and development in the behavioral and social sciences from all sources in 1967, compared with the total in the physical, biological, and engineering sciences (Table 1-2). A similar table, for 1962, appears in Appendix C (page 294). The estimated total of $803 million in 1967 compares with $384 million in 1962, a doubling over the five-year period. Other sciences also received greatly increased support over this same time, with the result that the proportion going to the behavioral and social sciences increased only from an estimated 2.5 percent of the total research and development funds in 1962 to 3.4 percent in 1967.

The federal government and industry provide the largest portion of the social science research and development dollar as Figure 1-1 and Table 1-2 show. The most accurate reported data are those for basic and applied research from the federal government; the other data are less reliable. The federal government data that are most open to question are for "development." Development accounts for a very large amount in the physical, biological, and engineering sciences and is a substantial proportion of the money for the behavioral and social sciences, even if, as estimated in Table 1-2, it is only 1 percent of the total of development funds. Reporting agencies have not specified development funds by field of science because development commonly requires the interplay of various skills provided by different disciplines. Development is somewhat easier to specify in the case of tangible products, such as weapons or transport planes; it is harder to specify in the social sciences. There are, however, products of social science activities that are better classified as development than as either basic or applied research, such as a specific plan for urban renewal, a decision on the site of a new power plant, the preparation of audiovisual aids for instruction, or a program for a computer. Product testing for marketing purposes is analogous to designing the physical product itself. Now that the Office of Education has established research and development centers, it has begun to report its development funds separately; with an increased interest in utilization of their research findings, behavioral and social scientists may become more interested in what costs of their work should be ascribed to development.

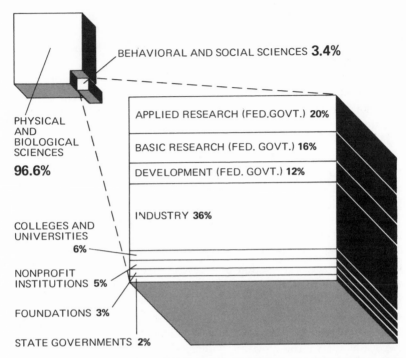

PHYSICAL
AND
BIOLOGICAL
SCIENCES

96.6%

BEHAVIORAL AND SOCIAL SCIENCES **3.4%**

APPLIED RESEARCH (FED.GOVT.) **20%**

BASIC RESEARCH (FED. GOVT.) **16%**

DEVELOPMENT (FED. GOVT.) **12%**

INDUSTRY **36%**

COLLEGES AND
UNIVERSITIES
6%

NONPROFIT
INSTITUTIONS **5%**

FOUNDATIONS **3%**

STATE GOVERNMENTS **2%**

FIGURE 1-1 AGGREGATE SUPPORT OF RESEARCH AND DEVELOPMENT IN THE BEHAVIORAL AND SOCIAL SCIENCES, 1967.

[Based on the data of Table 1-2.]

The growth trends of the various behavioral and social science disciplines within the universities, projected on the basis both of trends revealed by historical data and of judgments made by departmental chairmen, constitute useful information for the federal government, the universities, the foundations, the professions, and any others who seek to anticipate the future of the behavioral and social sciences and wish to participate in planning for their development and use.

2
THE BEHAVIORAL AND SOCIAL SCIENCES

The behavioral and social sciences have enlarged and diversified so much in recent years that there are many misconceptions about the "division of labor" among the various disciplines and about the range of topics within any one of these. To provide a brief overview of both the substance of these fields of scholarship and their methods, this chapter and the two that follow are devoted to illustrative examples of current and recent work. Although selected examples present the total fields somewhat out of focus, it is hoped that the advantages of concreteness may offset the inevitable distortions. (A more complete coverage of developments within the component disciplines surveyed is presented in the reports of the disciplinary panels separately published.*)

ANTHROPOLOGY

The major subfields of anthropology are usually listed as the following four: physical anthropology, archeology, social or cultural anthropology, and linguistic anthropology. Another specialty, applied anthropology, is occasionally listed as a fifth subfield.

Physical anthropology is closely related to anatomy, paleontology, and human genetics. It is concerned with the evolution of the human body, the antiquity of man, his primate precursors, and the evolution of his distinctively human qualities, especially his brain and the sensing and manipulative mechanisms controlled by it. Physical anthropologists study both fossil forms and the higher primates in their native habitats.

*A list of these is given on page xi.

Archeology is concerned with early man and his culture as preserved in the physical residues of earlier times, for example, art objects, burial mounds, utensils and weapons, shelters, and irrigation ditches. Its goal is the reconstruction of an earlier civilization whose only record the artifacts may be.

Social or cultural anthropology historically has been concerned with the organization, institutional arrangements, belief systems, and general manner of life of rather small and isolated groups of people, usually those called nonliterate because they have no written records. Studies of an American Indian pueblo, a tribe of Australian aborigines, or a group dwelling in the highlands of New Guinea are typical. More recently the methods of cultural anthropology have been extended to the study of villages on the edges of urban developments, and to such problems as kinship structure in more highly developed communities.

Linguistic anthropology arose as a specialty within the discipline because anthropologists studying isolated peoples had to develop grammars and dictionaries for their languages. The studies not only give information about the universals of human language, but also raise questions about the relationship between forms of language and thought, and about the diffusion of languages when cultural groups interact.

Applied anthropology finds problems to solve when one society becomes responsible for another, as in the administration of Indian affairs in the United States, the administration of trust territories in the Pacific, or this country's programs to assist development in new nations, as in Africa. The acceptance of technological improvements in agriculture and public health may depend on how they are presented in relation to cultural standards with which anthropologists are especially familiar.

But what of anthropologists at work? For a representative study in cultural anthropology, we may select an investigation of child-rearing practices in six cultures.* The team of workers spent a year together prior to going into the field to develop standard procedures for collecting data about an agreed-upon set of behavioral concerns. They were well aware of the difficulties that had been encountered by others in their attempts to make precise comparisons of different cultures when data had been gathered by unstandardized methods. Then, the

---

*Beatrice R. Whiting, ed., *Six Cultures: Studies of Child Rearing* (New York: John Wiley & Sons, Inc., 1963); Leigh Minturn and William M. Lambert, *Mothers of Six Cultures: Antecedents of Child Rearing* (New York: John Wiley & Sons, Inc., 1964).

investigators separated to do their fieldwork in places as far apart (both geographically and culturally) as villages in New England, Mexico, the Philippines, Okinawa, India, and Africa. Within each of the local cultures selected for study, they began with a census of the children between the ages of 3 and 10, and then, on a random basis, selected 24 of these children for intensive study in each place. The study, of course, included their parents.

The team turned up a number of differences in child-rearing practices, as anticipated; an advantage of this kind of study is that the range of practices is much wider than that within any single culture. One observation was that the mothers themselves faced very different problems of their own personal adjustments in the different cultures. Some mothers were essentially alone and isolated from near relatives, and some were confined in courtyards shared by other women with whom they had little in common. Others lived among congenial relatives, while still others lived among hostile persons suspected of bewitching a mother's children. Under each circumstance, how the mother dealt with her own problems affected what she communicated to her child as much as did her ideas about how to rear her children. Although American mothers face very different problems of economics, social adjustment, and health, it may be that their way of handling these problems affects their child-rearing practices more than what they are told about raising their children by pediatricians or by a manual on child training. Thus, for example, a mother who finds it necessary to seek employment outside the home is simply not there to give her child a warm welcome when he comes home from school, as much as she might believe it desirable to do so; she is as much a victim of circumstances as the mothers in the cultures studied.

The interdisciplinary nature of this research is worth mentioning because it illustrates how some kinds of complex problems have to be tackled in the behavioral and social sciences. The study of the mothers of six cultures was carried out jointly by anthropologists and psychologists; the anthropologists contributed their special skills in understanding a culture as a whole, and the psychologists their skills in studies of child development and quantitative techniques of appraisal.

ECONOMICS

Economics has become a highly complex theoretical and empirical science covering a broad range of topics, such as labor and

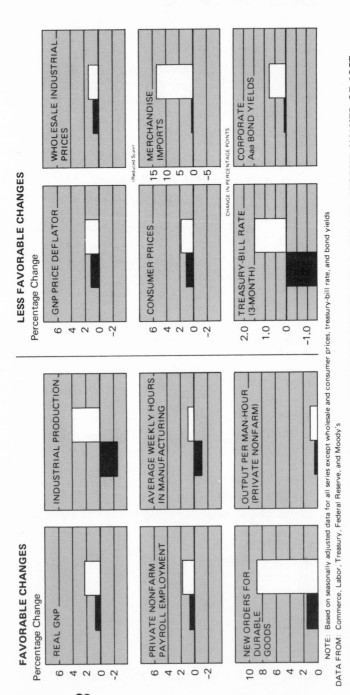

FIGURE 2-1 CHANGES IN SELECTED ECONOMIC INDICATORS WITHIN THE FIRST AND SECOND HALVES OF 1967.

[Source: Arthur M. Okun, *Economic Issues for the Future*, Seminar on Manpower Policy and Programs (U.S. Department of Labor, Manpower Administration, September 1968), p. 9.]

product markets, economic development in new nations, the consumption and saving behavior of households, agricultural production and marketing, and international trade. Its specialties refer in part to these topical fields, but there are others, such as economic history, econometrics, and economic theory. Managerial economics provides the basis for cost–benefit analysis and operations research in business firms and in government.

The manner in which economists have gone about their business is illustrated by the history of the work on the national income and product accounts, in which theory and empirical work have been combined to produce indicators of the state of the economy—indicators that extensively affect planning at the national level. Much of the early work on these accounts was done by nongovernmental research groups, in particular, the National Bureau of Economic Research. Their method of estimating national income was adopted in 1932 by the Department of Commerce, upon a resolution of the U.S. Senate; it has served as a basis for continuing the series under government auspices.

The Employment Act of 1946 created the Council of Economic Advisers and charged it with the responsibility for analyzing and interpreting economic developments and for recommending economic policies to the President that would promote the goals of "maximum employment, production, and purchasing power." Part of the research of economists has been directed toward improving the national income and products accounts within the government.

A set of economic accounts makes it possible to understand in a somewhat simplified form the enormous detail of economic activity going on in the nation. Periodic changes in these accounts, both in total amount and in amounts relative to the grand total, provide us with indicators as to how the economy is moving.

As an illustration of the manner in which economic indicators are used in assessing changes in the economy within a year, Figure 2-1 presents changes in a number of indicators between the first and second halves of 1967. On the left of the figure are the more favorable changes: rises in the gross national product, industrial production, employment, weekly hours in manufacturing, new orders for durable goods, and output per man-hour. But changes in economic indicators during the year were not all favorable; on the right of the figure are the unfavorable ones: a rise in the price deflator for the gross national product (meaning a general price inflation), as shown also by a rise in consumer prices and in wholesale industrial prices, and a rise in imports, which indicated an unfavorable balance of trade. The financial markets are represented by a rise in costs of borrowing money: higher treasury-bill rates and higher rates for corporate-bond yields. The forecasts and recommendations of the Council of Economic Advisers must be based on an understanding of the interrelationships among such indicators (and others) and on the changes in the indicators over time. The kinds of recommendations may be concerned with tax increases or decreases, with manpower policies, or with other factors affecting the economy over which the government has some control.

The development of the system of national accounts and its offshoots has provided a happy conjunction of basic and applied research opportunities, so economists can work at the forefront of their own science while contributing in a very practical way to the understanding and management of the citizen's daily life.

GEOGRAPHY

Geographers study the influence of spatial arrangements and environmental factors in determining the exploitation of natural resources, the settling and migration of people, the location of factories, and the behavior of markets. The older economic geography, which tended to plot the location of resources, has been superseded by a much more dynamic science of spatial organization.

While actual map-making (cartography) is now a relatively small part of the preoccupation of geographers, they retain skills in map and spatial analysis and in the visual presentation of data. Complex visual representation becomes a form of mathematical conceptualization, and the contemporary geographer uses a variety of mathematical devices for the study of gradients of property values, the overlapping of market areas, the flow of traffic, the diffusion of innovation, and numerous other processes in which social behavior is related to spatial arrangements.

As one illustration of a geographic research finding, we may examine a relationship discovered by geographers between the likelihood of floods in different areas and the awareness that precautions should be taken against them. When he sees homes and businesses stranded by floods in areas known to be subject to them, the observer may wonder about the stubbornness with which people cling to areas subject to such hazards (or perhaps about their helplessness to do anything to prevent the hazards). One approach to understanding their behavior is to study the probability of floods in a given area and the extent to which the people in that area are sufficiently sensitive to the problem to make preparations in advance. Table 2-1 shows the results of such a study.

While the data of Table 2-1 are interesting in themselves, they are not sufficient to permit generalizations about obstacles to the adoption of flood-control precautions. A summary of similar studies conducted on a larger scale, illustrated in Figure 2-2, shows flood frequency and critical levels at which "uncertainty" (no expected flood danger) and "certainty" (flood danger) arise.

It is not surprising that people facing floods more often are more

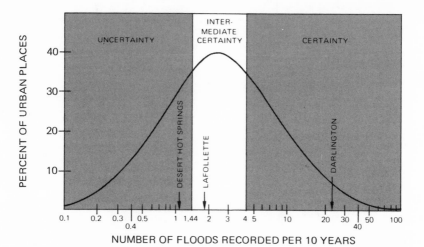

NUMBER OF FLOODS RECORDED PER 10 YEARS

FIGURE 2-2   GENERALIZATION OF STUDIES OF FLOOD PERCEPTION.

The distribution of flood frequencies at 496 places is such that an approximately normal (bell-shaped) distribution arises if the number of cases at each frequency is plotted on a scale of frequency expressed as the logarithm of the frequency of floods per a 10-year period. Surveys of the kind shown in Table 2–1 lead to the critical zones as shown by the vertical lines; floods of a frequency to the left of the line (as in Desert Hot Springs, California) are disregarded, floods to the right of the second line are regularly expected (as in Darlington, Wisconsin), while floods in the middle range (as in LaFollette, Tennessee) lead about equally to lack of concern and willingness to take precautions. [Source: Robert W. Kates, *Hazard and Choice Perception in Flood Plain Management*, Research Paper #78 (University of Chicago: Department of Geography, 1962), p. 87.]

TABLE 2-1 READINESS TO ADOPT FLOOD PRECAUTIONS RELATED TO FREQUENCY OF FLOODS

Concern about Floods and Readiness To Adopt Precautions	Location of Respondents		
	Desert Hot Springs, Calif. (1 flood per 10 yr)	LaFollette, Tenn. (2 floods per 10 yr)	Darlington, Wis. (24 floods per 10 yr)
No concern about floods	73%	17%	0%
Moderate perception of flood problem: no precautions	13	35	0
Greater perception of flood problem: no precautions	7	17	15
Ready to adopt flood precautions	7	31	85
Total respondents at each location	100% N=15	100% N=102	100% N=13

Source: Robert W. Kates, *Hazard and Choice Perception in Flood Plain Management*, Research Paper #78 (University of Chicago: Department of Geography, 1962).

likely to consider adopting flood-control measures. What is surprising is how short some peoples' memories are. If floods occur less frequently than once in 10 years, people are essentially unperceptive of flood danger or unresponsive to it; only when floods occur as often as once every year or two are they generally ready to take precautions.

HISTORY

Historians have tended to specialize in given areas at given times (e.g., Europe in the nineteenth century; China in the Ming dynasty) or they have specialized according to topical interests (history of science, history of the labor movement). These tendencies continue but are supplemented today by a great variety of specializations as perspectives and methods change. It is very difficult, therefore, to summarize the character and direction of historical research by one or two examples, however well chosen.

Such changes in perspective are reflected in the historians' treatment of pervasive themes, of which the subject of revolution may be selected as an example. Although historians commonly direct their attention to the past (the French Revolution of 1789 is a favored starting point), in recent years students of historic rebellions have looked increasingly at upheavals in the contemporary world; examining the present has sharpened their understanding of the past, and the earlier rebellions have helped to put the current ones in perspective. In this new concern with the act of revolt in its multitudinous instances and forms, a quantitative approach is being applied, in which sociologists have joined with historians.

It is possible to assess the number (and ages) of disaffected people who engage in revolts, the emergence of leaders, the relative sizes of opposing factions, and the resources available to them (food, money, munitions). By use of careful estimates of numbers involved and time trends, the quantitative methods of sociology are combined with those of history.

In all of this one can see not only a logical intellectual extension of the sphere of inquiry, but also an effort by the historical scholar to answer questions posed by his own time.

The overlap of interest between historians and other social scientists is evident also in the areas of demography and voting behavior. Around the time of the Second World War, demographic historians, working mainly in France and England, began inventing ways to get

detailed information on population changes from sources like geneal-
ogies and baptismal registers. Their results showed that many features
of modern population dynamics, such as voluntary birth control, had
begun to spread long before modern industry or massive industrial
cities took shape, a finding of considerable importance to the understanding of the Industrial Revolution and the industrialization of
new nations in the modern world.

In regard to voting behavior, we may note that historians have
always been interested in explaining why a particular candidate was
elected to office, but now, with better voting data available, historians
seek to classify types of electoral changes over time and to find common characteristics in these changes. They have noted that occasionally there are realigning elections in which voters shift their
loyalties markedly in a variety of ways at once (strong votes of one
party moving to the other or vice versa), on a relatively permanent
basis. Realigning elections have been rare in American history: the
early 1850's (especially 1854), the mid-1890's (especially 1894 and
1896), and the 1930's (1934 and 1936). Because of their significance
for historical change, elections in these realigning periods are now
receiving considerable attention.

With the increasing availability of quantitative data, whether in
the study of revolutions and revolutionaries, population problems,
voting behavior, economic changes, or other topics of historical interest, the historian, like other social scientists, relies more and more on
the assistance of the high-speed computer and modern statistical
techniques. Thus, while many historians continue to think of themselves primarily as humanists, the affiliation of other historians in
outlook and method with the behavioral and social sciences is
increasingly evident.

LINGUISTICS

A relative newcomer as a department in our universities
offering advanced degress of its own, the science of linguistics has
broad and significant connections with several of the behavioral
and social science fields, especially anthropology, psychology, and
sociology.

Language and speech are the most uniquely human forms of behavior, shared (if at all) only in the most primitive way by lower
mammals such as chimpanzees or dolphins. Communication in all

its functions (informative, exhortative, persuasive, derogatory, obfuscating, divisive, or unifying) and through all its media (the printed word, radio, television) plays such a pervasive part in modern life that anything we can learn about it is bound to prove valuable in the long run.

With the development of modern technology, great advances have been made in the study of the acoustic and articulatory bases of speech. The most important invention has been the sound spectrograph, which automatically analyzes the sound waves into the amplitudes at the component frequencies (Figure 2-3). This invention also has provided the basis for effecting artificial syntheses of speech and has been useful in teaching deaf-mutes how to speak. The deaf child attempts to utter the same speech sound as the teacher by matching the spectrogram produced by the teacher on one cathode-ray tube with that which he himself produces on another.

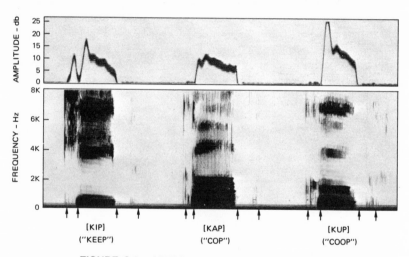

FIGURE 2-3   SPEECH SPECTROGRAPH.

Spectrograms of three words: "keep," "cop," and "coop" as spoken by an adult female. The phonetic transcription appears in brackets. The lower record shows the speech components according to frequency (the basis for pitch); the upper record, according to amplitude (the basis for loudness). Frequency is shown in kHz (1,000 cycles per second); amplitude in decibels. Note that the initial consonant is formed very differently in the three words, in anticipation of the vowel to follow. The vowels are readily distinguishable by their different frequency components, as well as by amplitude. Produced by the method of Carol Schatz. [Source: Courtesy of Dr. Dorothy A. Huntington, Stanford University.]

Applications of the findings and insights of linguistics to the solution of human problems have most often been in foreign-language teaching and in the creation of writing systems for nonliterate societies. Increasingly, however, linguistics is playing a role in dealing with complex social issues such as the language problems of urban Negroes in the United States. Many American Negroes use a variety of English sharply divergent from the dominant standard English—in some respects, a separate language is used alongside or in place of standard English. Its users are handicapped in securing an education. Full linguistic analyses of this kind of English and its patterns of use make it possible to accelerate and improve the learning of reading and other language skills by those who are held back by this divergent language. The same applies, of course, to other children, such as Puerto Ricans or Mexican-Americans, who are handicapped by the inability to use standard English.

Social class distinctions in speech are well known, both in grammatical usage ("them things") and in pronunciation. Here is an area of research in which linguistics overlaps sociology. For example, the initial consonant sound of "thing," or "three" may be made plosive (instead of labiatized) so that the speaker may say "ting" or "tree" in stigmatized forms of speech. These differences are clearly associated with social class in New York City, as shown in Figure 2-4. But this pronunciation varies with the context of speech, as well as with the social class of the speaker. Thus, when a lower-class person reads a word from a list he is more likely to pronounce it as an upper-middle-class person would than when he uses it in either casual or careful speech.

POLITICAL SCIENCE

Political science is concerned with government in all its aspects, in both theory and practice: political parties, interest groups, public opinion and communication, bureaucracy, administration, and international relations. The main subdisciplines have been political theory, politics, and administration, but as in all fields, there are new perspectives and new emphases to change old alignments. Shortly after World War II there came a vigorous development of new quantitative empirical methods associated with "political behaviorists." At first, this new approach was resisted by some who held to more classical political theory. Fortunately, the tensions that arose have

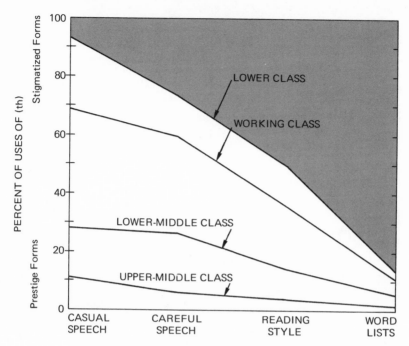

FIGURE 2-4   CLASS STRATIFICATION OF PRONUNCIATION.

The pronunciation of th as in thing, through, three, in New York City. Shown in percentages of prestige form th versus stigmatized form t, by social class and context. [Source: William Labov, "Stages in the Acquisition of Standard English," in Roger W. Shuy, ed., Social Dialects and Language Learning (Champaign, Illinois: National Council of Teachers of English, 1965), p. 83.]

largely disappeared, and now there is a recognized division of labor between the more classically oriented political theorists and the contemporary quantitatively oriented empiricists.

Facing governmental problems within the United States, political scientists have served importantly in proposing and improving city-manager forms of government and in other ways aiding in government organizations. They have contributed through election studies to the understanding of voting behavior and party allegiance.

The rise and fall of governments around the world during this century have presented many problems for research and theory. After the Allied victory in World War I, there was an upsurge of constitutional governments, but these were mostly short-lived, and a period of dictatorships, whether Communist or Fascist, preceded World War II. After World War II came the founding of many new nations, particularly in Africa and Asia.

Nation-building is now a fascinating problem for political scientists, some of whom have attempted to deal quantitatively with extremely difficult problems bearing on the rate of change as underdeveloped nations seek to modernize. People who are accustomed to being locally isolated and to living within a subsistence economy expect things to be done as they always were and tend to face life as their fathers did before them. But, through exposure to modern technology and practices, to the use of money, to trading with strangers, to dependence on distant markets, life and customs begin to change. Eventually there is a rise in literacy, the emergence of nonagricultural occupations, working for wages, urban residence, voting and other forms of political participation. These processes go on in measurable ways and constitute "social mobilization," through which people are prepared to accept the institutions of a modern state.* The correlations among these several processes constitute an indicator of political development. Once an indicator is available, it is possible to say something about the rates at which different developing groups are moving toward modern forms of political participation. Systematically collected data permit the calculation of rates of social mobilization, which replaces mere guesswork or hunches based on intuition. Movement of this kind is never very rapid; a typical rate calculated from empirical data is about 1.0 percent a year for the number of people in a developing nation who move from being classified as "nonmobilized" to "mobilized." This rate is perhaps twice as fast as calculations show it to have been in some European countries 100 years ago. Because of the slowness of some of these changes, the strife in some developing nations is likely to continue for many years to come, aggravated by conflicts between those who have adopted the new ways and those who have not.

PSYCHIATRY

Psychiatry is a branch of medicine dealing with mental, emotional, or behavior disorders; it might be thought of as an essen-

*Karl W. Deutsch, "Social Mobilization and Political Development," *American Political Science Review*, 55, September 1961, 493–514.

tially medical psychology. Its methods include psychotherapy, which is treatment by psychological means, whether in individual or group consultations or in environmental adjustments, and somatotherapy, or treatment through the body by way of drugs, hormones, electric shock, or surgery.

Psychiatry, as a well-established medical specialty, not only is a major user of the behavioral and social sciences, but also incorporates behavioral and social science into its thought and procedures.

Psychiatry is included in this report, not because of its medical role in the treatment of illness, but because of the social significance of mental hygiene, of child-rearing practices, of harmony within the family, of group conflicts as sources of emotional disturbance in individuals—all topics in which the psychiatrist and other social scientists share common concerns.

The scientific aspects of psychiatry have taken on unprecedented vigor since World War II, and particularly in the past decade. Many of its activities are interdisciplinary. For example, the serious problems of mental retardation have brought together workers from psychiatry, psychology, genetics, biochemistry, and pediatrics.

One line of research on mental retardation concerns an inherited biochemical abnormality that impairs brain development. Phenylketonuria is a typical example of one of these "inborn errors of metabolism," and it has been investigated genetically and biochemically more thoroughly than any other. This discovery, that some mentally subnormal individuals characteristically excreted in their urine large amounts of phenylpyruvic acid, was the first instance in which a specific biochemical abnormality was found to be closely linked with a severe mental impairment. Once the disorder had been recognized, additional cases were identified by screening patients in institutions for mentally retarded individuals. Phenylketonuria was then found to account for ½ to 1 percent of all severe mental subnormality.

Subsequent research was done along both biochemical and genetic lines. Biochemical research soon showed relations to particular substances that are important to metabolism and to their related enzymes, thus permitting a corrective diet for those whose phenylketonuria was detected before brain damage had been done. The genetics research showed that inheritance of the abnormality follows the pattern of a Mendelian recessive trait, but parents with a single appropriate recessive gene (not suffering from phenylketonuria) can be detected because they show, in a lesser degree, the same errors in metabolism.

These findings permit warnings to parents whose future children will have a high probability of showing phenylketonuria, and permit early detection and treatment when the condition is present. Unfortunately, the corrective diet may be harmful for infants falsely diagnosed as suffering from phenylketonuria, so that the tests, prescribed by many state laws, have to be made with extreme care and the results used with discretion.

Research on phenylketonuria (and other molecular diseases) has made fundamental contributions to genetics and medicine, has developed powerful techniques for human biochemical genetic analysis, and has pointed up sharply the relevance of biochemical approaches to brain function and behavior. An effective conjunction of basic science and clinical investigation has also made significant inroads on human suffering and disability. These advances in research on mental retardation have provided a valuable model for investigation of other serious disorders, including schizophrenia, depression, and a variety of stress reactions.

PSYCHOLOGY

Psychologists find research and service opportunities in many contexts: in colleges and universities, in industry and government, in clinical research and practice in hospitals and clinics, and in private practice. Along with anthropology, psychology has a biological heritage and a natural linkage with physiology, genetics, and medicine.

The biobehavioral emphasis in psychology has resulted in the establishment of many laboratories for the study of brain–behavior relationships. There the techniques of neuroanatomy, neurochemistry, and neurophysiology are used together with the special kinds of equipment that psychologists have developed for exploring their interests in sensory and cognitive processes, in learning, memory, and motivation. They may use birds, lower mammals, and primates as subjects of investigation. In addition, psychologists study human infants, growing children, and adults. Recent discoveries in brain mechanisms; the control of motivation through electrodes implanted in the brain or through chemical stimulation; new methods of studying the basis of learning and memory, of sleep and dreaming; and developments in behavioral genetics have created a general air of excitement in the biobehavioral laboratories.

The study of learning offers one illustration of the psychologist at work. Long a topic of interest to the psychologist in the laboratory, whether in lower animals or human subjects, the results today are contributing not only to increased knowledge of brain–behavior relationships, but also to the practical improvement of learning in schools. For example, the age-old problems of the effectiveness of rewards and punishments in learning have led to more precise study of how rewards operate. Studies of reward effectiveness have led investigators in a number of directions. Some, working with animals, have turned to the reward-related areas of the brain; electrical stimulation of some areas of the brain can serve as a reward in the same way that an attractive food does. Some investigators have shown that the effects of reward go beyond the learning of skills that use voluntary muscles; reward can be made to control such visceral activities as heart response or internal secretions in both animals and men. Among other findings, it has been determined that an act rewarded only a fraction of the times that it occurs may prove to be more strongly fixed than one regularly rewarded. Such basic laboratory studies provide the background for some important technological developments in education: programmed instruction and computer-assisted instruction.

Computer-assisted instruction in reading may serve as an example. The experiments to be described lean heavily on what has been learned through the studies of reward and through studies of memory and perception. In Figure 2-5 we see a child seated at his station (or terminal) with a display screen on his left, a cathode-ray display tube on his right, and an electric typewriter in front of him. He is wearing earphones to receive audio messages. With his electronic light pen he is now following an instruction to select the word describing the picture (a fan) on his left. Behind all this is a computer presenting messages to him, recording his responses, and deciding what he should do next.

An illustration of what the computer does is given in Figure 2-6, which is related to what is shown in Figure 2-5 but part of a different sequence. Here the learner is being taught to discriminate between the initial and final letters in a three-letter word consisting of a vowel between two consonants. In Part A he is asked for a total response, which, if successful, is "rewarded" by the commendation of Part D. If in Part A he makes an error in the final consonant, the computer sends him to Part C before he returns to Part A. If his error is in the initial consonant he goes first to Part B; whereas if his error is in both,

VISUAL PROJECTION   CATHODE-RAY TUBE   ELECTRONIC LIGHT PEN

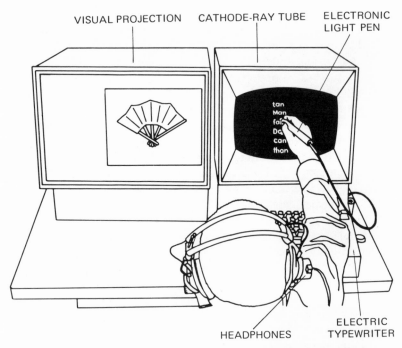

HEADPHONES

ELECTRIC TYPEWRITER

FIGURE 2-5   TERMINAL FOR COMPUTER–ASSISTED INSTRUCTION.

If the student touches the correct word ("fan"), he will be told of his success and move ahead; if not, he will be helped. [Source: After original photograph courtesy of Richard C. Atkinson, Stanford University.]

he goes first to Part B, then to Part C, and then back to Part A. When eventually successful in Part A he goes to Part D, where he gets reinforced and moves on to another sequence.

This is but a tiny segment of a very large program, but once the program is prepared and stored in the computer, individualized instruction can be given to very large numbers of children at once. In 1968 when the report from which these illustrations were taken was prepared, as many as 2,000 children were being instructed by this program simultaneously in Kentucky, Mississippi, and California using a single, time-sharing computer based in California.

Usually laboratory studies of learning have been confined to relatively short periods, but computer-assisted instruction is being carried out over several school years so that its actual feasibility will

PART A

CATHODE-RAY TUBE

Requested Response 1: Touch and say the word that belongs in the empty cell.

Correct Answer: (Branch to Part D)

Wrong Answer 1: No

rat = final → C → A
fan = initial → B → A
bat = other → B → C → A

Wrong Answer 2: No, touch and say ran
(Arrow appears by ran)

PART B

Requested Response 1: Touch the initial unit of the empty cell.

Correct Answer: Good.

Wrong Answer: (Arrow appears above the row letter r) No, this is the initial unit of the cell, so touch this. (Arrow now appears by the response letter r)

PART C

Requested Response 1: Touch and say the final unit of the cell.

Correct Answer: Good.

Wrong Answer: (Arrow appears above the column letter pair an) No, an is the final unit of the cell, so touch and say an. (Arrow now appears by the response letter pair an)

PART D

Requested Response 1: Good you have put ran in the cell. Touch and say ran.

Correct Answer: Good, ran. (Branch to next problem)

Wrong Answer: No, touch and say ran. (Arrow appears above the word ran inside the cell)

FIGURE 2-6 COMPUTER–ASSISTED INSTRUCTION IN READING.

Illustrated are the first steps in a decoding of simple consonant–vowel–consonant words, as explained in the text. [Source: Richard C. Atkinson, "Computerized Instruction and the Learning Process," *American Psychologist*, 23, April 1968, 229. Copyright 1968 by American Psychological Association and reproduced by permission.]

be known. Results already show it to be a good teaching method, and because the computer keeps accurate records, it is also a method of discovering ways to make learning more efficient. For example, it is already helping to solve a puzzling problem as to why boys have so much more trouble than girls in learning to read in the United States. The conjecture has been that boys develop more slowly than girls and that, perhaps, we are attempting to teach them to read too early. That this is not the answer is shown by the absence of sex differences in the reading skills of boys and girls when taught by the computer. A finding of this kind not only is of practical significance, but also bears on fundamental problems of the nature and development of sex differences in performance.

The basic science of the experimental and psychological laboratory and the careful psychometric and quantitative studies of individual development and social behavior have grown along with new methods that are widely applicable in education and industry and in studies of mental health. This complex, essentially pluralistic development of psychology not only has continued but also has increased in diversity as the number of persons identifiable as psychologists has increased.

SOCIOLOGY

Sociology embraces a wide range of subject matter, including the family, rural and urban life, race relations, religion, crime, political parties, populations, and social stratification. Sociologists employ many concepts to lend coherence to their accounts of social phenomena; some of these concepts are now familiar to people outside the field—for example, concepts of role, institution, social structure, norms, and conformity. Academic sociologists, to provide a firmer theoretical structure for their science, tended to withdraw for a time from concern with social welfare or social reform, which they left to the social-work profession and others. In this respect, the history of sociology contrasts sharply with that of psychology in that university psychology departments are staffed with both academicians and clinicians. More recently, academic sociologists have renewed their interests in applied sociology, but in ways different from the earlier social-welfare approaches.

Contemporary sociology continues to move toward the empirical, experimental, and quantitative, in keeping with other behavioral and social sciences. Among the more advanced quantitative fields in sociology is demography, the name given to the study of population densities, migration, and predictions of changes in the composition of the population. The survey is one of the oldest investigatory methods used by sociologists, and it finds a wide range of application.

As an illustration of data collection and analysis by sociologists, we choose a study on equality of educational opportunity, conducted in 1966.* This study is of interest for at least three reasons: (1) it demonstrates the desire of governmental bodies to be guided by the facts that social science methods can assemble, (2) it represents a very large-scale sociological investigation and makes use of survey techniques and highly complex analytical quantitative methods, (3) its acceptance (and criticism of it, as well) illustrates the problems of achieving social science responsibly related to policy.

The stimulus for the study was provided by the Supreme Court decision of 1954, which was based on the premise that separate schools for Negro and white children are inherently unequal. Ten years after this decision, Congress wanted to know to what extent desegregation had occurred. Section 402 of the Civil Rights Act of 1964 posed the problem as follows:

The Commissioner [of Education] shall conduct a survey and make a report to the President and the Congress, within two years of the enactment of this title, concerning the lack of availability of equal educational opportunities for individuals by reason of race, color, religion, or national origin in public educational institutions at all levels in the United States, its territories and possessions, and the District of Columbia.

The study, planned and completed within the specified two-year period, was of large scale. A total of 645,504 tests and other information concerning the schools were returned from school children, teachers, and principals all over the nation. As a specimen of the findings reported, consider Figure 2-7, which was derived by combining data from several figures of the original report.

Looking first at the more successful white-urban-northeast pupils, we note that they score higher than the general mean for their grades at the first-grade level and remain high throughout high school. The white-rural-south children score below the white-urban-northeast in first grade, but the differences are not great; they diverge somewhat as they get into the higher grades of school. Although both sets of Negro children score below the whites in the first grade, the Negro-urban-northeast pupil and the Negro-rural-south pupil are essentially indis-

*James S. Coleman et al., Equality of Educational Opportunity, OE-38001 (Washington, D.C.: U.S. Office of Education, 1966).

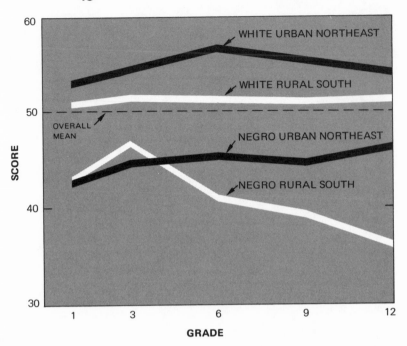

FIGURE 2-7   TEST SCORES FOR VERBAL SKILLS IN VARIOUS GRADES, ACCORDING TO RACE AND RESIDENCE.

The test scores are adjusted to a common mean of 50 at each age. [Source: James S. Coleman, "The Concept of Equality of Educational Opportunity," *Harvard Educational Review*, 38 (Winter 1968), 20, Figure 1—Patterns of Achievement in verbal skills at various levels by race and region. Copyright © 1968 by President and Fellows of Harvard College. Also in *Equal Educational Opportunity*, published by Harvard University Press, 1969.]

tinguishable in the first and third grades. Something happens thereafter, however, with the northern-urban-Negro child holding his place, and even increasing his relative standing, while the southern-rural-Negro child, on the average, falls farther and farther behind. It must be remembered that there are wide individual differences; there are always some white children scoring lower than the means for Negroes and some Negroes scoring higher than the means for whites. But the averages, particularly the increasing separation in scores of the Negro children in the rural South as compared with Negro children in the urban Northeast, indicate the impact of social influences upon learning.

The sociologists who studied equality of educational opportunity found some results in line with their expectations, but some that were surprising. They found school facilities to have somewhat less effect than expected, while other features—such as the predominant family backgrounds of the students in a given school or the predominant nature of fellow students—were more important than expected. The performance of the deprived child who happens to go to a school where the more favored families and students predominate, turns out to score higher than would otherwise be predicted.

The report has, in fact, stirred up a certain amount of controversy. Some critics have objected to the use of a score on verbal facility as the primary instrument for assessing educational achievement, because it is known that some groups have a language handicap; others are concerned about the use of districts (rather than individual schools) as the basis for assessing expenditures and facilities; still others believe there may be biases from nonresponses that always plague large surveys of this sort. Furthermore, the form of multiple regression analysis used in the study is a very complex tool and, when given a causal interpretation, can lead to faulty inferences. Some critics have argued that when the variables are entered in different combinations, different results are produced. No single study in an area as complex as this can settle all problems at once.

Another example of sociological research is provided by studies of social mobility. Except for societies with rigid caste divisions, there is always considerable mobility, both upward and downward. This has been true in Europe and Japan as well as in the United States (Table 2-2). Comparable studies show intermarriages across class lines to be roughly equivalent in frequency in all these countries. What holds true with respect to social mobility at any one time may not be true for all time, and this is one reason sociologists continue to do research in this important area. The opportunities for upward social mobility within the white population in the United States appear, by more recent studies, to be increasing rather than decreasing, but for nonwhites the evidence is that those born into families at the lower levels are likely to stay there, and those born into families at higher levels are likely to move down.

STATISTICS

Statistical methods are so important to U.S. social science that statistical specialties and statistical research are found in every

TABLE 2-2 SOCIAL MOBILITY: CHANGES IN OCCUPATIONAL CLASS FOR SUCCEEDING GENERATIONS OF NONFARM POPULATION

Country	Mobile Upward (fathers manual workers; sons nonmanual)	Mobile Downward (fathers nonmanual; sons manual workers)
United States	33%	26%
Germany	29	32
Sweden	31	24
Japan	36	22
France	39	20
Switzerland	45	13

Source: Seymour M. Lipset and Reinhard Bendix, *Social Mobility in Industrial Society* (Berkeley, California: University of California Press, 1959), p. 25.

one of the social science disciplines, and the teaching of statistics is a concern of all the disciplines in the training of graduate students. Because statisticians are also closely affiliated with mathematicians, many of their common concerns are represented in a mathematics report, paralleling this one, published by the National Academy of Sciences.* While statistics as a discipline has not been surveyed in this study, its contributions to the behavioral and social sciences, and the related ones of mathematics and computation, are covered in a special panel report. A short statement of these contributions appears also in Chapter 3 of this volume.

THE BROADER DOMAIN

Disciplines as defined by departments in universities, by professional societies, and by titles are always being formed and, less frequently, disappearing. The newest discipline in this survey, by this kind of definition, is linguistics, in which some 31 institutions have doctorate-granting departments that meet the criteria of the survey. Had it been our purpose we could have found a great assortment of PhD-granting departments with new names: behavioral science, demography, communications, social psychology, and social relations. Doubtless some new department names will become more general as the new disciplines crystallize, as they have in other fields (biochemistry and biophysics, for example). A growing area of social science promising to become a new discipline, but not included in this survey, is communications, which has tended to be separated from the familiar department of journalism as new mass media increase in importance. Communications as a field of study deals more with the contents and effectiveness of messages than with the details of speech and language (as does linguistics); with newspapers, radios, and television; and with the newer educational technologies (teaching machines and computer-assisted instruction). Some of the more important research on the impact of television on children has been conducted in such departments; these departments also become concerned with research bearing on the improvement of mass communications in developing nations.

When important social problems begin to command wide attention, as in the developing nations following World War II, or as in the

*The Mathematical Sciences: A Report, NAS Pub. 1681 (Washington, D.C.: National Academy of Sciences, 1968).

crises in American cities, research organizations develop on the margins of the established disciplines, bringing new types of collaboration and the redefinition of intellectual problems. Thus, research on population problems or urban renewal calls for economists, political scientists, sociologists, statisticians, city planners, architects, engineers, and interested citizens to work together to make the necessary studies and to evolve plans. Similarly, a new nation in Africa is likely to seek a wide body of experts to assist in ordering its economy and in improving its health standards and educational system. Out of this work come generalizations that can be used elsewhere; if the generalizations are carefully worked out and documented, they become contributions to the body of social science knowledge.

The professional schools such as business, education, law, medicine, public administration, and social work not only make use of the social sciences but also initiate their own research and instruction in behavioral and social science areas; they are represented in a limited way in our survey by psychiatry. Public health and medical economics programs are offered in the medical schools; industrial relations, management science, and marketing, in schools of business; and the many problems of law and society, in the law schools. Within schools of social work, doctorates are beginning to be offered more widely. Education is an enormous social enterprise, reaching into every community and every home. It is represented in this survey chiefly by educational psychology, but this does not by any means exhaust the social science impact of education, because the study of educational quality, reported earlier, is a sociological investigation, not a psychological one. The economics of education is also an active research area.

Some of the broader domain that is missed when exclusive attention is given to the component disciplines appears in the names of research institutes, which are neither in departments nor in professional schools —names such as human development, man–environment relations, urban studies, poverty and disadvantaged groups, coordination of public services, technology and society, and comparative study of new nations. The opportunities before the behavioral and social scientists in many instances lie in these borderline areas in which the disciplines overlap each other and neighboring disciplines.

Although unity among the behavioral and social sciences has not yet been realized, many of these joint efforts will bring individuals with different training into closer communication, and the result will be greater mutual understanding and, ultimately, a further reduction of the boundaries between the disciplines.

3
RESEARCH METHODS AND INSTRUMENTATION

The research capabilities of the behavioral and social sciences have been increased by the development of methods and instruments appropriate to the problems investigated. Consequently, a greater range of individual behavior and of institutional arrangements can be subjected to empirical study, and larger bodies of data can be analyzed and interpreted more rapidly.

DATA COLLECTION THROUGH NONEXPERIMENTAL OBSERVATIONS

The most distinctive method of science is the experimental method, in which, once a problem is defined, methods are devised for bringing the relevant variables under control and measurement, usually in a laboratory. But this is by no means the only method of science. Science begins with the observation of natural events, and these events have to be observed where they take place, as in the study of infants at home with their mothers or of legislative decisions in Congress. Many significant events of social life take place in the home, in the school, in the factory, or in the political arena, and behavioral and social scientists have had to find ways to make and refine their observations of such events. They have developed a number of methods for collecting data in the field, with a minimum of disturbance of the phenomena being observed.

Field Observation

In the field—where events are occurring now, or have occurred in the past—making relevant notes based on observation of behavior, or on the environment in which behavior takes place, is a long-established procedure in anthropology, history, sociology, and other areas of study. While biologists long have made fieldtrips (recall Darwin and the voyage of the *Beagle*), an upsurge of interest in naturalistic observations among anthropologists, psychiatrists, and psychologists has taken place owing to the careful field observations of a group of European biologists calling themselves ethologists. This group has observed that the social behavior of baboons, chimpanzees, and gorillas in their native habitats is so different from their behavior in captivity that only field observation can elicit the knowledge of intergroup accommodations and hostilities that lead to an understanding of the evolution of behavior. When the historian walks the field of an early battle, or follows the route of an early explorer, he discovers things that documents alone do not tell him. Firsthand observation of a riot by a sociologist gives him data that newspaper accounts may either omit or distort. Field observations, including those of archeologists, are expensive in man-hours, travel, and equipment. Modern motion-picture and sound-recording equipment greatly increases the accuracy of observations in the field, but such records taken over extended periods of time have to be processed and analyzed. Consider the costs and special problems of recording an unwritten language with all its nuances, as spoken by children and adults, in order that a written form can be provided, or a grammar and a dictionary prepared.

The Survey

The survey in its various forms (factual surveys, opinion surveys, market surveys, surveys of voting behavior) is not only the best known but also one of the most widely used research tools in the social sciences. It finds its place in anthropology, economics, geography, political science, psychology, and sociology. It is also one of the earliest social science tools, dating back to Sir Frederick M. Eden's survey, *State of the Poor*, published in England in 1791.

The technique of survey research proceeds essentially by the following steps: (1) Data are needed for some purpose, such as for an estimate of changes in the cost of living. The kinds of data required have to be established; for example, what goods shall be considered necessities of modern life? When a search of available sources shows that the information is not available, new data must be collected. The sources of the data required must be determined; for example, the retail prices in stores where consumers make their needed purchases. (2) A form of inquiry must be developed to secure accurate information at the source. Choices have to be made of instruments of inquiry, such as questionnaires, interviews, or financial reports (for the example used above, it could involve an actual checking of prices on store shelves). The data-collection procedure is usually tried out in a pretest to ensure that the data can be obtained in the form desired through the particular instrument selected. (3) A sampling procedure has to be designed. It is obviously impossible (were it possible, it would be wasteful) to price goods on every store shelf. Hence, a sample must be prepared to represent the stores in which people in communities of various sizes and in different parts of the country purchase their necessities. (4) Effective management is required in the conduct of a survey, making the necessary checks on the accuracy of the data at the source, and assembling the data in some central place. (5) Finally, the data are analyzed, estimates of error are made (both measurement errors and sampling errors), and then inferences are drawn. Clearly, the survey must be repeated at intervals in order to show what changes occurred. It is evident, even from this brief description, that a well-conducted survey is no simple matter, and if important decisions rest upon its conclusions, that every effort has to be made to ensure the most accurate results possible. Every degree of improvement in accuracy costs effort and dollars.

The importance of surveys for economic analysis is illustrated by the Monthly Survey of the Labor Force, which has been the basis for estimates of national unemployment since 1937. An annual survey of consumer finances has been conducted by the University of Michigan's Survey Research Center since 1947, initially with the support and cooperation of the Federal Reserve Board. These surveys have made it possible to assess the intentions of consumers to save or to spend in months ahead, and have permitted quite accurate predictions of planned purchasing for the year ahead of durable goods such as automobiles and air-conditioners. The Consumer Price Index, also based on a survey technique, serves the important purpose of measuring the aspects of inflation or deflation that affect the consumer; this index is tied to wages in some union contracts. These and other surveys of industry and agriculture have considerable significance for economic and social policies.

The Interview

The interview is a method of obtaining information directly from individuals; it is familiar in daily life and becomes an instrument of social science when it is used with precision. The standardized interview, in which those interviewed must answer a given set of questions and the replies are recorded by specially trained interviewers, is often used in surveys. The personal interview has an advantage over questionnaires and other means of obtaining information, because a skilled interviewer can follow up leads through supplementary questions, thus utilizing unanticipated comments of the respondent. Unstandardized interviews are used in a variety of settings, as in interviews between psychiatrists or clinical psychologists and patients, or in field interviews by anthropologists.

A number of methodological and technical problems arise in connection with interviewing. The whole question of "interviewer bias" or, more generally, "interviewer effects" has been studied in a number of contexts. The social class, race, or sex of an interviewer may affect the answers he obtains. If the interviewer allows his own opinions or beliefs to intrude into the interview, or if the phrasing of the questions provokes a particular frame of mind, the responses will be biased. Research has provided a rational and empirical basis for interviewer training and supervision. No well-directed survey organization would consider conducting a study without both intensive preliminary training for interviewers and repeated consultation, during the course of the study, with field supervisors.

The Case Study

Because of the complexity of the behavior of individuals and of institutions, it is often profitable to examine the impact of many concurrent circumstances on the course of their development. When one unit is selected for study and a "scientific biography" developed, the method is known as a case study. The method is familiar in the study of individual careers, educational or vocational advancement, illness, crime, drug addiction, growth of businesses, and cumulative court actions in particular kinds of legal cases. An Inter-University Case Program in political science and public administration has been in existence for many years and has led to the publication of volumes of cases useful to students. Historians often find that the biography of an individual or a study of a single institution can illuminate a whole class of simultaneous events.

From time to time, methodological disputes arise over the case method in social science. Most case studies are retrospective, and retrospective accounts tend to be selective in what has been recorded.

Without sufficient control over what is recorded and what is omitted, the danger of *post hoc ergo propter hoc* reasoning is often present; effects attributed to a dramatic event might have transpired even if that event had not occurred. Modern methods of data accumulation make new kinds of case studies possible, but run the risk of invasion of privacy, a subject discussed later in this report (Chapters 7 and 8). Any method can be used well or badly, and although the case method may have its weaknesses, when it is used well it can yield data that can be assembled to good effect in no other way.

Test Methods

The unstandardized test, in the form of a written essay examination, has been used in education for centuries, but the standardized test as a scientific instrument is a product of this century. Because it can be administered in a school, a factory, or an office, a great mass of data can be obtained without too great an inconvenience to those tested.

The difference between a *standardized test*, as used chiefly by psychologists and educators, and the more usual course examination is that the former has been carefully constructed in accordance with the purposes intended, with carefully designed, unambiguous questions, often graded in difficulty. Such a test meets criteria of *reliability* (degree of self-consistency on repeated tests or between tests with alternate forms) and *validity* (predictive value in relation to its intended purposes). Furthermore, a standardized test is provided with *norms*—that is, with empirically derived scoring standards—so that it is possible to tell where a score falls in relation to other scores. Test standardization has become a complex field of study. Through such agencies as the Educational Testing Service at Princeton, New Jersey, tests have become widely available for use in schools, colleges, and universities. In addition to the widely known intelligence test, many other tests for occupational abilities, attitudes, personality, and esthetic preference have been developed. Tests of personality, emotionality, and other nonintellectual traits have not been as fully developed as have the intelligence test or the tests of school achievement, but they have great promise.

The Longitudinal Study

The longitudinal study cuts across the methods of case study and of testing. The case study is retrospective and the test is contemporary; the longitudinal study collects contemporary information (as in the test) but it does so repeatedly, over time, so that in the end the history of a case has been built up from information that was contemporary when collected. The longitudinal method can be used for the study of organizations and institutions as well as for individuals. The advantage, of course, is that the contemporary information can be collected in standardized ways, avoiding retrospective omission or falsification; the disadvantages are the long time consumed and the amount of irrelevant information necessarily stored and processed. Consider, for example, what would be involved in studying the smoking habits of people who develop lung cancer late in life. A very large number of people would have to be studied at intervals over their lives to ensure ending up with at least a few with lung cancer. While abstractly this is the correct design, in practice it is easier to ask a sample of people with lung cancer and those without what their smoking practices were earlier, even if some errors of reporting occur. The same considerations apply to studying the early childhoods of people who later develop mental illness or become distinguished scientists.

Despite its difficulties, however, the longitudinal method is the only way of getting firm information, as, for example, on some aspects of the highly important problems of child development. A pioneer study of a group of gifted children was begun at Stanford in 1921, and continues today on these "children," who are now in later middle life or nearing retirement. The "promise of youth" could thus be ascertained. It has been found, for example, that while the bright children remained bright throughout their lives, their relative successes as effective adults were more closely related to personality factors (motivation or emotional stability) than to their intelligence. Without evidence collected when they were children, there would be no basis for these findings. Among other long-continuing studies are the Harvard Growth Study and two University of California (Berkeley) growth studies.

To retain the advantages of longitudinal studies, while avoiding the disadvantages, compromise methods are being developed so that overlapping age groups can be used; for example, three groups, of ages 0 through 5, 5 through 10, and 10 through 15, studied simultaneously, would provide a 15-year span in a 6-year study. By appropriate checks (including retrospective accounts for those begun at the later years) many of the advantages of the longitudinal study can be preserved without undue commitments of time by investigators (or by the supporting agencies).

The Analysis of Documents

Along with newly collected data, social scientists often depend on existing materials, especially documents of various kinds. This is especially true in history, in which the records of the past are studied for scholarly purposes. Historians developed methods of authentication of documents, an important step prior to their use as evidence, as early as the eighteenth century. Special techniques, known collectively as *content analysis*, have been developed in this century for the study of many forms of communication—their nature, their underlying meanings, and their changes through time.

Thus, for example, some shifts in political position can be detected in the number and frequency of emotionally toned words a speaker uses or the targets of his attacks. Political scientists have used content analysis of published documents, such as newspapers, with remarkably good results in analyzing societies, such as Stalin's Russia or mainland China today.

Simple counts of relevant words often lead to detection of political shifts that would not be noticed by a person listening to or reading a succession of speeches. This method also has other uses. It has been used, for example, to determine that James Madison, rather than Alexander Hamilton, wrote some of the *Federalist Papers*, whose authorship has been in dispute. This was done by counting the frequency of use of words in papers known to have been written by each man and comparing their frequencies with those in the disputed papers.*

THE EXPERIMENTAL METHOD

The experimental method is characterized by observations made under specially planned conditions, usually involving some intervention by the experimenter to obtain more precise control of the conditions under which his observations are made. It is for purposes of such control that most experiments are conducted in specially equipped laboratories.

It is a mistake, however, to conceive of an experiment exclusively as something done within the walls of a laboratory. The essential feature

*Frederick Mosteller and David L. Wallace, *Inference and Disputed Authorship: The Federalist* (Reading, Mass.: Addison–Wesley Publishing Company, Inc., 1964).

of an experiment is its design, and it does not matter whether the observations are made on crops growing in fields or on traffic moving along a highway. The design is experimental when some control is exercised, as in the selection of seeds planted in the plots or of traffic signs used selectively on comparable highways. Study of the effects on tooth decay of fluorine in drinking water illustrates how experimentation can be done in a naturalistic setting *if* some communities fluoridate their water while others do not. An endless variety of experiments of this general type can be done in the behavioral and social sciences, for example, in comparing different types of school practice, the treatment of prisoners, or the effects of variations in entrance fees on the use of recreational facilities. Experiments are under way by economists and sociologists to test various proposals for a guaranteed annual income or a negative income tax (providing an income supplement for a family below a stated income level instead of an income tax). Such experiments have to be done in the communities concerned, under circumstances as similar as possible to those that would be met were such proposals eventually adopted.

Everything that goes on in formal laboratories does not necessarily conform to standard experimental designs. The laboratory is a place, for example, where findings from archeological sites can be dated by carbon-14 methods, and where bone fragments can be identified by the physical anthropologist, neither of these requiring conventional experimental designs.

However, the more formal laboratory is a boon to science, because there precision instruments can be maintained and conditions can be controlled so that variations in some initial circumstances or conditions can be studied in relation to their outcomes, and lawful relationships can be established.

The Psychological Laboratory

As we shall see in Chapter 10, psychological laboratories are now the best equipped for laboratory experimentation among the behavioral and social sciences.* The development of psychological laboratories has been going on for about 100 years. Laboratories of comparative and physiological psychology include animal colonies, sometimes in laboratory quarters, sometimes in field stations of more

---

*Laboratories in departments of psychiatry have not been included in this comparison because clinical service in the hospital, including the costs of patient care, adds an element that is incommensurate with the activities of the other behavioral science disciplines.

naturalistic sort. The related laboratory equipment includes rooms for surgery and, when brain surgery is employed, the requisite equipment of microtomes for sectioning damaged portions of the brain and other equipment needed to prepare slides for detailed study. If the experiments involve hormones or other pharmacological agents (as many of them now do) equipment for biochemical analyses is also needed. An array of electronic amplifiers and recorders is used in connection with neurophysiology.

Much of this equipment is also used in biobehavioral studies of human subjects. While many of these devices were developed in the anatomical and physiological sciences, other devices—such as mazes, lever-pressing boxes in which animal learning is studied, choice-reaction apparatus—have been invented by the psychologists themselves. The computer has come to be an important aid in the actual conduct of experiments; for example, in presenting stimuli in some planned order to many animal subjects at once and in keeping track of the results. In addition, it is used increasingly for the continuous monitoring of physiological and behavioral variables, eliminating the tedium previously associated with this task and increasing the accuracy of outcomes.

Special apparatus for use with human subjects was developed early in connection with the study of speed of reaction, of sensory processes, and of learning and memory. New methods and instruments have evolved with the associated technical developments in light sources, sound sources, and time measurement. A modern tachistoscope (an instrument for the very brief presentation of visual stimuli, such as dot patterns, words, numbers, or pictures of objects) can now present stimuli to either eye at intervals of less than 0.001 second and up, controlling the "on" effects and "off" effects by maintaining constant illumination of the background. Such control is necessary in the study, for example, of masking effects of successive stimuli or of subliminal perception.

Other fields of psychology, such as child psychology and social psychology, have built upon psychology's experience in the laboratory and have developed laboratories of their own for types of inquiry not conventionally found within experimental psychology. Some psychology departments have their own nursery schools, which serve as child laboratories paralleling the animal laboratories. There is obviously an advantage in having children present regularly for studies of development of language, cognitive functioning, creative activity, leadership, and other social interactions.

Social psychologists have developed laboratories for studies of audience reaction, the emergence of leadership in small groups, reactions to persuasive messages, and a variety of other interactions. These are often equipped with intercommunication and registering devices—sometimes closed-circuit television—to provide adequate recorded material for subsequent analysis of the behavior that occurs in the experiments.

Laboratories in the Other Disciplines

The equipment used in psychology has been specified in some detail because psychological laboratories usually have the most varied apparatus. Laboratories are also widely used in anthropology, particularly in connection with the museums often associated with anthropology departments. As noted previously, the laboratory work need not be experimental in the formal laboratory sense, yet may use complex equipment in solving the problems presented by anthropological materials. Sociology departments, particularly in their social psychology research (which has developed alongside of or in collaboration with psychology departments), have often used small-group research or audience-response measures in laboratory settings. Political scientists have done some experimentation involving simulation of political conferences. The computer has become an aid in all fields; hence some kind of instrumentation is likely to be found in all departments. The special use of speech spectrographs in linguistics has already been mentioned (see Figure 2-3).

THE QUANTITATIVE METHODOLOGIES: THE MATHEMATICAL SCIENCES

Because the scientific method consists of a logic of discovery, ordering, and validation of knowledge, scientific research rests very heavily on techniques by which measurements are made and enter into computations. Thus, the behavioral and social sciences, like other sciences, rely heavily upon the mathematical sciences, especially mathematics, statistics, and computation. Mathematics, statistics, and computation are so intertwined with the social sciences that a portion of this survey deals with those mathematical sciences. Other mathematical sciences, for example, operations analysis, might be added; the emphasis of this section, however, is on mathematics proper, statistics, and computation.

Growth of the application of the mathematical sciences to the social sciences is reflected in the establishment of new journals, such as the *Journal of Mathematical Psychology*; in the publication of textbooks and monographs; in a growing concern about relevant questions concerning curricula in academic social science departments, such as concern about the mathematical backgrounds of entering graduate students; and in the activities of new organizational structures—for example, the Mathematical Social Science Board and the former Committee on Mathematical Training of Social Scientists of the Social Science Research Council.

Mathematics

Mathematics is important to the social sciences, as to any science, in two ways. First, mathematics provides instruments for manipulation and calculation. The most familiar example of this, of course, is ordinary arithmetic, but we are more concerned here with nonnumerical manipulations, such as calculus manipulations relating to rates of change (derivatives) and algebraic manipulations of complex relationships. Such manipulative uses of mathematics are employed throughout the social sciences; often they are resisted at first but, later, taken for granted. Examples are the extensive use of calculus in theoretical economics and the use of the algebra of relations in anthropology and linguistics.

The second function of mathematics in the social sciences relates to the construction and analysis of formal mathematical models for particular fields of study. An example is the axiomatization of the concept of utility, an endeavor that interests psychologists, economists, and sociologists.

The historical development of mathematics has been closely connected with its applications in the physical sciences. There are indications that applications in the social sciences are now beginning, in turn, to have an influence on mathematics (for example, game theory or linear and more general programming), and it is likely that we will see further influences, in both directions, between mathematics and the social sciences.

Statistics

The great variability of people, and groups of people, together with difficulties in measuring their characteristics, have required the use of statistical methods in the social sciences almost from their start. Some important statistical concepts, like that of factor analysis, have come directly from social science settings, in this case, from the measurement by psychologists of individual abilities.

That statistics are used throughout the social sciences is evident from the examples of social science investigations described in Chapter 2; every one of those examples has important statistical aspects. In some examples, like that of the Coleman report (discussed in Chapter 2), statistical problems and analyses are crucial.

In one sense, "statistics" refers to collections of numerical facts about population, trade, and so forth. It is important, although not easy, to collect such facts carefully and accurately, but "statistics" today has a much more comprehensive meaning. Present-day statisticians use a wide variety of methods and create new devices for reaching conclusions from the necessarily imperfect observations of any science. In addition, statisticians are concerned with the effective design of surveys and experiments. In their thinking about design and analysis, statisticians typically rely upon mathematics, and, in particular, upon the theory of probability.

A critical concept in statistics is the fallibility of observations. The census enumerator who asks a citizen's age sometimes gets a wrong answer because of memory lapse, vanity, or carelessness of the respondent. The psychologist measuring intelligence, or other characteristic, by a standardized test knows that if he could give the test twice to the same person (with the effects of memory and practice removed) he would usually obtain two different results. Two important questions are: What is the magnitude of observational fallibility? and What can be done to mitigate and minimize its effects? In connection with these two questions, census statisticians and psychological statisticians have done much research in efforts to understand and mitigate the fallibility of observations.

Another central statistical concept is that of sampling. It is often impossible or inefficient to obtain data on all members of a population. Even when there is a legal requirement to do so, as in the case of the U.S. Census, special sampling is carried out to help fill in the gaps of the Census and to obtain census-like information between full censuses. A major advantage of sampling is that highly trained observers can be used for the enumeration, whereas, complete coverage of a sizable population almost inevitably requires a large staff and, thus, employment of generally less experienced enumerators.

Sampling inevitably entails fluctuations in the data collected in successive samples, and much statistical study has centered on understanding these fluctuations. Contrary to some popular impressions, huge samples are not, as a rule, needed to reduce sampling fluctuations to reasonable levels. To determine the number of Americans who see a dentist at least once a year, a properly chosen sample of a few hundred, or at most a thousand, would give an answer sufficiently precise for many purposes—provided the respondents gave accurate answers. Also, contrary to some popular impressions, the sample size needed for a given level of accuracy does not usually depend on the size of the population. For the same accuracy in obtaining the dental information, one would use approximately the same sample size for the population of Chicago as for the entire population of the United States.

Perhaps the most widely used and influential statistical methods are those associated with sample surveys, and some of the best-known surveys are of public opinion, especially public opinion on politics. Here, problems of *nonsampling* error become serious; concern for obtaining truthful answers increases when the questions depend on revealing preferences for political candidates. Lying, refusing to answer, and misunderstanding of the question are among the difficulties faced by opinion surveyors. To surmount these difficulties, special experimental surveys are needed along with cooperation from social scientists and statisticians. One must keep in mind that political public opinion polls are more useful for understanding basic political phenomena, such as age differences in voting patterns or shifts in party loyalty, than for predicting who will be elected President next week.

As a smaller-scale example of the use of statistics in the social sciences, one may cite the role of statistics in exploring social attitudes by observation of behavior rather than by asking questions. One instance of this dealt with the seating of students in college classrooms. The basic observations were the numbers of pairs of adjacent seats occupied by Negro and white students. If such adjacencies were more common in one school than another, this would imply something about differences in social attitudes. But clearly one cannot look simply at the number of adjacencies; the total numbers of students and the proportions of Negro and white students would also clearly affect the results—quite aside from social attitudes—and the use of statistics in this study was to provide a yardstick that would eliminate, at least in part, the effects of different class sizes and different proportions of Negro students. A second use was to aid analysis of the resulting modified numbers of pairs of adjacent seats, for example, to help

TABLE 3-1 INCREASING COST OF COMPUTERS PER HOUR; DECREASING COST PER COMPUTATION

Means	Technical Innovation	Time To Do One Multiplication	Cost of Machine per Hour	Cost of 125 Million Multiplications [a]
Desk calculator	Mechanical	10 sec	$ 0.20	$2,150,000
Harvard Mark I	Electromechanical	1 sec	12.50	850,000
ENIAC	Electronic	10 ms [b]	25.00	12,800
UNIVAC I (Type D)	Large memory	2 ms	50.00	4,300
UNIVAC 1103 (Type C)	Magnetic core	500 μs [c]	70.00	1,420
IBM 7094 (Type B)	Modern transistor	25 μs	140.00	132
Stretch (IBM 7030; Type A)	Parallel circuits	2.5 μs	320.00	29

[a] Assumes need of two operators per machine at $6 per hour each, except for desk calculator, which requires only one operator.
[b] ms = millisecond (1/1,000 sec).
[c] μs = microsecond (1/1,000,000 sec).
Source: *Digital Computer Needs in Universities and Colleges*, NAS-NRC Pub. 1233 (Washington, D.C.: National Academy of Sciences–National Research Council, 1966), p. 105.

decide whether an apparent difference between two schools arose by chance or was clearly real.

Statistical questions arise in many discussions of public policy. How accurate are unemployment statistics, military statistics, crime statistics, or automobile-safety statistics? Can one sensibly interpret statistics on relative standards of living among different countries? A central difficulty here is the human tendency to accept cited statistics as absolute truth, or else to condemn all statistics. Greater stress is needed—in and out of government—on the study of the accuracy of collected statistics. No serious program of data collection should be without a parallel program directed toward understanding and improving accuracy. No publication of collected statistics should be without a discussion of the magnitude of possible errors.

Computation

The amazingly rapid growth in the available capacity and speed of computational equipment over the last 20 years has profoundly affected research methods in the social sciences (Table 3-1).* Mathematical and statistical analyses, on a scale formerly almost inconceivable, are now standard. For example, enormous data files can now be maintained, revised, and searched automatically in a small fraction of the time and of the cost required only a few years ago. Complicated simulations of social processes for which reasonable mathematical models exist can be run through in very short time. Similarly, lengthy regression or correlation statistical analyses can be carried out quickly and in variations (including several transformations of the variates).

The changes have been so rapid that they are by no means fully understood or digested. Formerly, each of a limited number of tables constructed from sample data was run off and examined by the researcher before he decided which tables to publish; now, automatic methods of data processing exist that allow the investigator to ask machines to examine a very large set of tables and to choose from these the ones that are most informative. Those chosen for publication come from this subset. Thus, high-speed computers make it possible to come much closer than before to examining every possible result from a sample survey.

---

*Even a table as recently published as this one is by now outmoded by new computers such as CDC-6600, IBM 360-85, or UNIVAC 1108.

Some social scientists have made excellent use of the new computational facilities in, for example, enormous input-output analyses of current economics; while others have explored the great potential of the machine for computer-guided teaching. But some attempted uses have been expensive failures or, still worse, unrecognized failures. The computer is a glorious slave, but it is a slave that will do only what it is told.

Society is facing problems of a different kind because of modern computational abilities. An important example comes from our ability to store and manipulate great quantities of data. The pressure to extend and combine government files on individuals is growing, partly because of potential economy, and partly because of the opportunities thus provided for better understanding of society, thus permitting more sensible social actions. These advantages must be balanced against the dangers of invasion of individual privacy arising from centralized machine files, a problem that is discussed further in Chapter 7.

It would be a serious mistake, however, to allow rightful cautions to prevent our celebrating the gains to the behavioral and social sciences that the computer has already brought and that it will bring in the future. Some of the emphases in later chapters on large-scale social research relate directly to the new-found capacity to store, retrieve, consolidate, and draw inferences from masses of data.

4
BASIC RESEARCH
IN THE
SCIENCES OF BEHAVIOR

Science, as we have observed, has a dual function. It serves man's search for the tools he needs to cope with his environment; at the same time, it satisfies his strong urge to explore and understand the world around him—an urge that in our time has taken man to the moon. In justifying the claims they place on society for support of their work, scientists, quite understandably, stress primarily the benefits that can be derived from the application of scientific knowledge to the problems of society. But, it would misrepresent science as a whole and its human significance to put exclusive emphasis on application and to ignore the curiosity and intellectual drive that provide a major part of the fascination of science for scientist and layman alike. Indeed, we must eat and be clothed. But we need also to explore, to understand, to perceive, and to admire the beauty and intricate construction of the natural phenomena around us.

The behavioral sciences share with the physical and biological sciences this dual concern for application and understanding—for mastering phenomena and standing in wonder of them. In this chapter, we should like to give some examples of lawfulness and pattern in human and social phenomena. Some of these examples have important practical implications, which we shall mention. However, the principal purpose of the chapter will be to illustrate how the application of scientific method to human affairs can reveal underlying order in the midst of superficial randomness and complexity—to show that man is a part of nature, not just a contingent intruder into an otherwise lawful world.

69

WHAT CAN WE REMEMBER?

How much can a man hold in memory for a short time, without painstaking "memorization"? The answer, which is surprisingly consistent over many different kinds of tasks and quite consistent among different persons, is that he can retain in short-term memory about seven "chunks" of information, a chunk being any unit of information that is thoroughly familiar to him, such as a number, a familiar word, or the name of a friend. This limit of seven chunks of immediate retention explains some familiar everyday phenomena; for example, that most of us can—though not easily—keep in mind a phone number from the time we look it up to the time we dial it. It also explains the "magic" in certain memory tricks; for example, by recoding data, information can be compressed into fewer chunks, and thus more items can be retained. The digit sequence 1, 4, 9, 2 decreases from four chunks to one if it is recognized as 1492, the year Columbus discovered America. It is now fairly well established that unusual feats of short-term memory rely primarily on mastery of such recoding techniques, rather than on highly special individual "talents."

Performance of many daily life tasks depends on this capacity limit of short-term memory. It is the main limit on doing simple arithmetic without paper and pencil, on speed of operating a desk calculating machine, on a pilot's retention and use of information from instrument-panel displays, and on a pianist's sight-reading performance. Discovery of the seven-chunk memory limit and its high degree of constancy over tasks has provided machine designers and methods analysts with a key piece of information about the capabilities of the human operator. Tasks can be designed so as not to impose excessive memory demands on the operator, and the design limits can be approximately set in advance without elaborate and time-consuming trial-and-error experimentation.

Exploring the processes and mechanisms underlying the seven-chunk limit led to the discovery of other unsuspected memory mechanisms—for example, the so-called Sperling visual memory. In this experiment, an array of five rows of five letters each is exposed on a screen for a fraction of a second. Five seconds after the array has disappeared from the screen, the subject is asked to reproduce the letters. The result can be predicted from the seven-chunk rule: if the letters make up five-letter words, he can usually reproduce all; if they are random sequences of letters, he can reproduce little more than one row. Next, an array is exposed as before, but one tenth second after its disappearance, the subject is asked to reproduce the letters in a specific row—the fourth row, say. He will usually respond without error. Thus, he must be able to hold all twenty-five chunks, not just seven, for a very short time. The time turns out to be of the order of a second, and the memory mechanism that retains the visual display for this time is usually called the Sperling memory, after its discoverer.

When aural rather than visual memory is explored in depth, equally interesting but quite different phenomena appear. Some of the most striking experiments involve feeding information to the two ears separately. When a string of digits is recited to one ear, and a string of letters, in alternation, to the other, the listener finds it easiest to recall all the digits, then all the letters, rather than to recall the interwoven series in the order in which he heard them. But the result is the same, even if the letters are not presented to one ear and the digits to the other, but if, instead, they are allocated at random. It continues to be easier to recite digits first and then letters, than to recite the itemized series in temporal order, or even to recite the items presented to one ear first and then those presented to the other ear. These experiments show that, even at the moment of listening, a great deal of sorting out and processing is being imposed on incoming messages before they are "heard" or stored in temporary memory.

It should not be supposed that these simple memory phenomena apply only to simple tasks like remembering digits or letters. Human performance in much more difficult symbolic tasks—for example, in solving algebra problems—has now been analyzed in considerable detail, with the finding that limits of short-term memory play a major role in successful performance. A major factor in success is application to the task of a strategy that does not require retention of more than seven chunks. How do successful problem-solvers acquire their strategies, and why don't the unsuccessful ones acquire them? The answers to those questions would have obvious applications to practical problems of learning and teaching. They have not yet been answered, but they suggest an exciting and important direction for future research on human problem-solving.

THE SIZE OF THINGS

Puzzling regularities in nature, seemingly arbitrary and coincidental, are actually tell-tale clues to underlying lawful processes that the scientist seeks to reveal. One such regularity that was observed in a considerable number of apparently unrelated phenomena was the so-called rank-size law. Finding mechanisms to explain this apparent similarity among widely diverse phenomena was a provocative challenge to theorists. Some answers have been found, and like answers to most good questions, these have led to new phenomena and new questions.

The rank-size law is best explained by describing how it was first observed. In the late nineteenth century, several linguists discovered a surprising regularity in the relative contributions of very frequent words and of rare words to any body of text. It is well known that certain words, like "of," occur rather frequently, while other words, like "conundrum," occur quite infrequently. Of course, the frequency of any specific word may vary widely from one text to another. Suppose, however, that you arrange the various words that occur in a particular text in the order of their frequency of occurrence—first the word that occurred most often in that text, then the word that occurred next most often, and so on. The observed regularity—which holds to a surprisingly good approximation—is that the tenth word on your list will occur about one tenth as often as the first word, the hundredth word about one hundredth as often as the first word (or one tenth as often as the tenth word), and so on. Why should this be? Why should the balance between frequent and rare words be exactly the same in the daily newspaper as in James Joyce's Ulysses, the same in German books as in English books, the same in most (not all) schizophrenic speech as in normal speech?

Moreover, the mystery goes farther. If the largest cities of the United States are arranged according to their size, as reported in the 1960 census—New York first, Chicago second, Los Angeles third, and so on—they can be seen to obey the very same rank-size law, to a fairly good approximation. If two cities have ranks j and k, respectively, in the list, their populations will be approximately in the ratio k/j. For example, in 1960 Philadelphia ranked fourth in size with 2,002,512 persons and San Francisco ranked twelfth with 740,026. The rank-size law states that Philadelphia's population ought to be twelve fourths as large as San Francisco's, that is, three times as large, and it very nearly is.

These are not the only phenomena that obey the rank-size rule, or slight variations of it; scientific authorship is another. If the authors who published in a scientific journal over a 10-year period were arranged in the order of the number of articles each published, with the most-published author placed first, the publication frequencies would approximate the rank-size rule. The sizes of nations belonging to the United Nations, when arranged according to population, will also approximate the rank-size rule.

What do word frequencies have in common with city sizes, or what does either of these have in common with scientific publications? Nothing specific, but a great deal in general. Although there is not complete agreement among social scientists on how these regularities are to be explained, several specific, plausible mechanisms are now known that lead to definite predictions of the distributions that are actually observed. We can only sketch here one kind of explanation that has been proposed for the city-size distribution.

Cities grow by the net balance of births over deaths. Within a single economic domain, permitting relatively free trade and movement, they also grow by migration from country to city and from one city to another. Let us make the simplest assumptions: birth and death rates are essentially independent of city size; on the average, the attractiveness of a city as a "target" for migration is proportional to its size; and on the average, the probability of any given family or individual migrating from a city is independent of that city's size. It can be shown, by a straightforward application of probability theory, that under these assumptions, the cities in the domain under consideration will tend to distribute themselves according to the rank-size law; this law describes the most probable equilibrium distribution of population.

There are a number of ways, other than simple observation of the size distribution, by which the mechanisms presumed to operate under this theory can be tested directly. A few such tests have been made, with positive results, but others must be made, for the rank-size law has obvious practical import. In connection with our current concern for the growth of cities, for example, it tells us something about the control of city size if free migration of persons is permitted as a fundamental right.

There are other significant applications of the theory. It has long been known that business firms in the United States, England, and other countries have size distributions that conform more or less to the rank-size law, except that size decreases less rapidly with rank than in the situations described previously (that is, the ratio of the largest firm to the tenth largest is generally less than ten to one). One puzzling fact has been that the degree of industrial concentration, as measured by how rapidly size falls off with rank in the distribution, changes slowly or not at all, even during periods of frequent mergers. Recently, it has been shown mathematically that, under certain assumptions about the sizes of the firms that disappear by merger and those that grow by merger, mergers will have no effect on concentration. Moreover, the assumptions required for this mathematical derivation fit the American data on mergers reasonably well. Thus, a line of scientific inquiry that began with a linguistic puzzle over word frequencies has led to an explanation of an apparent paradox relating to industrial concentration in the United States.

HOW IDEAS SPREAD

Processes like those used to explain the distributions of city sizes and of business firm sizes are examples of *diffusion processes*, which have wide application to human affairs. We live in a society that depends heavily on new advances in technology and on securing the adoption of those advances throughout the society. Generally, this diffusion does not take place by governmental fiat but depends on individuals—farmers, businessmen, physicians, and engineers—learning about new ideas or techniques and being motivated to adopt them. The social sciences can look at the broad phenomena of diffusion; they can also dissect the phenomena and peer into the processes of learning and motivation that energize them.

Diffusion theories, not wholly unlike the theory applied to city migration, have been used to explain the adoption of hybrid corn by American farmers, the use of new antibiotics by physicians, and the spread of such diverse products as diesel locomotives and beer cans. These diffusion phenomena have been a fruitful meeting ground for psychologists, sociologists, and economists, and an equally fruitful area of convergence for methods of inquiry—sample surveys of opinions and behavior, interviewing, statistical analyses of census data and other public records, sophisticated mathematical model-building, careful observation, and hard thought.

Consider the adoption of new drugs, for example. One can imagine several distinct processes: a physician's information and impetus to adopt a new drug could come from his exposure to public media—medical journals, meetings, and advertisements of pharmaceutical companies—or from individual professional contacts with his colleagues. When these different possibilities are translated into mathematical models, it is seen that they lead to different time-patterns of adoption of innovations. Hence, time-series data on adoptions permit us to discover the relative importance of the different processes. In almost all cases where such studies have been carried out, they have shown that the major part is played by "opinion leadership"—by persons thought knowledgeable and reliable, exercising their influence through direct personal contact.

The opinion leadership explanation is not at all inconsistent with explanations that emphasize economic motivation. If information diffusion depends heavily on channels of trusted communication, the patterns of speed of adoption, particularly of industrial and commercial products, fit expectations derived from economic theory. Large firms, because they can accept the risks and pay the information-acquiring costs, tend to adopt new technologies sooner than do small firms; innovations promising large profits spread more rapidly than those offering marginal advantages, and so on.

Our awareness of the role of opinion leadership in the adoption of new practices and new viewpoints came initially not out of studies of technological change, but out of research on how voters make up their minds in an election campaign and how opinions are molded in communities. In the 1930's and 1940's, social scientists interested in processes of influence and persuasion found that it was difficult to obtain financial support for basic research on consumer decision-making, but that it was somewhat easier to obtain support for research on voter decision-making. Fortunately, there was good reason to suppose that the same fundamental mechanisms were involved in both processes, and thus advances in our knowledge of one could contribute importantly to our understanding of the other.

Voting research provided clear-cut evidence for at least three important phenomena: the opinion leadership already mentioned, "cross-pressures," and attention mobilization. Opinion leadership means that, in most practical affairs, recipients of communications evaluate them in terms of the reliability of their sources, as well as by analysis of contents. Reliability of a source depends on perception of common interests and values, as well as assessment of its technical competence.

A second major set of findings obtained from voting research was that persons subjected to conflicting pressures from their social environments tended to withdraw from the conflict situation—not to vote, for example. If they did not withdraw, they often misperceived the situation in ways that reduced the dissonance between conflicting forces. Such persons, for example, would tend to see the candidate for whom they intended to vote as agreeing with them on issues on which, in fact, he did not.

A third major set of findings demonstrated that changes in voting intention during a campaign had less to do with persuasion, as that is usually understood, than with directing attention to particular issues and values. Voters did not often change their minds about particular issues; rather, they often shifted their attention from one set of issues early in the campaign to another later in the campaign. Because they might agree with one candidate on one issue but with another candidate on another issue, shifts in attention caused shifts in voting.

None of these findings is peculiar to human behavior in voting situations; all of them appear equally clearly in consumer behavior and technology diffusion. It is a historical accident that much of the early research that disclosed these phenomena was research on voting behavior. Potential applications of our knowledge of social-influence processes are not limited to the particular areas in which the knowledge was originally obtained. We have, today, the foundations of a theory that tells us how human beings of ordinary intelligence and information cope with a complex environment in which they are expected to make many difficult choices, are faced with competing and conflicting claims, have incomplete and imperfect information, and encounter more issues than they can consider at any given moment.

Because the operation of our economic, political, and social institutions rests on the behavior of such decision-making human beings, it is reassuring to have it verified that we are neither boobs, vulnerable to cynical manipulation, nor geniuses, capable of sustained flights of intellectual and moral virtuosity. Human behavior, even in complex social situations, begins to be understandable in terms of the capabilities for remembering, learning, and responding that are being revealed by research on simple human tasks in the psychological laboratory.

FATHERS AND SONS

Study of the diffusion-like processes can be applied to more detailed examinations of influence and decision-making, as we have just seen. It can also be expanded into an examination of broader social processes, some of them extending over generations. One of the important aspects of any society concerns the amount and kinds of opportunities it offers to the members of each generation and the dependence of those opportunities on their parents' positions in the society.

The kinds of data needed to assess individual opportunities are available in only a few societies. Ingenious methods have been used—particularly analysis of biographical data—to get some picture of social mobility in the United States at earlier periods, or in the U.S.S.R. since the revolution. In the United States in recent times, the data about our population gathered by the U.S. Census Bureau have made possible more adequate analyses. In one study, for example, the occupations of individuals in 1962 were related to their educations, the nature of their first jobs, and their fathers' educations. Father's occupation, on the average, had little influence on son's occupation after the effects of the other two variables (father's education and nature of the first job) had been allowed for. On the other hand, differences in amounts of education and in types of first jobs were predictable, to a considerable degree, from father's education and father's occupation.

Thus, this study revealed a two-step process wherein family influenced occupational opportunity indirectly through opportunity to enter the occupational structure in a favorable way but not directly once the structure was entered.

Questions about social mobility and opportunity can be answered not only for whole populations, but also for groups within populations. For example, differences in ethnic origins among white immigrants to the United States affect occupational achievement only indirectly through their effect on educational attainment. In the black minority, on the other hand, a substantial part (at least 20 or 25 percent) of the difference in mean income between black man and white appears to be attributable to job discrimination, for it remains when the black and white men compared have the same educational attainments and the same family circumstances.

Thus, with continually improving data and methods of data analysis, we begin to obtain a factual picture of the movement of people in our society, from the generation of the fathers to the generation of their children. We begin to understand more objectively the degree and limits of the attainment of equality of opportunity; and we provide the basis for a deeper explanation of the processes—like education—through which movement in society is achieved.

THE USE OF RESOURCES

Of all the social sciences, economics has made the most extensive and deepest use of formal deductive analysis, sometimes but not always mathematical in its researches. Abstract models of economic phenomena serve both as approximate descriptions of some real-world phenomena, and as normative patterns from which to measure real-world departures. Consider, for example, the theory of public goods—technically defined as goods whose consumption by one person does not reduce the amount available for consumption by others. For example, a lighthouse whose beam can be seen for 20 miles is a public good; if one boat is guided by the beam, this in no way diminishes the value of the lighthouse to a second boat, or a third. If the lighthouse is maintained by subscriptions from boat owners and there are enough subscribers to assure its operation, it will be difficult to enroll additional subscribers, because they can refuse to contribute, secure in the knowledge that the services of the lighthouse cannot be denied them without also being denied to subscribers.

Goods and services of this kind cannot be sold on the market and may need to be provided by government without charge and financed by taxation. In this and similar kinds of economic analysis, the basic theory of free competitive markets serves as a norm 'for studying the conditions under which such markets can or cannot be expected to operate satisfactorily as mechanisms for allocating goods and services. Public goods are examples of situations in which the market mechanism has to be supplemented by other devices, and economic theory helps sort out such situations and suggests guides to appropriate public policy.

Economic analysis often leads to conclusions that are far more surprising and less obvious than the one just cited. The factor–price-equalization theorem, first published in 1948, is an excellent example of a discovery in the pure theory of economics that initially may conflict with our intuitions about the matter. For instance, suppose that each of two countries produces two commodities with the use of two factors of production, such as land and labor, and that one commodity requires more land per unit of labor than the other. Moreover, one of the countries has relatively more land, and the other, relatively more labor. In the absence of trade between the countries, the price of labor will be lower, relative to the price of land, in the country where labor is relatively abundant. Will this continue to be true if international trade in commodities is permitted between the two countries without allowing migration or interchange of either labor or land? Mathematical analysis shows that the answer is "No." If trade in commodities is introduced, prices will have to shift until the ratio of the price of land to the wage of labor in the one country is equal to the ratio in the other. Even more surprising, the total output of the two countries (in sum) will now be as large as it would be if movements of labor had been allowed. This is the factor–price-equalization theorem.

Now the proof of the theorem demands that certain strong conditions—not mentioned previously—remain constant. Among other conditions, tariffs and other barriers to trade must be absent, and there must be no transportation costs. In the real world, these conditions are not met, and relative factor prices differ substantially from one country to another. Yet the theorem provides the same kinds of insights into the mechanisms of international trade that are provided by theorems in mechanics that assume "perfect vacuums" and "frictionless planes." They are useful limiting approximations to the real states of affairs, giving us a measure of the consequences of departing from those limiting conditions.

GAMES IN REAL LIFE

Shakespeare described life as a play; others have thought of it as a game. It remained for von Neumann and Morgenstern, a mathematician and an economist, to take the game notion seriously and to construct a formal, mathematical theory of games as a tool for illuminating such phenomena as bargaining between monopolistic or semimonopolistic firms or the forming of coalitions in politics. Throughout American political history, no political party has been able to maintain a stable level of support substantially above the 50 percent mark for any length of time. Most of our history has seen a very close division between the major political parties, and occasional "landslide" elections—almost never giving the winner as much as two thirds of the popular vote—are usually soon followed by a swing of the pendulum back close to an even division.

Something similar is apparent in the operation of European parliamentary governments. Successful parliamentary coalitions usually tend to include just enough groups to give them lean majorities; seldom, under democratic conditions, do oversize coalitions remain stable. Unless we are to attribute these observed facts to coincidence, they must have an explanation somewhere deep in the machinery of democracy. Game theory shows how an explanation of the "minimum-size principle" can be derived rigorously from simple assumptions. The basic idea is that minimum-size majorities have all the power they need to govern; the price they must pay (in terms of concessions and compromises on issues) to attract or to retain additional adherents will be greater, the theorem shows, than anything the core group can hope to gain from the additional strength.

The practice of examining the institutions of society as if they were sets of rules often leads to interesting insights, challenges to commonly held assumptions and cherished beliefs.

For example, most people readily accept, as a social goal, the notion of social actions to obtain "the greatest good for the greatest number." It is a mathematical commonplace that it is possible to maximize two functions simultaneously (here the functions are the amount of good and the size of the number) only under rather unusual and severely restricted conditions. To illustrate this point, in distributing a sum of money to several individuals, it is likely that the greatest good could be done by giving all the money to a very few of the most needy; whereas helping the greatest number would mean giving a little to everyone, possibly so little as to do very little, if any, good at all.

Theoretical economists have long been concerned with one particular set of rules, namely those whereby the value preferences of individuals are put together in a collective social choice—a "welfare function," economists term it. The nature of the welfare function in a democratic society is of particular interest because of the difficulties of adding (or otherwise combining) the value preferences of many individuals in such a way as to get a clear choice among alternative social or economic policies. Ideally, such a choice would be determined solely by the preference orderings of the individual members of society, and not on the wishes of a single individual (a dictator). Likewise, if everyone in the society prefers one alternative, then that is the society's choice. The social choice ought to depend only on the ordering of alternatives among actually available options, not on irrelevant matters. It also seems reasonable to make the assumption that preferences must be transitive (that is, if Alternative A is preferred to Alternative B, and Alternative B is preferred to Alternative C, then Alternative A is preferred to Alternative C). These conditions seem entirely plausible as a statement of the social-choice mechanism for a democratic society. The mechanism is a sort of computing machine into which the preference orderings of every individual in the society are fed, and from which emerges the society's choice among available alternatives. It can be shown mathematically, however, that it is not possible to have a social-choice mechanism that operates in this fashion for all possible sets of individual orderings. A democratic social-choice mechanism cannot insist on such clear and strong conditions.

If the range of individual choices is restricted in certain ways, then a social-welfare function can be defined that meets the conditions. But fixing the trouble misses the main point, which is that attempts at constructing a satisfactory social-choice mechanism can be illuminated by precise mathematical analysis. By making social principles and political ideals explicit and operational, we make them subject to mathematical analysis that can sometimes tell us what is and what is not logically possible. Given logical possibility, then social desirability must decide acceptance.

WHAT THE GLANDS TELL THE MIND

Economics tends to be interested in man in his most rational moments; clinical psychology is perforce often involved in dealing with him when he is being most irrational—though Freud has taught that we must always look for and seek to understand the method in madness. Some of the most interesting human phenomena of concern to the social sciences are those that bring man's reason into conjunction with his emotions and motivations. Our earlier example of man's tendency to reduce dissonance between conflicting forces by withdrawing from situations that present conflicts among strongly held values or beliefs typifies such meeting points.

A classical problem in psychology relates to how people identify and label their own emotions. It might seem obvious that such diverse feelings as fear, rage, joy, and sorrow must represent different bodily reactions in the glandular and sympathetic nervous systems. Careful physiological research casts doubt on this, showing that many of the same bodily changes occur in very different emotional states. Our bodies seem to have far too few patterns of physiological response to account for the rich variety of emotions and moods that we experience psychologically. This paradoxical situation suggested to psychologists that they must look elsewhere than to the glands and sympathetic nervous system for a full explanation of emotion and feeling. One place to investigate was the brain and its thought processes. Perhaps the specificity of emotion had something to do with the individual's "labeling" it congruently with the particular situation in which he perceived himself to be and in which he experienced it. Perhaps whether the tears were the tears of laughter or sorrow depended on whether his thoughts told him he was in a happy situation or a sad one.

How could such a hypothesis be tested? Because emotions involve the arousal of certain physiological states, the use of drugs to arouse the emotions under controlled experimental conditions might permit manipulation of the physiological response independently of the social situation in which it occurred. If the hypothesis were correct, the specific emotions experienced by a subject might then depend on the emotional states of other persons around him.

The experimental facts showed this result. Individuals receiving injections of a drug (epinephrine bitartrate) that excites the sympathetic nervous system reported feeling euphoric in the company of others who were behaving in an excited, carefree way and angry in the presence of others who acted as if they were annoyed, irritated, or enraged.

In addition to euphoria and anger, fear can also be produced experimentally by combining physiological arousal with fear-inducing cues. Fear often causes people to avoid behaviors that have fear-evoking consequences. Conversely, it has been shown experimentally that by using drugs to depress the sympathetic nervous system, fear reactions may be reduced so that, for example, students in this condition will take greater risks of being caught at cheating in examinations.

The findings on the physiological bases of fear have been explored further for their possible relation to some forms of criminal behavior. Experiments have shown that so-called sociopathic criminals in prisons exhibit low levels of anxiety and have great difficulty in learning to avoid painful stimuli. Because it is generally thought that fear is a key factor in learning to avoid pain, it seemed reasonable to investigate whether criminal sociopaths could be helped to learn to avoid painful events by administering a sympathetic-nervous-system excitant to make them moderately anxious. Prior to the treatment, the sociopaths had shown themselves as capable as normal persons of learning rewarded behavior, but as greatly inferior to normal persons in learning to avoid pain. When injected with the excitant, sociopaths showed a dramatic improvement in learning to avoid pain, whereas normal persons did not.

The "obvious" interpretation of these results is that the sympathetic nervous systems of sociopaths are less reactive, less responsive, than those of normal persons to emotion-arousing stress and to epinephrine. The facts show that this obvious interpretation is wrong. The nervous systems of sociopaths are *more* responsive to stress than are those of normal persons and more sensitive to epinephrine. In fact, the sensitivity of sociopaths is so great as to be indiscriminate; they react autonomically to harmless as well as frightening events, and hence their reactions do not help them to distinguish situations that are labeled painful, dangerous, or frightening and do not help them learn to avoid such situations.

Work now going forward seeks to extend these findings to other relations between internal physiological states and the psychological interpretations of them. For example, in people of normal weight, experiments show that changes in internal physiological states associated with hunger (for example, increased gastric motility) cause changes in the amount of food they eat. Among obese persons, the physiological cues to hunger exercise much less control over their eating habits. Their eating appears to be stimulated mainly by external cues—the tastiness of the food, the sociable nature of the eating situation, the length of time since the last meal, and other facts extrinsic to the organism. The obese have not learned to label their internal bodily states correctly.

THE VARIETY OF MAN'S CULTURES

The balance of commonalities and diversities among human societies is a major theme of inquiry in the social sciences. In history, it leads us back to the study of earlier societies and ways in which they resemble or differ from our own. In sociology and anthropology, it leads us to inquiries into the functional needs that all societies must meet for their members, if they are to survive and flourish, and the innumerable ways in which these needs are met. In psychology, it leads to the study of individual differences drawing upon a sophisticated methodology of testing and analyzing test results. In political science and economics, it leads to comparative studies of the political and economic institutions among the world's many nations.

Part of this inquiry is taxonomic—it seeks to describe and to classify the kinds of existing phenomena and where they are found. As in biology, a thorough descriptive knowledge of the basic systems with which the science deals must precede and accompany more abstract inquiry and the development and testing of hypotheses. But the continuing comparative study of cultures and institutions has already gone far, in many directions, beyond simple taxonomic description.

By opening our eyes to all the world's cultures, anthropology has taught the lesson of cultural relativity. It has shown that most of the customs that seem "quaint" or "primitive" represent, in fact, understandable adaptations of behavior to particular physical environments and particular courses of cultural development. It has greatly enhanced our ability to enjoy esthetically the products of other cultures without necessarily wanting to imitate those cultures or to adopt their values.

The concept of cultural relativity has led to interesting experiments on how people form their beliefs in our society. In many, if not most, cases, our beliefs depend quite as much on the information provided by our social environment as on the evidence of our own senses. All of us now believe that the earth is round. Until we saw photographs of it taken from space, few of us knew any evidence in support of that belief —just why Columbus was right and his critics were wrong.

Even when facts are presented to our senses, our social surroundings may cause us to doubt them. Experiments tell us that when a group of people are asked to judge the relative lengths of two lines and when a majority of judges are unanimous (deliberately) in announcing objectively wrong answers, a lone individual is likely to modify his judgment to conform with the majority and to report the longer line as shorter. It is not clear from the evidence whether the situation affects the individual's perception or just his willingness, or ability, to report it. In either case, the majority opinion exerts a social pressure toward conformity. Another striking finding in this research is that the social-pressure effect occurs when a lone individual is opposed by a unanimous majority, but if the individual has even one "ally," the effect disappears almost entirely.

These experiments are significant in measuring some of the limits of social influence on perception of "objective reality." In many spheres of life, criteria of correctness are purely social. The only test of correctness in speaking a language is whether a certain way is the way "it is spoken." In the light of this conventional character of all language, it becomes challenging to discover whether there exist any fundamental limitations on the modes of human communication— whether there are "language universals."

The question of language universals is one of the liveliest domains of social science today. Anthropologists, who have been major contributors to our knowledge of the world's languages, use the vast body of grammatical information they have collected to ask whether there are any languages that do not contain "verb-like" elements and "noun-like" elements. In the light of present evidence, it appears that there are not. The modern school of structural linguistics has made great strides toward constructing general, formal theories of grammar that would help explain such universals, to the extent that they exist. To complete the circle, advances in structural linguistics have given new impetus to the psychological study of language behavior, so that today we have the rudiments of description of the "grammar" used by a child during his first months of speech and some predictions about what people remember from sentences that are read to them.

FREE TRADE IN IDEAS

A number of the examples cited in this chapter have shown how curiosity in exploring striking or puzzling phenomena has led the social scientist to a deeper understanding of matters of considerable practical importance. As in all international exchange, this kind of trade in ideas between basic and applied science flows both ways. Some of the good ideas for basic research arise from inquiries of the most immediate and practical sort. The roots of the study of short-term memory, discussed earlier, lie partly in the need during World War II to improve human performance of vigilance tasks, such as watching air-defense radar scopes. Economics has always drawn many of its research problems from the need of governments to fix policies for raising revenues, maintaining employment, or modifying tariffs.

A striking example of this reverse flow is provided by the practices of parole and parole prediction. John Augustus, a Boston cobbler, in 1841 volunteered to assist offenders if the court would release them to his care. Before his death, he and his friends are said to have supervised some 2,000 parolees. In our century, observation of the operation of the penal system led sociologists to ask whether the probability that a parole would be successful could be predicted from the characteristics and histories of prisoners. Correct prediction would test the validity of theories of the motivation of criminals. The prediction schemes that have resulted from asking these questions not only have contributed to our basic sociological knowledge, but also have led to the development of practical parole-prediction techniques that are part of the administration of parole systems in many jurisdictions today.

The success and utility of parole prediction have led to similar questions about marriage. Could the likelihood of success of a marriage be predicted from information about characteristics of the prospective partners? What light would such predictions cast upon the institutions of marriage and the family and upon the social psychology of husband–wife relations? One product of these researches has been to provide marriage counselors with additional tools to help them in their guidance activities.

A vast body of social science research rests on the data of the Decennial Census, an institution created for the purely pragmatic purpose of allocating representatives to the Congress. There is no end to such examples. The lesson of the examples is that the basic and the applied components of research, properly construed, do not compete but, rather, they reinforce each other. Good basic research, leading to answers to fundamental questions, soon finds practical applications. Thoughtful attention to the world of practical problems raises basic research questions of the most challenging kind. The everyday world provides the scientist with an ever-renewing source of fresh research problems, while fundamental inquiry provides him· with a stream of ideas to apply to the problems of the world.

Any basic science has an inner logic of its own, which for considerable periods of time, guides inquiry, defines problems, and discloses opportunities. This inner logic does not imply irrelevance to the practical world; it may, however, imply patience in allowing the science to unravel its internal puzzles without demanding that relevance always be instant or direct.

CONCLUSION

This series of examples has illustrated the many faces of the social and behavioral sciences. Even such a brief, island-hopping survey reveals the greatest diversity. The social sciences sometimes rely on qualitative description and sometimes on sophisticated mathematics. Sometimes they turn to the laboratory for the methods and data of experiments, sometimes to sample surveys and opinion polls, sometimes to the methods of the interview, and sometimes to patient observation and interpretation. Sometimes they appear preoccupied with plodding descriptions of facts—facts that appear very dull and even superficial when viewed in isolation. Sometimes they soar to heights of abstraction that leave factual details well behind. Sometimes they moralize, but at their best, they seek to understand before evaluating.

What, then, do the social sciences hold in common? They hold in common the belief that man and his institutions are a part of nature; that as in the rest of nature, all kinds of patterns and order and beauty are to be found if we learn where and how to look; and that discovery and understanding of patterns in human affairs are as exciting and as important to our insight into the world's meaning as are discovery and understanding of the patterns in material things, in living organisms, or in the abstractions of mathematics. Finally, they share the belief that improvement in the human condition is achievable only in the measure that we achieve understanding.

5
SCIENCES OF BEHAVIOR
AND THE
PROBLEMS OF SOCIETY

Over the years, social scientists have made many contributions to the improvement of society. The city-manager form of government was developed and spread largely through the efforts of political scientists. It brought professional management into the operation of American cities, vastly improving efficiency in many instances. The social security system was very largely the work of American economists. In both world wars, psychologists developed methods of testing the aptitudes and abilities of military recruits; these were a great improvement over the hit-or-miss methods used previously to assign men to jobs or to training.

It is easy to overlook the contributions of social science to society when social science has led to a successful solution of a specific problem, for the problem may then disappear and be quickly forgotten. Consider, for example, the problem of demobilizing an armed force of nearly 10 million men and women following World War II. The eagerness of the citizen forces to return to civilian life was a potentially serious source of unrest and trouble. Everyone wanted to be released as soon as the shooting stopped, to return home, to find work, to continue education, and to be free of military discipline. How could an orderly and logistically feasible demobilization be arranged?

Sociologists in the Information and Education Division of the Army conducted sample surveys of troops in the United States and abroad to test various possible schemes. The essence of the problem was to discover what soldiers considered a fair system, for the validation of the scheme's success would lie in its acceptance by troops who were about to be demobilized. Out of these surveys came the "point system," which gave credit for longevity of service, overseas duty, combat performance, and other factors whose relative weights were determined by the carefully sampled opinions of troops themselves. The scheme was a success. The enormous armed force was returned to civilian life with dispatch, in good order, and with almost no unrest—in contrast to demobilization protests and riots in other armies and in earlier American ones. Moreover, the same surveys, inquiring into postwar plans, also provided an early and accurate appraisal of the demand for education, for which the GI Bill of Rights later provided.

More recently, the spectacular success of the income-tax reduction of 1964 was a major contribution of social science to the national welfare. In 1964, the nation faced a budget deficit and a high unemployment rate. The Council of Economic Advisers, basing their views on Keynesian theory and modern econometric measures, urged the President to reduce taxes. As a consequence of the tax reduction, unemployment began to fall and gross national product rose, between 1964 and mid-1965, at a rate of $10 billion a quarter (see the upper portion of Figure 5-1). The effect on consumer spending (see the lower portion of Figure 5-1) was similarly dramatic: an increase unmatched in our peacetime history. Finally, the best available estimate is that the cumulative net gain in federal receipts, added to the gain for state and local receipts, nearly equaled the $13 billion of tax reduction.

The tax policy adopted in 1964 is precisely opposite to the course the United States followed in 1932, when the country also faced a budget deficit and a high unemployment rate. Then, the United States raised excise taxes and introduced several new taxes. The unemployment rate rose further and the depression was prolonged. The difference between 1964 and 1932 reflects the substitution of systematic social science for the obvious "common-sense" solution.

A great deal of social science results in the disproof of common-sense knowledge, folklore, and superstition, and the development of systematically obtained and rationally tested knowledge to replace them. For example, consider the following generalizations, together with their alleged explanations, of how soldiers behaved during World War II: (1) "Better-educated men showed more psychoneurotic symptoms than those with less education." (The mental instability of the intellectual as compared with the more impassive psychology of the man-in-the-street has often been commented on.) (2) "Southern soldiers were better able to stand the climate in the islands of

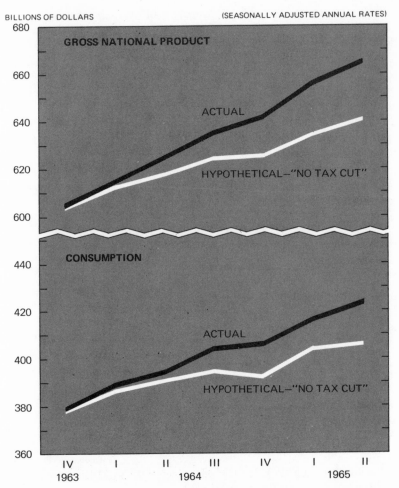

**FIGURE 5-1   GROSS NATIONAL PRODUCT AND CONSUMP-
TION, ACTUAL AND HYPOTHETICAL.**

[Source: Arthur M. Okun, "Measuring the Impact of the 1964
Tax Reduction," in Walter W. Heller, ed., *Perspectives on Economic Growth* (New York: Random House, 1968), p. 48.]

the South Pacific." (Naturally, for southerners are more accustomed
to hot weather.) (3) "White privates were more eager to become
noncommissioned officers than were Negroes." (To be sure, lack of
ambition among Negroes is almost proverbial.)

This list of "obvious" findings, explainable by common sense, suffers from one fatal flaw: each of those statements is the *opposite* of what was actually found. It was found that poorly educated soldiers were much more neurotic than those with high education, southerners showed no greater tolerance for the South Pacific climate than northerners, and Negroes were much more ambitious for promotion than were whites.*

This sort of disconfirmation of "what everybody knows" goes on continually in the behavioral sciences, and the discredited ideas steadily disappear from popular culture. It is hard to remember some of the beliefs that were once entertained about society and even harder to credit their acceptance; for example, that sun spots caused business cycles, that dreams foretold the future, or that punishment for mistakes was a more effective teaching technique than rewards for correct performance. It used to be considered unpatriotic to talk of social classes in the U.S. society and the pervasive influence of life style on motivation, ability, and values; character structure of the individual is only beginning to be generally appreciated. In this as in numerous other ways, the insights of the behavioral sciences, as well as their very concepts, have penetrated the public understanding of social issues and have raised the level of sophistication in discussion of them. Poverty is no longer treated as a characterological defect nor criminal behavior as a hereditary trait. It is increasingly recognized that hortatory speeches and moral warnings are not effective means of changing individual behavior or the dynamics of a social system.

One of the persistent questions addressed to social scientists is, in fact, how to make information and educational campaigns most effective. Recent sociological research on the acceptance of birth-control measures in an underdeveloped country has shaken some stereotypes about information and persuasion campaigns. A direct-mail campaign was no more effective than merely putting up posters and meeting with neighborhood leaders. Personal visits by trained nurse-midwives who provided information, contraceptive supplies, and guidance to married women were two to three times as effective in winning acceptance. On the other hand, it made almost no difference in the rate of acceptance if considerable extra effort was taken to ensure the presence and participation of the husband. Finally, it is clear that, among the ordinary population, a great deal of influence takes effect

*Adapted from Paul F. Lazarsfeld, "The American Soldier—An Expository Review," *Public Opinion Quarterly*, 13, Fall 1949, 377–404.

outside the planned professional home visits. In fact, only 40 percent of the acceptances of birth-control measures in the first 8 months were the direct result of home visits. Yet those professional visits were necessary to prime the communication process and start it off.*

ADVANCING THE ART OF SOLVING SOCIAL PROBLEMS

Many of the useful results of social science have emerged from attempts to solve basic problems. Gains within the disciplines advance the art of solving social problems by providing better techniques of analysis and by sharpening the conceptual tools of social science. However, the solution of social problems demands combinations of skill both from within and from outside the social sciences.

Social problems come in all sizes and many varieties, but some are inordinately persistent: prejudice and discrimination against minorities, poverty and inadequate levels of living, ignorance and inferior education, mental illness, violence and crime, and, the fundamental problem of all society, the resolution of deadly conflicts among factions within it. Other social problems are more recent and traceable in some part to man's own efforts to improve his lot. The automobile, a great modern convenience, causes massive traffic jams that make living unpleasant or exhausting and contributes to the pollution of the atmosphere. Neighborhood interest and influence in schools runs head-on against an organizational device designed to protect teachers' interests. New drugs alter frighteningly the psychic structure they were intended to explore experimentally. Computers seem to threaten the preservation of privacy, possibly even individuality. All these are social problems in the sense that they cause apparently needless pain, effort, fear, unpleasantness, or deprivation to the human beings in whose interest society exists. Which problems should social scientists tackle? How can they *contribute* to their solution?

The operative word is "contribute," for behavioral scientists alone cannot solve social problems. Almost all such problems are found in a political and economic context, which means that legitimate power and material resources must be brought to bear before a solution can occur. Social scientists can contribute, not by attempting to take

---

*Bernard Berelson and Ronald Freedman, "A Study in Fertility Control," *Scientific American*, 210, May 1964, 29–37.

power or allocate resources—which are decisions of the polity—but by analysis, by careful dissection of problems into components, and by assessing the probable consequences of alternative courses of action. Ideally, a team of behavioral scientists would be able to clarify the several issues that together constitute a social problem, to identify the effective factors that cause or maintain the pathological processes, and to predict correctly the consequences of each alternative course. The social scientists need not act like philosopher kings nor need they merely supply data or make measurements at someone else's direction. Rather, they can bring to bear a conceptual–analytic apparatus, methods for measuring variables, and techniques, such as simulation and gaming, for extrapolating the consequences of various action strategies for the total system. Although they can bring objectivity to the study of the problem, they need not confine themselves to suggesting alternative solutions but may select a preferred one and be able to give convincing arguments and evidence for that choice. The value of social science in the public debate on a social problem can be determined by the soundness of the evidence, the defensibility of the arguments, and the costs and benefits to be derived from the recommended strategy.

The contribution of the social sciences is not to replace public debate and legitimate political processes, but to supplement them by additional information and rational evaluation, to substitute verified findings for conventional wisdom, and to test what may be erroneous opinions that are taken to be "common knowledge."

THE BEARING OF THE BEHAVIORAL AND SOCIAL SCIENCES ON POLICY

Responsible leaders who participate in the making of governmental, business, or professional policy often seek expert advice concerning the formulation of policies or the outcomes to be anticipated. Depending on the state of the sciences bearing on these decisions, an expert can draw upon firm knowledge and can propose how the relevant information can be obtained, or he can merely express his opinions as a (presumably) wise citizen. Value judgments may be involved in his advice, but when the scientific base is well established, his judgments become less controversial and their bearing on policy more precise. For example, if an epidemic is threatened and the medical authorities recommend mass inoculation, their value judgments are that health is better than illness and that some invasion of privacy is justified for the common good. Some fraction of the population (for example, Christian Scientists) may not accept the common value and may resist inoculation, but, on the whole, the medical authorities will not be charged with proceeding on a false understanding of the disease process. Whatever the conflicts of value may be, the public is usually ready to accept the *technical* soundness of the advice of the engineer or medical authority, even though they may not agree with him about the desirability of his recommendations. The basis of their disagreement is likely to be that they differ on the relative weights assigned to the various values to be served. However, the public is not so ready to accept the validity of the technical advice of the behavioral or social scientist. This is not only because of the less-established scientific position of the social sciences but because the problem areas are more likely to involve directly some passionate concerns of the individual.

Rather than point to the differences between the roles of the social scientists and the natural scientists in relation to policy, we stress the strong case that can be made for their essential similarity. When given specific responsibility, most scientists tend to be cautious; they are accustomed to having their research efforts published in such detail that others can check their findings, and they do not like to make predictions without a basis in evidence and theory. Thus, scientists who work on applied problems tend to see the complexity of problem-solving and are not likely to be impatient for quick solutions. This has led one social scientist to remark:

The maturity of a science may be measured not only by its power but by its discrimination in knowing the limits of its power. And if this is so, the layman does not need to worry lest the social sciences, as they become more scientific, will be more likely to usurp political authority. On the contrary, they will stop short of trying to solve completely our major political problems not because they are unlike the natural sciences, but to the extent that they are like them.*

The Council of Economic Advisers provides an excellent illustration of how social scientists, in their scientific capacity, can contribute to policy formation. Their recommendations are of a scientific character in that they purport to apprise the President of the consequences of various alternative courses of action under consideration. Given an agreed-upon goal, delineations of consequences may be abbreviated to

---

*Don K. Price, *The Scientific Estate* (Cambridge, Mass.: The Belknap Press of Harvard University Press, 1965), p. 111.

read like policy recommendations, but they contain a scientific core whose validity is independent of the evaluation placed upon the consequences of a proposed course of policy.

Neither the policy recommendations of the Council of Economic Advisers nor the scientific analysis on which they rest are, or should be, beyond dispute. However, to an increasing extent, it is recognized in Congress and elsewhere that the results of an economic analysis cannot be ignored or bypassed because they are inconvenient to one's policy preferences. Either the scientific validity of the results must be successfully challenged or the value judgments governing their use must be denied. Where an effective value consensus exists, the economic analysis may exercise great influence. The 1964 tax reduction is a case in point.

The success of the Council of Economic Advisers does not depend on its neutrality with respect to social issues. It accepts the goal of full employment and the later-recognized goal of price stability as desirable objectives of its recommendations. The significance of its recommendations for policy rests on two grounds: first, they are made on the basis of fact and tested theory, and second, the economic advisers are willing to take responsibility for suggesting policy.

When social goals are agreed upon—as in the relief of suffering, the reduction of crimes of violence, satisfaction in useful work, and the constructive use of leisure time—the function of the scientist is to find the most effective way to move toward these goals. Even so, desirable goals compete for scarce resources; for example, money for health comes from the same taxes as money for education. Hence, issues of goal-conflict inevitably arise. Furthermore, not all social goals are agreed upon, and how some measure of consensus on goals is achieved is in itself a research problem. It is in the definition of goals and the resolution of goal-conflict that the social sciences may have a unique opportunity for service, because their methods permit research on these processes.

RESEARCH ON THE POLICY PROCESS

The behavioral and social sciences are like the other sciences in having sources of information and methods for finding answers to questions that bear upon policy. The behavioral and social sciences differ from the other sciences in their concern for understanding the processes of policy-formation itself: defining the problem, directing attention to it, identifying the motives and goals of those affected, and observing how negotiations are carried out, how innovations are introduced, and how action is eventually undertaken. These developments are the subjects of what is sometimes called *managerial science*, or in other contexts *policy science*, and they are now reasonably well advanced and well understood by those who are concerned with the applied problems of business and government.

Studies of a wide range of decisions (federal budget-making, businessmen's decisions to invest abroad, the Congressman's role and participation in foreign-trade policy, capital budgeting in business, and community highway location) have shown a number of common properties that deny a simple model of rational decision-making. Some of these common properties are:

1. *Negotiating*, rather than seeking to reach an unequivocally "best" solution, is invariably involved, either explicitly or implicitly. Usually, when those with one set of interests are benefited, some others suffer frustration or setback.

2. The solutions do not arise directly out of the alternatives emerging from research; therefore, the task is not that of choosing between readily available alternatives, but of *inventing* or *designing* a viable course of action that may blend several of the originally formulated alternatives.

3. The *phrasing* or *rephrasing* of proposed courses of action in terms that are meaningful to the participants is of great importance. If these statements of intended action prove unacceptable, new courses of action may have to be invented.

4. Finally, in a real-life situation the policy issue is embedded in a context of other issues, is *competing* for the time and attention of the persons involved, and has higher or lower priorities, depending on the character of its relation to those other issues.

An important point is that solutions to social problems that are based on research alone, no matter how sound, are not automatically accepted. For example, there is little doubt of the general advantage to be gained from a universal language, but there are countertendencies that have led to the establishment in recent years of a number of local languages as the official languages of new states. Regulation of population growth—until some better balance is established between food (and other resources) and people—is certainly desirable but it is resisted in many quarters. It would not be difficult to add to the list of recommendations based on the behavioral and social sciences that have not straightaway become a part of accepted policy because the means of overcoming obstacles to their introduction or undesirable side effects have not been found.

Resistance to innovation requires that behavioral scientists give some attention to understanding social change as a process, and resistance to innovation as a social and psychological problem is worthy of study in its own right. The experience of numerous agencies in introducing change based on social science research (in areas like child care and employer–employee relations) provides a vast archive for research on the process of innovation through legislation, education, testing, and demonstration.

Some behavioral scientists believe that the most efficacious way to study social change is to conduct experiments in producing change in the context of actual community life. This kind of experimentation was initiated during World War II, when food needs of the armed forces made it desirable to increase civilian consumption of less-favored meats—hearts, kidneys, brains, and so forth. Several different techniques were tried for changing the meat-purchasing and meat-serving behavior of housewives. The most effective techniques were not patriotic appeals or rational lectures on nutrition, but group discussions that frankly explored resistance to unfamiliar meats, indicated ways of cooking and serving them that made them more attractive, and most important, ended with an explicit commitment on the part of each housewife–discussant to try serving one or more of these meats to her family.

Institutional arrangements are subject to invention and design, just as machinery is. Computers are now widely used in the industrial design of machinery; they may eventually be helpful in the design of instrumentalities to serve policy.

With these intellectual and scientific developments, it is not surprising that new research institutes have been set up with policy and planning as major objectives. We shall return to a discussion of these in Chapter 12.

PLANNING

Man can relate the past to the present and, on that basis, plan for the future. It is inevitable that he should plan; planning and prediction are inherent in sciences that tend to ascribe some lawfulness to events, even though there are serious limits to that lawfulness. The future is not entirely capricious, or one could make no sensible plans at all.

Something like a planning body had been recommended by the commission appointed by President Hoover, which issued its report *Recent Social Trends* at the end of his term in office (1933), in readiness for President Roosevelt. The proposal was for a National Advisory Council, which would be ". . . able to contribute to the consideration of the basic social problems of the nation." Roosevelt, under the authority of the National Industrial Recovery Act, established a National Planning Board in 1933, which later became the National Resources Planning Board. A *Plan for Planning*, issued in 1934 by the first board, called for cooperation between natural and social scientists; both the Social Science Research Council and the National Academy of Sciences supported this call for more effective planning. After World War II, policy-planning and program-evaluation units appeared in several federal departments, including Treasury, Interior, Labor, and Health, Education, and Welfare.*

The National Planning Association, in existence since 1934, is a private nonpartisan planning organization. It has as its objective the study of methods for full utilization of the productive resources of the nation for the greatest possible benefit to the American people. It attempts to bring basic knowledge to bear on problems faced by public and private leaders by relating their actions to broad national goals and economic trends.

Other privately established agencies, Resources for the Future, established in 1952, and the Committee for Economic Development, established in 1943, are also representative of the acceptance of some aspects of the planning function outside the government.

The uneasiness about planning that was felt up to and during World War II has tended to dissipate since the end of the war. Industrial corporations found it advantageous to plan for plant location and development as they increasingly analyzed and tried to forecast demand in national and international markets. New nations have emerged, and planning for development has been given high priority. In more-established nations, as in the United States, there is no longer one central planning board; planning goes on in many agencies, and

---

*For a useful discussion of the history of social science in relation to government, see Gene M. Lyons, *The Uneasy Partnership: Social Science and the Federal Government in the Twentieth Century* (New York: Russell Sage Foundation, 1969).

urban and regional planning are accepted as essential. When the Marshall Plan started operation in Europe in 1948, all member countries of the Organization for European Economic Cooperation began some national economic planning.

Economic planning is perhaps the most familiar, and accepted, but there are other kinds of planning, including forecasting and projection, general social planning, regional and urban planning, resource planning, and welfare planning. There is clearly a role here for the behavioral and social scientist, although as the disciplines are organized, they seldom (except for economics) provide explicit training for filling this role. This does not mean that we lack competent planners. It does mean, however, that we must do more training of students for planning and provide more of the kinds of experiences in the course of training that make the planning functions attractive.

PARTICIPATION IN FORMULATING SCIENCE POLICY

In view of the rapid developments within the behavioral and social sciences and the desirability of participation by behavioral and social scientists in multidisciplinary roles with life scientists, physical scientists, and engineers, national policies affecting science and technology should take account of those sciences as a matter of course. All the relevant types of expertise should be used in policy and planning, and we believe that the behavioral and social sciences should be more fully represented than they are now in bodies that advise on science policy matters within the Executive Office of the President. The first behavioral scientist to be appointed to the President's Science Advisory Committee (PSAC) was appointed in 1968, and we encourage further broadening of PSAC's scientific perspective in this direction.

RECOMMENDATION: INCLUSION OF BEHAVIORAL AND SOCIAL SCIENTISTS IN SCIENCE POLICY ADVISORY BODIES

The Committee recommends that more behavioral and social scientists be appointed to the President's Science Advisory Committee (PSAC), thus broadening the spectrum of its scientific capabilities so that PSAC can deal most effectively with the full range of matters brought to its attention. These include the social and economic effects of technological change, and the role of the federal government in strengthening scientific developments in all fields, including the behavioral and social sciences.

Further, the Committee recommends that the professional staff of the Office of Science and Technology (ost) be enlarged to include more behavioral and social scientists, and that ost have the same responsibilities for governmental programs in the behavioral and social sciences that it now exercises in the physical and biological sciences, including the review of government support for the continuing growth of these sciences and special problems with regard to their application to government programs and processes.

It will be noted that these recommendations correspond closely to the recommendations made earlier by the Advisory Committee on Government Programs in the Behavioral Sciences, and the Special Commission on the Social Sciences of the National Science Board.*

*The Behavioral Sciences and the Federal Government, nas Pub. 1680 (Washington, D.C.: National Academy of Sciences, 1968); National Science Board–National Science Foundation, Knowledge Into Action: Increasing the Nation's Use of the Social Sciences, Report of the Special Commission on the Social Sciences, nsb 69-3, 1969.

6
ASSESSING
THE STATE OF
SOCIETY

Social science aims to provide an explanation of observed and measured social phenomena. If these aims are to be achieved, two steps are desirable. The first is to find some way of measuring significant aspects of the state of society and the changes in them, and the second is to bring the interpreted results to the attention of a wider public through a periodic report.

SOCIAL INDICATORS

There have recently appeared several independent proposals from both private and public sources, including Congress, to develop what have come to be called "social indicators"—measures of aspects of social behavior and the quality of life. A measure of job satisfaction or a measure of "alienation" among the young would tell us things about the state of the society that cannot be captured in economic indicators. Changes in educational indicators might show the response of the educational system to deliberate attempts to improve its functioning—that is, to investment in education, changes in laws regarding school attendance, and so forth—or its response to long-run changes in the society's requirements for employability. Parallel indicators for health, welfare, crime and delinquency, housing, the status of minority groups, and other social conditions have been suggested. The general idea is to provide indices of social change in important areas of life, and estimates of the current well-being of the population.

Such indicators could serve several purposes. They would be warning signals of dangerous or undesirable trends in the nation, such as increases in crime or poverty, that could call attention to the need for remedial action before the problems reached a critical stage. They could help assess the performance of our social institutions and of special programs or policies established to remedy social ills and to move toward a more ideal society. They could serve as the basis for more informed and enlightened forecasting and action by both public and private agencies.

A system of social indicators could provide all these things, if it could be brought to a sufficient degree of power and precision. Social scientists agree that present knowledge can meet this demand only in part and that social science techniques and tools are not yet fully sufficient to the task. But the way to improve knowledge and technical capacity is to make a start—to try out some indicators and to work at improving them.

Several questions must be resolved. What data will serve as indicators of what states of the social system? This is only partly an empirical question—that is, one that can be answered by gathering and analyzing more facts. It is also a theoretical question whose answer rests on a better understanding of how society works, how its component processes interact, what its members want for themselves, their families, and their communities. The analogy with the system of national economic accounts should not be pressed too far, because the creation of a social counterpart of gross national product is not likely to be achieved in the near future. Social indicators lend themselves less readily to aggregation than do economic indicators. Most contemporary theories of society suggest that an array of social indicators must be developed to relate to a variety of particular social subsystems: housing, political participation, education, health, science, and so forth. The conceptual basis of such indices would take into account general human and social values, such as satisfaction, accomplishment, enjoyment of life, enlightenment, and self-expression through participation in the affairs and institutions of the nation. To be sure, more adequate data series would be needed, including some data that are not now collected; but the decisions as to what data to collect can be made only if we develop both some basic conceptual models of how the society works and some notions of what objectives or goals are most important in assessing the social state of the nation.*

*For useful introductions to the problems of developing social indicators, see Raymond A. Bauer, ed., *Social Indicators* (Cambridge, Mass.: The M.I.T. Press, 1966); "Social Goals and Indicators for American Society," *The Annals of the*

Most social scientists who have considered the problem think it would be worthwhile to pursue the objectives set forth for such a system and agree that, if developed appropriately, it would be useful for both social research and social planning.

RECOMMENDATION: SOCIAL INDICATORS

The Committee recommends that substantial support, both financial and intellectual, be given to efforts under way to develop a system of social indicators and that legislation to encourage and assist this development be enacted by Congress.

For the immediate future we believe that responsibility for the development and improvement of social indicators could be located within an agency of government, perhaps in the Department of Health, Education, and Welfare. Not only is the responsibility appropriate to many of that Department's missions, but also a commendable start has already been made on this difficult task. A general statistical office might be created at the secretarial level, incorporating the now disparate activities of the Center for Health Statistics, the Center for Educational Statistics, and the statistics-gathering activities of the Social and Rehabilitation Service. Provision would, of course, have to be made to ensure that indicators relating to other important aspects of society, such as housing and transportation, would also be included.

Alternatively, provision might be made for the Bureau of the Census, in the Department of Commerce, to assume this responsibility. This agency has a primary concern for social data collected on a large scale, has traditionally dealt with data that go beyond the more particular interests of the Department of Commerce, and has, over the years, developed excellent working relations with behavioral and social scientists throughout the country.

Still another possibility might be to place responsibility for the development of social indicators in the Executive Office of the Presi-

---

American Academy of Political and Social Science, 371 and 373, May and September 1967; U.S. Senate Committee on Government Operations, *Full Opportunity and Social Accounting Act* (3 parts), Hearings before the Subcommittee on Government Research, 90th Cong., 1st sess., 1967; Eleanor B. Sheldon and Wilbert E. Moore, eds., *Indicators of Social Change: Concepts and Measurements* (New York: Russell Sage Foundation, 1968); and U.S. Department of Health, Education, and Welfare, *Toward a Social Report*, January 1969.

dent. Such an arrangement would avoid the difficulties that might arise from locating responsibility for the indicators in a single operating agency.*

The difficulties of the task are such that it will take years to refine the indicators and to realize the full range of their usefulness. Conceptual development is as important as the need for new and better data. We warn against premature expectations of utility and caution against short-cuts that could produce misguiding results that ultimately might be both expensive and harmful.

One problem is the absence of a common basis for measurement in the social area comparable to the dollar in the economic area. This lack does not mean that we cannot make useful indices about aspects of social life, but merely that comparisons among the various indicators will require judgments different from those called for in purely economic matters. Suppose that the indices show that control of crimes of violence is improving but that control of theft is not. How shall judgments of police performance be made? Is it more important to control violence or to protect property? Such judgments must be matters of public debate, not scientific decision. We can count lives lost in highway accidents, work days lost by the common cold, grade level of school attainment, patients in mental hospitals, or persons in jails or on parole. Regardless of the unit of measurement, a firm baseline, once established, can be used to appraise gains or losses. Although some methods of aggregation may be developed, a common unit, which would permit comparison of one indicator with another, is not on the horizon at the moment.

Although some form of aggregation is desirable, so that there will not be a confusing array of indicators, aggregation is by no means an essential sign of a useful indicator. In fact, once successful indicators are found, disaggregation may become of telling importance; that is, local indicators may be instructive in showing how the social benefits of our society are distributed among different segments by region, community, ethnic group, age, sex, or occupation. Just as economic indicators require some disaggregation, because unemployment falls unequally on different groups or because the annual income that indicates the poverty level in a city differs from that in a rural area, so, too, the impact of social programs will fall unequally. On such im-

* [While this was in proof the Office of Statistical Policy in the Bureau of the Budget was assigned responsibility for the assembly and dissemination of a coherent system of social indicators.]

portant matters as social participation and cohesion versus isolation and alienation, disaggregated indicators may be particularly important.

The need for fundamental research on techniques of measurement is essential if we are to develop indicators that relate in a valid way to important states of society and conditions of individuals and that, at the same time, are sensitive to change over relatively short time spans. Economic indicators reflect changes taking place currently. The desired social indicators should become precise enough to reflect annual changes.

PROSPECTS FOR AN ANNUAL SOCIAL REPORT

Mention of social indicators usually raises the issue of an annual report, similar to the annual report from the Council of Economic Advisers.

It is important that such a report be produced on an annual basis, for at least two reasons. First, whatever is socially important is always in flux, and rates of change are usually as important as the absolute level of an indicator; only with frequent data points in time can these changes be detected and appropriately taken into consideration in policy decisions. Second, issuing an annual report will further encourage development of indicators that are sufficiently precise to reflect the kinds of changes that take place over short periods of time. It is much less difficult to devise indicators that show changes over long periods of time than to devise those that can measure changes over the short run. The concerns of our society are current, and useful indicators will have to reflect very recent changes in human aspirations and fulfillments.

Social indicators will be best developed if there is a lively interest in them among both social scientists and government officials, as well as among other leaders who will have responsibility to judge the import of what the indicators show concerning changes in the state of our society. Thus, the indicators must be subjected to criticism, for conflicting conclusions may sometimes be drawn from them (or faulty conclusions, or no conclusions at all). With better data, and better social indicators developed from them, successes and failures in education, health, housing, transportation, and other programs would be more precisely defined. Although various agencies could make use of the indicators without a central summarizing report, such a report would provide the basis for establishing priorities, important because social policy always is implemented through selective allocation of available resources.

The federal government has shown an interest in the development of a social report, and a preliminary version of such a report, *Toward a Social Report*, appeared in January 1969. This is, however, primarily a demonstration of the possibility of finding useful social indicators, and we do not believe that the time is ripe for a full-scale annual social report from the government.* Hence, we favor the development, on a trial basis, of an annual social report by behavioral and social scientists in the private sector. By beginning now, on a private basis, we could lay the basis for assessing the quality of present indicators (particularly with respect to annual gains or losses), and for identifying weaknesses in present data and kinds of new data that may be required.

RECOMMENDATION: A PRIVATELY DEVELOPED ANNUAL SOCIAL REPORT

The Committee recommends that behavioral and social scientists outside the government begin to prepare the equivalent of an "Annual Social Report to the Nation," to identify and expedite work toward the solution of problems connected with the eventual preparation of such a report on an official basis. Support for this endeavor should come from private foundations as well as from federal sources.

Several considerations have led us to recommend that a social report be tried out on a private basis. The principal consideration is the desirability of avoiding premature solidification of the effort in official administrative forms. Furthermore, a federal agency, which would need to justify its past use of public funds and to convey a sense of competence to the Congress in its annual budget appeal, would probably be more reluctant than a private group to admit that its early attempts had been relative failures.

* [On July 13, 1969, after this report was already in the hands of the printer, President Nixon announced the establishment of a National Goals Research Staff, to issue a public report, to be delivered by July 4, 1970, and annually thereafter "setting forth some of the key choices open to us, and examining the consequences of these choices." The statement above, that the time is not ripe for a full-scale annual social report, should not be construed as in any sense in opposition to policy statements to be issued by the new National Goals Research Staff. The need for more research on social indicators, and ultimately a social report based on more substantial data, still holds].

Second, under private auspices, an annual social report is less likely to be caught up in partisan justification and attack on governmental social measures. A privately subsidized report can be more objective in analyzing social phenomena that seem to index the success or inadequacy of governmental programs to affect crime, poverty, welfare, education, employment, or health.

Third, private initiative may make it easier to develop indicators in those behavioral areas in which the federal government is traditionally constrained, particularly religion and politics. Deeply seated suspicion of governmental interference with fundamental rights may make it more practical to explore the value of such indicators under private auspices.

Another reason for proposing experimentation with an annual social report on a private basis is to engage more fully behavioral and social scientists outside the government. If they take some initiative, they are likely to become more deeply involved in this important task and make it more central to the research and training in their disciplines.

The Committee proposes that it would be appropriate for either the National Research Council or the Social Science Research Council (or the two jointly) to take the initiative in developing a proposal that would provide for a substantial effort over 5 to 10 years, producing several annual reports on a trial basis, making use of indicators developed in government agencies and perhaps devising others of its own. Initially the report might be given only limited circulation for professional criticism. Experience would suggest appropriate recommendations regarding the continuance of such a report and the auspices within the government or outside it. Precedents already exist in the annual *Economic Report* and in the *Manpower Report*; once a social report became better developed and defined, it could readily take its place with these.*

A COUNCIL OF SOCIAL ADVISERS?

An adequate annual social report doubtless will call attention to problems requiring action. Once such a report is established, we would expect behavioral and social scientists to be involved in con-

---

*See, for example, *Economic Report of the President*, Transmitted to the Congress January 1969; and U.S. Department of Labor, *Manpower Report of the President*, Transmitted to the Congress January 1969.

sidering its implications, in offering constructive proposals for solving some of the problems already shown to exist, or in indicating possible means of avoiding difficulties that are foreseen.

Such advice is already regularly sought by the government. A number of federal agencies have science advisory groups that help them to plan research and review policy related to their missions. The President occasionally, and especially in times of crisis, appoints an ad hoc commission, such as the Commission on National Goals, the Commission on Civil Disorders, or the Commission on Law Enforcement and the Administration of Justice. Such special groups may be necessary to cope with the immediate pressures generated by critical events. And yet, some of the problems to which these Presidential Commissions have addressed themselves fall in areas of social malaise that might have been identified before reaching crisis proportions. Thus, Recent Social Trends showed that many of the problems that we became aware of in the 1960's were already on the horizon in 1933; the massive distortions of the depression called for crisis remedies, so that the long-term significance of "trends" was overlooked. Had such a report been established on a more permanent basis, we might have been more aware of the problems that were developing in the post-depression and postwar years.

While we would applaud the eventual creation of some sort of social science advisory group at the highest levels of the government, we are not prepared at this time to recommend the establishment of a council of social advisers. The analogy often made between the Council of Economic Advisers and a council of social advisers is incorrect. The Council of Economic Advisers has chosen to tie full employment to the stability of the economy and to a desirable level of economic growth, in accordance with economic theory. It has at hand a direct means of inducing changes in the economy, chiefly through recommendations regarding taxation and government spending. Unfortunately the aims to which a council of social advisers might address itself, such as improvement of the quality of life, cannot be stated as precisely and unequivocally as the economists' goals of full employment and economic stability. Furthermore, means for implementing the economic advisers' recommendations, corresponding to fiscal and monetary policy, would not be as apparently available to a council of social advisers.

When social indicators are better established, and an annual report shows that the indicators do indeed signal changes in the quality of life that deserve attention, then a high-level body concerned with policy statements on these matters would be desirable. Even if aggregate indicators of the quality of life are less likely than aggregate indicators of the economic state of the nation, specifics with respect to education, crime, and natural resources are likely to be of great value, and some guidelines toward priorities should emerge. Even if overall correctives, such as taxation and monetary policy, are not at hand, the government does indeed have many policies bearing on health, education, recreation, housing, and other matters within the purview of an eventual council of social advisers.

We therefore recommend immediate and sustained action with regard to social indicators and an annual social report, postponing until some future time the establishment of a permanent council of social advisers.

7
THE POTENTIALS
OF LARGE-SCALE
SOCIAL RESEARCH

The development of a system of social indicators will be
a difficult and costly undertaking, perhaps on a scale that social science
research has not often achieved. To be effective, it will have to be
comprehensive in scope and unquestionably accurate. These requirements imply the need for both manpower and machine capacity to
handle great quantities of data, and foresight in planning. Where data
on a large scale are needed, meticulous care will be required in determining what data are to be collected, in preparing the plans for
their collection, and in working out problems of storage and retrieval.

LARGE-SCALE DATA IN THE SERVICE OF SCIENCE
AND POLICY

The U.S. Census provides the historical example of large-
scale data that have proved to be immensely useful to social scientists
who generally have not participated in their collection. Without it,
demography, one of the best developed of the social science fields,
would be in a far more primitive state. The Census is expensive
(costing some $140 million in a Census year) and illustrates the cost
of collecting data on a large scale.

The Brookings Econometric Model of the United States (initially
constructed under the auspices of the Social Science Research Council) is a product of social science research of wide scope, based on a
great many data gathered by others, and thus not requiring a very
large team of research workers for construction of the model itself.
The model is the result of an effort to improve and go beyond the

kind of national accounts represented in the computation of the gross national product, which are so important in the thinking and recommendations of the Council of Economic Advisers. By the end of 1968 this model contained several hundred equations designed to provide a quantitative explanation of the manner in which various features of the economy interact. The larger scale of this model, as compared with earlier models, makes possible a more detailed treatment of sectors of the economy, which is more precise and, therefore, more useful for policy planning.

The Human Relations Area Files were organized originally by a group of anthropologists at Yale University, who began by assembling all available ethnological data (especially on nonliterate cultures); these data are classified under a number of rubrics to permit cross-cultural generalizations about child-rearing practices, taboos, family structure, political organization, and so forth. Data for a sample representative of all known cultures, historical and contemporary, were to be included, and the files now contain an abundance of this material. The files are duplicated at a number of university centers in this country and abroad; they have been used not only by anthropologists but also by psychologists, sociologists, and political scientists in their researches. One study, based on data on 80 cultures that had been gathered by anthropologists in the Area Files, illustrates the advantages of a program of this sort. It was found that for those cultures in which male children were subjected to various sorts of physical stress during the first two years of their lives, the adult males averaged 2.7 inches taller than the adult males in those cultures in which the male infants were not so stressed, even though the racial backgrounds of the cultures were matched as carefully as possible. These somewhat surprising results are being checked by contemporary studies in Africa, for they appear to have implications for child-rearing that should not be overlooked. Apparently, an appropriate amount of physical stimulation may be a good thing in infancy.

The American Institutes of Research, in their large-scale "Project Talent," are accumulating an extensive file of data on high school students of various abilities, obtained through aptitude and intelligence tests. With these data and followup data on future academic and vocational careers, it should be possible to determine the effects of schooling and abilities on career achievement.

Congress has occasionally felt so strongly about the need for better information on a social problem that it has, by legislation, authorized research on a scale that would not otherwise have been undertaken.

In accordance with an authorization passed in 1955, the Joint Commission on Mental Illness and Mental Health was created to conduct research and to make recommendations for improving mental health facilities throughout the nation. Its report, *Action for Mental Health* (1961), presented a comprehensive plan for federal and state programs to strengthen the nation's mental health resources, and the results have been seen in new programs, particularly at the local level, with reductions of emphasis upon residential care for the mentally ill in large state hospitals. A second example of work resulting from congressional action is the report entitled *Equality of Educational Opportunity* (already described in Chapter 2) based on an instruction by Congress to the Commissioner of Education.

These examples point out that when social science research is directed to problems in areas of social concern, whether in economics, mental health, or education, it is likely to become large in scope. Our concern is to consider how social scientists can best prepare for the demands likely to be made on them in the future.

THE CRITICAL IMPORTANCE OF DATA

Although one may speculate about the eventual role of the behavioral and social sciences, it is already clear that a great deal of responsibility for social and economic policy rests with the collectors and users of social data.

The factual basis of the "war on poverty" may be found in the 1960 Census, which showed that more than 10 million families had annual incomes of less than $3,000, and in the subsequent data on income distribution obtained by the Current Population Survey, which further refined the picture of low-income families. In a very important sense the reawakened awareness of poverty was stimulated by these facts.

A conservative estimate places an annual value of $5 billion on the grants-in-aid that federal government agencies distribute to local communities and states according to formulae based on Decennial Census statistics. The importance of these data is enormous and, regrettably, their applicability is constantly and increasingly threatened by outmoding, sometimes with curious results. The legislation for one antipoverty program, for example, specified the basis of grants to communities to be the number of families with children in which annual income was below a specified amount as reported by the Decennial Census. The seven-year-old data pointed to, among other places, a number of metropolitan suburban communities whose character had changed considerably since 1960.

The Consumer Price Index serves as the basis for wage adjustments in some contracts of unions with management. Farmers receive subsidies based on indices of farm prices. Obviously, the data that serve such purposes must warrant the confidence placed in them.

Planning, forecasting, and evaluating the effects of programs require extensive and detailed data. City planners, confronted with the task of designing urban transportation systems, need detailed data on the journey to work—that is, the commuting patterns of residents of urban areas, including residents of both the inner city and the suburbs. To be of any real value for planning highway and rapid transit systems, such data must be provided in great detail, preferably block by block within the city for both origin and destination. Large-capacity computers together with the conceptual equipment of urban geography permit handling of the masses of detailed data that block-by-block reporting provides for large cities. Housing agencies, as well as banks and other financial institutions, require block-by-block data for use in community development, urban renewal, and similar programs.

Many other social purposes are served by social research that requires detailed data about individuals (although, as we shall point out, these individuals need not be identified). For example, personal information about individual states of health (including numbers of days spent in bed with respiratory illness) was essential for measuring the course of the Asian flu epidemic of 1957–1958 and in deciding not to launch a mass immunization campaign. The planning of educational programs and facilities depends on accurate information about families, including age and educational level of parents, ethnic composition, migration, and employment patterns. Highly detailed data about families enable demographers to develop more precise models of behavior that are valuable predictors of such varied matters as the fiscal requirements of the social security and welfare systems, the supply of draft-age men, the housing market, and the demands for education and employment.

The assessment of the outcomes of deliberate interventions in social processes will also require detailed accurate information, and an increasing number of federal programs incorporate a requirement for their evaluation. What will be the socioeconomic effects of the labor-force provisions of the Immigration Act of 1965? Will it greatly change the ethnic composition of some cities? Some rural areas? Will it affect particular occupations differentially? Will it affect technological change in particular industries? More detailed data on both corporate and individual expenditure and savings patterns would have been an enormous help in making a more comprehensive assessment of the economic effects of the 1964 reduction in federal income taxes. It is equally true that detailed data of the same sort would permit a greatly refined evaluation of the 1968 income-tax increase. Accurate information about individual incomes is impersonally useful in calculation of "lifetime earnings," a statistical datum that is acceptable in some states as legal evidence in compensation litigation.

THE MULTIPLE USE OF DATA, AND PROBLEMS RAISED BY ASSEMBLING DATA ON INDIVIDUALS

These developments in the scale of social research, and other promising ones, depend in large measure on modern techniques for processing data, especially those involving computers. A computer's capacity to make readily available a vast amount of information about a social unit (a person, firm, school system, or nation) makes it possible to perform complex analyses with far greater speed and accuracy than ever before.

The source of this greater capacity is not only the more dependable memory of the computer and its ability to perform complex routines without error at high speed, but also the possibility of analysis by individual units rather than by aggregates. "Microanalysis" (based on detailed descriptions of individual units) is sensitive to changes in assumptions and to variations in specific parameters, whereas aggregated data often obscure relations among basic variables.

An example may make this advantage clearer. The tabulations of U.S. income taxes, published annually in *Statistics of Income*, are quite complete. Nevertheless, it is difficult to use them for any purpose other than the specific purpose for which each was originally prepared. From these tabulations, for instance, it is possible to estimate approximately the effects on individuals and corporations of a change in the structure of tax rates. The approximate nature of the estimate is attributable to the necessity, in tabular material, to group individuals who are more or less alike in some characteristics. The wider the limits of a classification, the larger the error of estimate may be; the narrower the limits, the more accurate. Some years ago, experts on taxation were able to estimate only approximately the effect that broadening the tax base had on tax revenues and were unable to say how the built-in flexibility of the tax would be affected. A few years later, the same experts were able to produce much more accurate estimates by using a sample of the data from 100,000 income-tax returns coded on magnetic tape for use in electronic computers. The data were, of course, carefully coded to make sure that there was no possibility of identifying a particular taxpayer. The computer program for processing these data permitted a research worker to compute tax liabilities of individual taxpayers under alternative rates and exemptions and under varying rules with respect to personal deductions and exclusions from taxable income. The computer-based model could deal rapidly and efficiently with complicated assumptions about differential changes in income among different income classes, marital statuses, geographic areas, and other categories. If data from other sources could be combined with these income data, it would become possible to forecast the effect of tax policies on consumption and savings, as well as to conduct studies of the varying impact through time of personal income taxes on individuals with different time patterns of income. Such studies would be of enormous value in the development of rational and equitable tax structures; they could remove much of the uncertainty in forecasting the consequences of alternative programs. These advantages can be maximized only if data are collected and matched at the level of the individual (person, firm, or other taxable unit) with, of course, full guarantees of nonidentifiability.

Nonidentifiability is essential to the protection of the reporting unit from unwarranted intrusion into privacy, from burdensome requests for information, and from having the data about the reporting unit used illegitimately or to its disadvantage. This problem becomes paramount when a great many diverse data are collected about a single individual. When different sorts or sources of data are matched for the purpose of meeting the data needs of a complex model of some social process, it may appear as though the interests of the researcher were in the singular affairs of individual units. Quite the opposite is true. The social scientist does not need to know the identity of an individual unit. His only reason for using a name or a code number is to be sure that two or more pieces of information from different sources are accurately matched—for example, that Firm A's 1967 profits are matched to its 1968 profits, not to those of Firm B. Many research purposes require that two or more kinds of information about the same individual be compared, but it is not necessary to know the name and address of the individual or any other "identifying" information that would enable his friends, enemies, employers, or colleagues to recognize him. If a name or an identifying number is secured by the social scientist, it is for purposes of matching or followup, as in longitudinal studies of individual development. It is important to keep clear the sharp distinction between the needs of the social scientist for detailed but anonymous data (mostly facts supplied directly by the individual) and those of the credit- or police-dossier builder, to whom identity is paramount (although at present he depends largely on reputation and statements of third parties).

Social scientists recognize the danger in misappropriation and misuse of data originally gathered for legitimate administrative or research purposes. They endorse safeguards of confidentiality and anonymity and the same prohibition on identification of respondents that the U.S. Census employs. The Census has been highly successful in protecting the anonymity of respondents. Many social scientists would welcome statutory protection of the confidentiality of communications between researcher and respondent. Such legal protections do not extend to survey or to psychological-test data, but the ethical codes of the relevant professional groups are directly concerned with the preservation of respondent anonymity. Except when tests or questionnaires have been subpoenaed (a risk the social scientist deplores), social scientists have an excellent record of keeping faith with their respondents concerning anonymity.

The aim of behavioral and social science is to understand human behavior and society and to predict the consequences of changes in persons and their environment. Such changes may be attributable to the introduction of programs, policies, or other deliberate interventions (from any sector of the society) in on-going social processes. Understanding and prediction can come about only if concepts and theories are based on dependable evidence and if accurate data can be used in forecasting and evaluation. The values to society of accurate and adequate data are abundant, not only for developing stronger behavioral science, but also directly for the guidance of public policy. This point was recognized by a special panel appointed by the Office of Science and Technology.* It is said of individual rights:

The individual has an inalienable right to dignity, self-respect, and freedom to determine his own thoughts and actions within the broad limits set by the require-

*Executive Office of the President, Office of Science and Technology, *Privacy and Behavioral Research*, February 1967.

ments of society. The essential element in privacy and self-determination is the privilege of making one's own decision as to the extent to which one will reveal thoughts, feelings, and actions.

Of society's need for knowledge through research, the report says:

If society is to exercise its right to know, it must free its behavioral scientists as much as possible from unnecessary constraints. Yet behavioral scientists, in turn, must accept the constructive restraints the society imposes in order to establish that level of dignity, freedom, and personal fulfillment that men treasure virtually above everything else in life.

A NATIONAL DATA SYSTEM

If the behavioral and social sciences are to grow toward the more developed and more useful stage we envision, they will require greater access to data collected nationally both routinely and for special purposes. A great many government agencies besides the Census Bureau now collect data of particular interest to social scientists (see Table 7-1). These data represent a substantial investment of human and material resources by both collecting agencies and respondents. It is important, therefore, that the data be used as fully as possible for the purposes of social research and that potentially useful data not be destroyed because their original purpose has been served.

This concern for the preservation and use of economic data led a committee of the Social Science Research Council in 1965 to propose the establishment of a federal data center.* They also proposed the development of standard procedures and uniform practices by statistics-collecting agencies for the retention of material and for making it available under rules for preventing disclosure of respondent's identity. The committee's recommendation for a center was based on its assessment of the formidable problems of coordination among agencies in the decentralized federal statistical apparatus in this country and on recognition that outside requests for data imposed a severe burden on the data-processing facilities and the manpower of operating agencies.

*Richard Ruggles, chairman, "Report of the Committee on the Preservation and Use of Economic Data to the Social Science Research Council, April 1965," in U.S. House of Representatives Committee on Government Operations, *The Computer and Invasion of Privacy*, Hearings before the Special Subcommittee on Invasion of Privacy, 89th Cong., 2nd sess., 1966, pp. 195–253.

TABLE 7-1 FEDERAL STATISTICAL PROGRAMS: OBLIGATIONS FOR FY 1968

Programs by Broad Subject Areas	FY 1968 Actual (in millions of dollars)
Labor statistics (Departments of Agriculture, Interior, and Labor; National Science Foundation)	27.1
Demographic and social statistics (Departments of Agriculture, Commerce, Justice, and Health, Education, and Welfare; National Science Foundation; Office of Economic Opportunity)	39.3
Prices and price indices (Departments of Agriculture, Commerce, and Labor)	6.6
Production and distribution statistics (Departments of Agriculture, Commerce, Defense, Interior, and Transportation; Civil Aeronautics Board; Interstate Commerce Commission)	31.7
Construction and housing statistics (Departments of Commerce, and Housing and Urban Development; Federal Home Loan Bank Board)	3.5
National income and business financial accounts (Departments of Agriculture, Commerce, and Treasury; Federal Trade Commission; Securities and Exchange Commission)	10.1
Total, principal current programs	118.3

Source: Bureau of the Budget, *Special Analyses of the Budget of the U.S., FY 1970*, 1969, Table F. 1, p. 71.

A year later, a task force of the Bureau of the Budget on storage of and access to government statistics found the decentralized statistical apparatus both inadequate—in the sense of failing to do things that should and could be done—and inefficient—in the sense of not doing what it does at a minimum cost and not getting the most for what it spends.* This task force also recommended establishment of a national data center with responsibility for integrating and storing in accessible form all the large-scale systematic bodies of demographic, economic, and social data generated through federal agencies. Again, the recommendation recognized the need for statutory protection of respondents against disclosure.

Neither of these study groups (nor others working at the same time) anticipated the amount of public concern (and misunderstanding) over the purposes and the unanticipated potentialities of a national data center; and neither seems to have devoted very much attention (understandably, for their time and resources were quite limited) to some of the technical problems of both matching and protecting the security of machine-readable data. Furthermore, after these reports were issued, there appeared some technical papers that questioned the necessity of a center and of assembling physically all the statistical material in one place.

The Congress has reviewed the various proposals for a national data center, and opinion is divided on the best action to be taken. In the spring of 1967, the Joint Economic Committee of the Congress held hearings on the basis of which it concluded that the statistical programs of the federal and state governments were not sufficiently integrated or coordinated and that further integration would help the design and administration of government programs. The committee concluded that problems of privacy were serious but soluble and recommended that "work should proceed toward the establishment of a national statistical servicing center."†

The House Committee on Government Operations, on the other hand, gave a more cautious endorsement. Viewing the dangers to privacy with alarm, this committee recommended that the Bureau of

---

*Carl Kaysen, chairman, "Report of the Task Force on the Storage of and Access to Government Statistics" (October 1966), in U.S. Joint Economic Committee, *The Coordination and Integration of Government Statistical Programs*, Hearings before the Subcommittee on Economic Statistics, 90th Cong., 1st sess., 1967, pp. 195–205.

†U.S. Joint Economic Committee, *The Coordination and Integration of Government Statistical Programs*, Report of the Subcommittee on Economic Statistics, 90th Cong., 1st sess., 1967, p. 9.

the Budget not only submit detailed plans for a national data center to the Congress, but also that it explore fully the problem of protection of privacy. The committee also recommended that standing committees of the Congress be given access to the national data bank, to give it equal capability with the executive branch in evaluating legislative proposals.*

We are convinced that the problems of making nationally collected data more useful while protecting the privacy of individual respondents can, in principle, be solved. These problems, however, should not be underestimated; accordingly, we make two recommendations designed to improve the national data base and to make the behavioral and social sciences more useful for public-policy and private-planning purposes.

RECOMMENDATION: A NATIONAL DATA SYSTEM

The Committee recommends that a special commission be established to investigate in detail the procedural and technical problems involved in devising a national data system designed for social scientific purposes; that it recommend solutions for these problems and propose methods for managing a system that will make data maximally useful, while protecting the anonymity of individuals.

We believe that such a commission will need two or three years to make its study and will require a full-time professional staff, as well as an advisory committee to coordinate ideas from the social sciences with those of federal agencies, computer specialists, and responsible lay members. We believe that the commission could be organized either within federal agencies or under the aegis of a private body, but that federal financing, as well as full cooperation, will be required for its success.

Among the early tasks of the special commission would be:

1. To inventory all relevant data, both historical and contemporary, in the federal system.

---

*U.S. House of Representatives, *Privacy and the National Data Bank Concept*, H.R. 1842, Thirty-fifth Report by the Committee on Government Operations, 90th Cong., 2nd sess., 1968.

2. To develop procedures to enforce uniform disclosure standards so that the legal requirement of confidentiality would be met.

3. To cooperate with state and local governments to perform similar tasks for data generated at those levels of government.

4. To devise methods to assemble and integrate data and preserve it in usable form.

5. To set standards in cooperation with others for further data-collection efforts.

In making this recommendation we support three earlier reports.*

Recommended adjustments in the existing federal data system, if accepted, will not be sufficient to meet fully society's needs for social data. One reason is simply that certain kinds of information are not collected at all now. For instance, although the Uniform Crime Reports maintained by the FBI provide data from local and state police departments on crimes reported to them, these reports probably seriously understate the total amount of crime—especially larceny and assault. A more sensitive indicator of the amount of crime could be obtained from a sample survey of the general population to learn the rate and type of victimization, for studies by sociologists have indicated that a victim often does not report a crime to a police agency.

The present federal statistical system is inadequate also because many of its agencies collect data, for administrative or regulatory purposes, in terms and categories that suit these purposes but are inappropriate for research purposes, or are mutually inconsistent. For example, social security records are collected on an individual basis, consumer expenditure studies on a household basis, and internal revenue records partly on both. It may be possible to integrate information from these several sources by appropriate matching procedures. For certain purposes, new or additional collection of data may be essential.

Our belief that governmental data-gathering, and the accumula-

---

*Richard Ruggles, chairman, "Report of the Committee on the Preservation and Use of Economic Data to the Social Science Research Council, April 1965," in *The Computer and Invasion of Privacy*, 1966, pp. 195–253; Carl Kaysen, chairman, "Report of the Task Force on the Storage of and Access to Government Statistics" (October 1966), in *The Coordination and Integration of Government Statistical Programs*, 1967, pp. 195–205; *Communications Systems and Resources in the Behavioral Sciences*, NAS Pub. 1575 (Washington, D.C.: National Academy of Sciences, 1967).

tion of large masses of now scattered data, would significantly strengthen the social sciences led us to make the previous recommendation, looking toward a national data system. However, we believe privacy to be so important an issue that we offer another recommendation.

RECOMMENDATION: PROTECTION OF ANONYMITY

The Committee recommends the establishment within an appropriate agency of the federal government, or as an interagency commission, of a high-level continuing body, including nongovernmental members, to investigate the problems of protecting the anonymity of respondents, to prescribe actions to resolve the problems, and to review the dangers that may arise as new techniques of data-matching are developed.

Information technology is advancing so rapidly that we do not believe that an *ad hoc* commission could foresee the problems far enough ahead to make the necessary recommendations. We believe that the benefits of science are potentially so great that we must find ways to continue to capitalize on its advances. Yet, it would be intolerable to allow these advances to create limits on freedom.

OTHER DATA ARCHIVES

Social scientists also use many data that are not collected by government. A number of private data archives have been established to serve as repositories of these data. A principal type of archive stores the results of public opinion polls that, when studied over time, may indicate changes in social values and beliefs.

Most data stored in archives were collected independently and were not intended to be cumulative. They are, therefore, not directly comparable. Occasionally, secondary analysis of these data will produce derived data in time series. For example, different data sets can often be used to compare public opinion on the same subject at two different times. But probably the most cumulative and comparable studies to date are those relating to federal elections. There is a considerable variety of political data: election statistics, legislative roll-call votes, and data on political elites. Large numbers of health and welfare data also exist.

These archives have been used primarily for training purposes at the graduate and undergraduate levels. Courses have been developed at a number of institutions on quantitative data analysis and the methodology of secondary data analysis, as well as on substantive areas, such as legislative behavior and public opinion. As more young professionals are trained in these new courses, social scientists will know better what to include in the archives and how better to use them.

In 1967 there were at least 25 such archives, ranging in size from 40,000 to 12 million cards containing data.*

One reason for the appearance and proliferation of social data archives at this time is the computer, which permits quick and accurate analysis of large masses of research data. The capacity of the computer and the possibilities of compact storage on microfilm, microfiche, and other such devices pose problems of what to store. While machine-retrievable data are much more useful than old-fashioned hand files, they do not relieve the archivist of the burden of deciding what materials will be of most use to future social scientists. Intelligent decisions cannot be made in the absence of experience, which is just beginning to accumulate. We consider nongovernmental data archives to be highly desirable, and, therefore, make the following recommendation.

RECOMMENDATION: NONGOVERNMENTAL DATA ARCHIVES

The Committee recommends that continuing support be made available by federal agencies and private foundations to consortia of universities and other private nonprofit organizations for the necessary development and professional staffing of data archives.

Having made this recommendation, we offer a caveat. The number of data archives has increased rapidly, without sufficient concern in all cases for the quality of data being stored. Proper storage requires certain skills and resources to assure the adequacy of the data being stored and satisfactory methods of access and distribution. The nature of the data-collection effort must be made clear in all cases, and consolidation achieved wherever possible. Sufficient staff must be provided to assure and increase the proper utilization of stored data.

---

*"Social Science Data Archives in the United States, 1967" (New York: Council of Social Science Data Archives, September 1967).

While urging support, we also urge close cooperation between the granting agencies and the archival groups in the social science community to prevent fragmentation, waste, and haphazard accumulations. While these efforts are in their infancy, progress should be deliberate enough to permit looking ahead as far as possible. Later correction of error, as in the recataloging of a library, becomes increasingly difficult and costly.

There are many other kinds of archival problems, to which the historians are perhaps most alert. Historical materials, often at local levels, have proved to be of immense value: personal documents, notarial and vital records, organizational documents, and "fugitive materials"—political posters, "underground" newspapers, and the like. We recommend supporting efforts in the direction of greater use of such materials.

RECOMMENDATION: HISTORICAL ARCHIVES

> *The Committee recommends that historians and other social scientists give special attention to the intellectual and technical problems of sampling, preserving, and indexing such fugitive material as may prove of interest to historians and other social scientists of the future.*

Special attention should be paid to the collection of materials that cannot be obtained from ordinary library or museum sources. We have not attempted to estimate the costs connected with these nongovernmental data archives. The funds required can best be estimated on the basis of proposals submitted. In view of the many uncertainties and the degree of innovation involved, it would probably be helpful to obtain funds for pilot studies prior to major commitments. Once an archive is established, the obligation mounts to continue it.

The support of university libraries will be mentioned later (Chapter 10), but we wish here to note the archival function of the library. Libraries are national resources, containing many, if not most, of the recoverable data from the past; hence, their support should receive primary consideration in connection with archives. With modern reproduction methods, many kinds of documents (pamphlets, posters, and so forth) that are difficult to file on library shelves can now be cared for more easily in libraries.

We may call special attention to the work going on to develop social science information systems. Such systems represent integrative types of data dissemination, and the proposed centers often have clearinghouse functions. This topic has been extensively treated in another report.*

SURVEY RESEARCH FACILITIES AS NATIONAL RESOURCES

National surveys provide a primary source for many of the data to be used in the development of social indicators, in a national data system, and to be stored in the recommended archives. They also serve many other purposes of social science research. Accurate survey data are not easy or cheap to collect, and survey research depends on the existence of organizations able to carry on high-quality work at the national level. A survey-research facility requires a central staff that is capable of designing and selecting national samples of respondents; able to design, pretest, and "debug" questionnaires or interview schedules; and equipped to code, tabulate, and analyze raw data, as well as to write reports. In addition, a survey research center needs a field staff of conscientious interviewers who are selected, trained, and supervised in their work by another part of the central staff. Such organizations are difficult to establish and expensive to maintain, yet without them many research tasks in applied, as well as basic, social science would be difficult or impossible. The large-scale surveys to which this report has frequently referred would not have been done, or at least they would have been long delayed, if high-quality facilities had not been available to meet critical needs for data. These centers are the social science equivalents of observatories or accelerators. Attention should be directed, therefore, to the organization and maintenance of national centers for survey research.

The Bureau of the Census is an effective national resource, but the demands made on it within the government itself are already so heavy that it cannot be expected to extend its services much farther to the nongovernmental research community.

Researchers requiring survey facilities are being served by a number of independent agencies, both profit and nonprofit. Notable among the nonprofit agencies are the National Opinion Research Center,

*Communication Systems and Resources in the Behavioral Sciences, NAS Pub. 1575 (Washington, D.C.: National Academy of Sciences, 1967). See also, Scientific and Technical Communication: A Pressing National Problem and Recommendations for Its Solution, NAS Pub. 1707 (Washington, D.C.: National Academy of Sciences, 1969).

associated with the University of Chicago, and the Survey Research Center, associated with The University of Michigan. A number of state-university-related survey centers and a few regional ones also provide services.

These facilities face a major difficulty in that most of their work has to be done on grants or contracts. As a result, their work flow is uneven, thus making it difficult to maintain a high-level staff. In addition, present government regulations require cost-sharing on research grants to universities. These centers, however, have only limited independent funds to be used for such purposes, and because their work is likely to be of large scale and expensive, their host universities are reluctant to furnish the required share.

As the behavioral and social sciences move into increasing demands for regional or national data, the Committee believes that some method will have to be found for providing sustaining funds for the needed survey research centers.

8
VALUES, ETHICS, AND PRIVACY

Behavioral and social scientists, because of their concern with the organization of human societies, human behavior, and the quality of life, necessarily deal with human values; they find that ethical problems are inescapable. People have strong views on matters with which social scientists deal, such as the effectiveness of various forms of government, styles of leadership, or appropriate relationships between majority and minority groups. Because these personally held views are based wholly or mainly on value judgments, it is difficult for some to see how social scientists can go about their work with the same objectivity and detachment expected of other scientists. Objective study is the scientist's role, however, and as a scientist the behavioral and social researcher must be guided only by the evidence, not permitting his personal preferences to influence the outcomes of his research. This is by no means easy, and the more relevant his work is to problems of policy, the more difficult his task becomes.

OBJECTIVITY IN THE BEHAVIORAL AND SOCIAL SCIENCES

Science is a public affair; it deals with communicable information that can be verified by competent individuals. This constitutes the objectivity of science.

Debates over appropriate scientific methods are valuable in sensitizing social scientists to the misunderstandings and fears relating to their science; but the methods of the biological and physical sciences have led to so much firm knowledge and to so much control over natural phenomena (including matters that affect the lives of human beings, as in the case of nutrition and medicine), that they provide proven models for other sciences to follow. Moreover, the scientific successes already achieved in the behavioral and social sciences through the use of familiar methods of science are great enough to demonstrate the validity of these methods as applicable to behavior.

Although openness and objectivity make scientific methods highly efficient tools for arriving at consensus, they contain some hazards that the opponents of science recognize. Some fear, for example, that on the basis of a scientist's recommendation undesirable developments, such as the despoliation of a natural beauty spot in locating a factory, might occur—not because the scientist is lacking in objectivity, but because he may be insensitive to values outside the sphere of his science. Therefore, the scientist must recognize that applications of his science are limited in their adequacy at any one point in time, and those who apply scientific findings cannot take into account all of their social consequences. The social scientist must be unusually sensitive to the values inherent in what he proposes, particularly hidden values of which he may be unaware. Furthermore, the social scientist cannot be given full responsibility with respect to the policy judgments into which his findings enter. The policy-makers responsible for making such judgments would do well, however, to make as much use as possible of the knowledge that the behavioral and social sciences provide. Greater danger lies, not in science, but in the pitting of one man's subjective judgments against another's, when the only way to resolve the conflict is through suppression of minorities. Objectivity, however imperfect, implies a less arbitrary exercise of power than does subjectivity.

THE STUDY OF VALUE-LADEN TOPICS

Research, as such, is neutral with respect to values, but this does not prohibit the scientist from being concerned with values: what values have achieved consensus, what value-conflicts hold back agreement, what consequences men's values have for the individual and society. One can study the effect of religious belief without accepting (or denying) the validity of that belief; one can study the distribution of race prejudice without being either a "racist" or a "reformer." There are difficulties inherent in the study of this kind of problem because of the sensitivities involved, but in principle, the task is no different from that of studying any other phenomena.

Within a framework of accepted values and goals, the behavioral and social scientist may not appear to be neutral. Even when the neutral stance is achieved and maintained, the social scientist may readily be misjudged as favoring one set of values over another. Yet, explaining the conditions that have led to a riot in a city is not the same as condoning the riot, and measurable psychological differences between ethnic groups are facts, not denials of the democratic doctrine of human equality. There are times, however, when the scientist becomes an advocate of some procedure on the basis of his evidence and the probability that adopting the procedure will help to meet a desired end. Here his roles as scientist and as citizen become difficult to distinguish, and it is out of such situations that the more serious ethical conflicts arise. Social scientists are aware of these problems. A scientist who offers advice on the basis of scientifically grounded experience, exposing his evidence and reasons and subjecting them to full discussion, is not denying the neutrality of the scientific process, even though he himself may be making value commitments.

THE PROBLEM OF PRIVACY AND INDIVIDUAL RIGHTS

We have already considered, in Chapter 7, the possible invasions of privacy that might be engendered in a more advanced system of national data storage and retrieval. The assumption was that the data already existed, so that it was their coordination and possible misuse that threatened the individual.

The behavioral and social scientist faces this problem in collecting data, whether through questioning individuals or through their participation in his experiments. The indispensable principle is that such participation should be based on the informed consent of the participant, but this principle is sometimes difficult to apply. For example, to satisfy this principle in anthropological research, it might be necessary to get the consent of an entire society or, in a study of prediction of grades in a university, of the whole student body. Problems arise in gaining informed consent in studies of children or of mentally incompetent persons. Sometimes laboratory studies require concealing for a time some of the purposes of an experiment, in which case obtaining informed consent is not feasible.

These problems have puzzled social scientists and the agencies that support their research. The Office of Science and Technology established a panel on privacy and behavioral research, to which reference has already been made (Chapter 7). In its report, *Privacy and Behavioral Research*, the panel stated propositions along the following lines:

1. Participation in behavioral investigations should be voluntary and based on informed consent to the extent that this is consistent with the objectives of the research.
2. It is fully consistent with the protection of privacy that, in the absence of full information, consent be based on trust in the qualified investigator and the integrity of the institution under whose auspices the research is conducted.
3. The preservation of confidentiality, once consent has been obtained or institutional justification for the research received, is the responsibility of the investigator.

Professional organizations of behavioral and social scientists accept these propositions and bring effective force to bear to assure that they are observed. There are borderline cases, however, and the ethical questions in such cases are settled, in part, by a give-and-take process in which accommodation between protection of privacy and obtaining necessary information is gradually achieved.

One of the very troubling cases, found chiefly in psychology and sociology, is the kind of experiment that involves deception as to its purpose, or as to what is going to be done to participants or to others as a consequence of the participant's activities in the experiment. Such experiments by psychologists have occasionally involved threatened pain, fear, or humiliation. In sociological research, the deception is more likely to involve observation of participants by an investigator who gains access to them by posing as someone else. Experiments involving such practices are generally frowned upon, not only because of potential harm to those who participate in them, but also because of the damage done to the social sciences when the nature of the experiments is revealed. The protection offered the deceived participants comes through a careful postsession (a debriefing as it has come to be called) in which the scientific purposes of the experiment are explained. Even if participants go away happy and unharmed, and perhaps wiser for their experience, the ethical problems are not thereby completely obliterated.

At the extreme, some of the necessary limitations of experimentation are quite obvious. It is important to discover, for example, the effects of prolonged malnutrition upon mental activity, emotions, and the processes of recovery. A deliberate experimental design for such research offends our sensibilities, yet conscientious objectors volunteered to serve as subjects in such an experiment in World War II, on the valid grounds that what was found in observation of them could be used in the rehabilitation of starving persons known to be in concentration camps at the time.

Because the issues involved in these matters are so important for the behavioral and social sciences, we believe there should be mechanisms for review of research projects that will assure protection of the privacy of those involved. We therefore offer the following recommendation.

RECOMMENDATION: INSTITUTIONAL REVIEW TO PROTECT THE RIGHTS OF SUBJECTS

The Committee recommends extending the procedure, originated by the Surgeon General of the Public Health Service in July 1966, setting up institutional review panels, outside as well as within the disciplines, for review of research procedures for their adequacy in protecting the rights of subjects against deception, embarrassment, or invasion of privacy.

The Surgeon General's order applied to projects involving the use of human subjects when funds of the Public Health Service were involved. We believe that the provisions should also be applied to research supported by funds from other agencies and by nongovernment funds. These review procedures would help in the articulation of principles and guidelines, which could then be fed back into the training of research scientists and into the professional codes of the disciplines.

These considerations apply to the research uses of data on individuals, and not to the clinical or service use. When questions are asked in an interview for employment, or for admission to a clinic, or in the course of private consultation, new ethical issues arise. The protection of the individual's right to privacy raises a different set of questions in these circumstances, for here his identity is central, and questions of protection concern who has the right to know, rather than more technical problems of concealing personal identity in research reports.

There are many threats to privacy, of course, that are unrelated to behavioral and social science research. Surveillance by private agents, credit organizations, and mere curiosity seekers is insidious, in sharp contrast to organized scientific efforts, which have ethical controls built into them. Modern electronic eavesdropping devices, remote television cameras, and many other products of modern technology threaten privacy in their own ways. The story is not entirely new: tapping of telegraph lines was common in the Civil War.*

The advances of science themselves sometimes pose ethical problems concerning the rights of individuals, dramatized in 1968 by the beginning of heart transplantation, and perhaps soon to be raised again in connection with possible control of genetic factors.† Whatever the origins of the advance in knowledge (whether in the synthesis of a new drug, in surgical techniques and immunology, or in the control of an individual's genes) the problem soon becomes one of social and ethical concern, and the kinds of controls needed to protect the rights of individuals will have to be considered by policy-makers. They will need the benefit of all the knowledge that is available in making the important decisions that will be required.

ETHICAL ISSUES AND CODES OF CONDUCT

Although we have urged certain official actions to protect the privacy and anonymity of individuals about whom data are gathered, ethics is far too subtle and sensitive a matter to be dealt with by formal legislative procedures alone. In a profession, ethics are communicated by the established members and inculcated in new members by example. The range of experience of any one member, or even a few members, of a profession is limited; therefore, the accumulated experience tends to be collected in codes of ethics. The American Psychological Association set out in 1948 to develop a code of ethics on the basis of actual experiences of its members: situations in which it had proved puzzling to know what to do, or in which there were conflicts between courses of action, each justified in its own right. Hence, without the kind of moralizing that sometimes goes into codes of ethics, a number of guidelines were formulated in

*The history of invasion of privacy is well documented in Alan F. Westin, *Privacy and Freedom* (New York: Atheneum, 1967), a book that also gives a full account of the effort of legislatures to deal with the problem.
†See, for example, U.S. Senate Committee on Government Operations, *National Commission on Health Science and Society*, Hearings before the Subcommittee on Government Research, 90th Cong., 2nd sess., 1968.

1953, with case studies appended, so that those entering the field would be exposed to issues that had arisen in the experience of others. Other societies in the behavioral and social sciences have also developed, or are in the process of developing, ethical codes: the American Association for Public Opinion Research, the American Political Science Association, and the American Sociological Association, to name a few.

The primary purpose of the codes is to protect the public in the demands made upon it and in services received, and thus, indirectly, to enhance confidence in and respect for the profession. Because new ethical problems are always arising, if the codes are to be more than pious statements they will require frequent revision to keep them abreast of specific new issues that behavioral and social scientists will be facing in the future.

RESEARCH AS A PUBLICLY SHARED ENTERPRISE

Because the objectivity of science is made possible by its open communication system, in which the results that either confirm or deny a scientist's hypotheses are reported, it is understandable that scientists dislike any restrictions against free communication. This is a different matter from the communication of information about identifiable persons: personal information is privileged, but scientific results are preferably public.

In some circumstances scientific information does not flow freely. This is often the case within industry, where products under development are hidden from competitors. It may obtain in the course of development of a patentable invention, where the patent rights belong to the person who seeks them first. Conflict with respect to copyrights is less frequent, because ethical restraints against plagiarism are strong.

There are other complexities in the free flow of information, such as the publishing of scientific studies in many native languages, publication lags, and inadequate indexing, which have concerned many investigators, but these are not deliberate constraints. The most deliberate, and in some ways most troubling, frustration of free information flow relates to security classification (in its various degrees of restricted, confidential, or secret) of research by government arising out of national needs. We do not propose an elaborate discussion, because the issues have been much debated, but we do wish to state a position in the following recommendation.

RECOMMENDATION: ON SECURITY CLASSIFICATION OF RESEARCH

The Committee recommends that, wherever possible, behavioral and social science research be carried out on an unclassified basis with normal rights of publication by the investigator.

The Committee further recommends that, when it is necessary to classify research for purposes of national security, it be carried out separately from the instructional or degree-granting processes of universities, and preferably in research institutes or other settings entirely outside of universities.

Although we prefer unclassified research, we recognize that some types of behavioral and social science research, entirely legitimate and essential to the national interest, must be classified for reasons of national security. We deplore the conduct of such research in universities because it necessitates obtaining clearance for students who are research assistants or are undertaking their studies in the areas of investigation being classified. We would not wish to see the federal government deprived of the services of the talent that resides in the universities, but we insist on the inappropriateness of classified research within the teaching and training functions of the university.

Behavioral and social scientists working in foreign areas or consulting with foreign colleagues are often suspected of engaging in concealed missions, such as gathering intelligence for the government, which adversely affects their work as scientists. While this, too, is a complex matter that has been much discussed, we wish to express concern, particularly with respect to deception practiced in the name of behavioral or social science. Espionage agents, soldiers, diplomats, and other government representatives engaged in adversarial tasks abroad should be prohibited from posing as social scientists. And social scientists should restrain any desire to assist the government by engaging in activities incompatible with their role as scientists.

The Foreign Affairs Research Council (FAR) was established in 1966 by the Department of State to assess the foreign policy implications of research financed by agencies of the government engaged in foreign affairs or in defense activities. In January 1968, it issued a set of guidelines against deception with which the Committee is in accord.* These guidelines include the following two statements:

When a project involves research abroad it is particularly important that both the supporting agency and the researcher openly acknowledge the auspices and financing of research projects. . . . The government has the responsibility for avoiding actions that would call into question the integrity of American academic institutions as centers of independent research and teaching. . . .

We welcome these statements from official government sources, which suggest a sensitivity to the ethical issues we have been discussing.

IMPROBABILITY OF DANGERS INHERENT IN A STRONG BEHAVIORAL AND SOCIAL SCIENCE

Objectivity in the behavioral and social sciences, as stated earlier, does not prevent the study of controversial topics. It is possible to study the parties to a controversy without taking sides in it, although the consumer of social science research may not always see it this way. It is important to reemphasize that objective research does not always receive an objective reading and review.

In matters relating to policy, the behavioral and social scientist must not only assemble data but also evaluate them in the light of a balancing of conflicting goals and be willing to make recommendations to administrators and policy-makers. He attests to his objectivity (1) by presenting data impartially, (2) by stating the premises for his judgments, and (3) by seeking arrangements whereby evaluative reviews will prevent his being forced into a dogmatic type of prediction in an uncertain world.

The fear that use of a scientifically based social science will so mechanize life that man will be turned into a machine, and that all life will be regulated like the assembly line of a modern manufacturing plant, is not well founded. The social scientist is as concerned as anyone else with the quality of life. He does not expect to be the one to set policies; he expects only to be listened to when policies on which his scientific judgment has relevance are being formulated. He is more concerned to warn against infringements on freedom— not to promote them. He is caught in the same ethical dilemmas as others in our times, but hopes to encourage those processes whereby all voices can be heard.

*FAR Horizons, Vol. 1, No. 1, January 1968. (Department of State)

9
STUDENTS AND
DEGREES

The demands for personnel with advanced degrees in all fields of the behavioral and social sciences provide a wide range of choice for the able student. Thus, it is desirable that he learn about career opportunities as early as possible, and that the fields competing for his services make known their requirements for personnel. For these and other reasons, university departments concerned with producing doctoral candidates are interested in what happens in the secondary school and the undergraduate college. Candidates for the behavioral and social sciences typically choose their areas of specialization later than their colleagues in other fields of science, as shown in Figure 9-1. Very few of them enter their specializations earlier than do those teaching in engineering or the physical or biological sciences. Only history, which is taught widely in high school, is chosen early nearly as often as are natural sciences. It appears that lack of behavioral science in the secondary school may in part account for the delayed career choices.

The preparation of materials to provide students in high schools with appropriate introductions to the behavioral sciences has been encouraged recently by the Office of Education, the National Science Foundation, and a number of private foundations. Substantial projects are under way in anthropology, economics, geography, and sociology to provide intellectual stimulation and to invite students to consider each field for its career opportunities. It does not seem feasible or desirable, however, to establish disciplinary courses in high school paralleling those at the college level. The Committee endorses efforts to devise appropriate curricula to introduce students to a broad spectrum of the behavioral and social sciences without primary emphasis on one or another discipline.

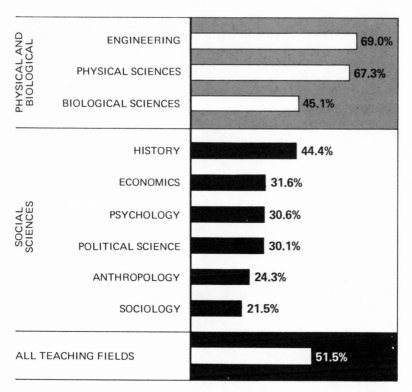

FIGURE 9-1   PERCENT OF FACULTY IN EACH FIELD OF SPECIALIZATION IN UNIVERSITIES AND FOUR-YEAR COLLEGES WHO DECIDED ON THEIR AREA OF SPECIALIZATION BY THE END OF THEIR SECOND YEAR OF COLLEGE.

[Source: U.S. Office of Education, *Teaching Faculty in Universities and 4-Year Colleges, Spring 1963,* oe-53022-63, 1966, Table 15, p. 90.]

BACHELOR'S DEGREES

The number of bachelor's degrees granted in the behavioral and social sciences grew very rapidly between 1957 and 1967, as shown in Table 9-1. (See also Figure SR-2, Summary and Recommendations.) A projection has been made for the future, reflecting the rate of increase over the last 10 years.* Such figures always involve

*Details and alternative models for projection are given in Appendix D.

TABLE 9-1 BACHELOR'S AND 1ST PROFESSIONAL DEGREES ACTUALLY AWARDED IN 1957 AND 1967 AND PROJECTED FOR 1977, BY FIELD OF STUDY

Field	Degrees Awarded		Projected 1977[b]
	Actual		
	1957[a]	1967[a]	
Anthropology	350	1,825	11,200
Economics and agricultural economics	7,393	13,829	24,500
Geography	699	2,163	5,500
History	11,692	31,793	91,000
Political science	5,874	17,733	61,600
Psychology and educational psychology	6,191	19,542	61,400
Sociology and rural sociology	6,383	17,751	49,900
Other social science	10,572	19,959	13,800[c]
Total:			
Behavioral and social sciences	49,154	124,595	318,800[d]
All fields of study[e]	340,347	594,862	1,024,000[f]
Behavioral and social sciences (percent of all fields of study)	14%	21%	31%

[a] Actual values obtained from the Office of Education.
[b] For projection method, see Appendix D.
[c] The computed difference between the projected total and the sum obtained by projecting individual fields.
[d] Detail may not add to total because of rounding.
[e] All fields of study in total U.S. degree-granting institutions.
[f] Projected from Office of Education reports of actual degrees, 1958 to 1967, by methods used in projecting behavioral and social science degrees.

uncertainties about future economic and social conditions, but if present trends continue, behavioral and social science bachelor's degrees will have increased greatly not only in absolute numbers but also in relative numbers, up from 14 percent of all bachelor's degrees in 1957 to 31 percent in 1977.

ADMISSION TO GRADUATE STUDY AND FINANCIAL AID

The number of students applying for graduate study in all fields has been growing rapidly. A study of seniors graduating in 1961 showed that about 80 percent of the behavioral and social science majors hoped to enter graduate work "eventually." A follow-up showed that of all seniors, 64 percent of the social and behavioral sciences bachelors had actually enrolled for graduate work within three years of graduation.*

A related study, following the later careers of the class of 1958, showed that except for economics majors, where the percentage was lower, more than 50 percent of male undergraduate majors in the social sciences had gone on to graduate work within five years of graduation.† The averages were smaller for the women majors: only about 25 to 35 percent of them went on to graduate training. Of course, much of this graduate study is in professional schools or in other fields of study and does not result in graduate degrees in the social sciences themselves. The details of movement between undergraduate majors and doctorates are shown in Table 9-2. Of those who have both AB and PhD degrees in these disciplines, 20 percent shifted their areas of specialization between the undergraduate and graduate degrees. As to movement between social sciences and other areas, there was a net loss in the exchange only in education; in all other areas more persons came from the other areas to social science for the doctorate than went to the other areas from the social sciences. This supports the observation concerning late attraction to the social sciences.

*James A. Davis, *Undergraduate Career Decisions* (Chicago, Ill.: Aldine Publishing Company, 1965), Table A-2.2, p. 234; and Alan S. Berger, *Longitudinal Studies on the Class of 1961: The Graduate Science Students*, Report 107 (Chicago: Ill.: National Opinion Research Center, January 1967), Table II.1, p. 49.
†Data furnished by Mrs. Laure M. Sharp. For a fuller account, see Laure M. Sharp, *Five Years After the College Degree, Part I: Graduate and Professional Education* (Washington, D.C.: Bureau of Social Science Research, Inc., June 1965). (Mimeographed)

TABLE 9-2 SPECIALIZATION CHANGES BETWEEN BACHELOR'S DEGREE AND DOCTORATE

Fields in Which Undergraduate Majors in the Behavioral and Social Sciences Were Awarded Doctorates			Fields in Which Doctorate Recipients in the Behavioral and Social Sciences Were Awarded Bachelor's Degrees		
Field	Number	Percent	Field	Number	Percent
Same social science field for			Same social science field for		
BA and PhD	12,159	58	BA and PhD	12,159	56
Changed to:			Came from:		
Different social science	3,118	15	Different social science	3,118	14
Education	3,720	18	Education	891	4
Humanities	709	3	Humanities	2,046	9
Biological sciences	214	1	Biological sciences	835	4
Physical sciences	141	1	Physical sciences	956	4
Other professional	815	4	Other professional	1,368	6
			Field unknown	697	3
Total	20,876	100	Total	22,070	100

Source: *Doctorate Recipients from United States Universities, 1958–1966*, NAS Pub. 1489 (Washington, D.C.: National Academy of Sciences, 1967), Appendix F.

Only 54 percent of newly entering graduate students in the behavioral and social sciences received some form of financial aid other than loans in the autumn of 1965, while 69 percent of entering graduate students in other science fields received some financial aid. In the second and later years of graduate study 70 percent of the behavioral and social science graduate students received financial aid, as compared to 83 percent in non-social science fields. Psychology graduate students fare better than those in other social science fields; 76 percent received aid, whereas only 68 percent of the students in other social science fields (excluding psychology and history) received aid.*

In addition to receiving a smaller proportion of financial aid in 1965, graduate students in the social sciences were receiving stipends averaging only about 80 percent as large as those of their counterparts in the biological and physical sciences.† (Government agencies provide the same size stipend for students in all fields. It is the relatively smaller amounts available to graduate students in the social sciences from university and private sources that reduce the overall average.)

In view of the need for support of more graduate students we are led to the following recommendation.

RECOMMENDATION: SUPPORT OF GRADUATE STUDENTS IN TRAINING

The Committee recommends that graduate students in the behavioral and social sciences be given financial aid in the same proportions and in the same amounts per student as students in other sciences. To achieve this equality it will be necessary to increase grant assistance in some fields (e.g., history) beyond that commensurate with sheer growth in number of students.

Were support to be increased to place students in the behavioral and social sciences on a parity with those in other science fields, an immediate annual increase of approximately $25 million would be required. This would mean a total graduate student financial aid outlay of $100 million per year, a sum that would have to be increased

---

*The source of these data is National Science Foundation, *Graduate Student Support and Manpower Resources in Graduate Science Education, Fall 1965–Fall 1966*, NSF 68-13, June 1968, Table IV-d, p. 35.

†U.S. Office of Education, *The Academic and Financial Status of Graduate Students, Spring 1965*, OE-54042, 1967, Table 17, p. 30.

each year to take care of increased numbers of students, assuming maintenance of support at the same level.

The "efficiency" of graduate training is of some concern. Although the time required for a PhD is commonly stated as three years, the median registered time is 5.3 years in the social sciences (excluding history) and the average actual elapsed time before acquisition of the PhD is 8.0 years beyond the bachelor's degree; for history the periods are 5.7 and 8.9 years, respectively. These periods are for those who finish; approximately 41 percent fail to complete all the requirements. There are many reasons for these long delays between the AB and the PhD, but finances play a large part; graduate study is often interrupted in order for students to earn money for self-support. Some federal agencies, such as the National Institute of Mental Health, National Science Foundation, and Office of Education, and some foundations (notably the Ford Foundation) have sensed the need to provide for more years of predoctoral support to help students complete training sooner. We offer the following recommendation as an endorsement of these trends in support.

RECOMMENDATION: FOUR- TO FIVE-YEAR GRADUATE SUPPORT

The Committee recommends that the practice of providing assured support for graduate students in good standing for periods of four to five years without reapplication be more widely adopted by federal agencies and private foundations. The Committee further recommends that graduate student support include funds for the direct cost of research by predoctoral students, in addition to tuition and subsistence.

A recent study of NDEA Title IV fellows showed that they completed their doctorates in less time than did a comparable group of students who were supported on a year-by-year basis or who did not receive stipends for graduate education.* The total time required may vary, of course, from field to field. In anthropology, and some parts of history, political science, and sociology, a period of five years appears to be a minimum when fieldwork, including the requirement

*Laure M. Sharp and Barton Sensenig, III, *Study of NDEA Title IV Fellowship Program, Phase I* (Washington, D.C.: Bureau of Social Science Research, Inc., March 1968). (Mimeographed)

of learning native languages, is part of doctoral programs. University departments should make every effort to keep the time spent on degree programs within bounds dictated by necessity.

MASTER'S DEGREES

Just as the social science bachelor's degrees are an increasing proportion of all bachelor's degrees, the master's degrees in these fields have become an increasing proportion of all master's degrees (Table 9-3; see also Figure SR-2, Summary and Recommendations).

The situation of the master's degree in the conventional social science fields is anomalous. Many departments in leading universities will not accept students for graduate work unless they indicate interest in obtaining the doctorate. At these institutions the master's is given either in recognition of a certain amount of work on the way to the doctorate, or as an "also-ran" degree for students who prove unsuited for doctoral training. On the other hand, largely outside these institutions, the master's degree is being awarded more frequently than ever, and those holding this as their highest degree find many satisfactory professional employment opportunities.

The kinds of opportunities open are indicated by those who report their employment to the National Register of Scientific and Technical Personnel. In selected social science fields (Table 9-4), educational institutions appear to be the largest employers of both master's and doctoral degree recipients, although other kinds of employment are widespread. In view of the growing demand for social science knowledge and expertness, particularly for capacity to apply social science for public purposes, it is likely that the market for holders of the master's degree will continue at a high level.

DOCTORAL DEGREES

Doctorate production in the behavioral and social sciences has risen rapidly as in other fields of science, although, unlike the bachelor's and master's degrees, the share of all doctorates has remained essentially constant between 1957 and 1967 and may decline slightly by 1977 (Table 9-5; see also Figure SR-2, Summary and

TABLE 9-3 MASTER'S DEGREES ACTUALLY AWARDED IN 1957 AND 1967 AND PROJECTED FOR 1977, BY FIELD OF STUDY

Field	Degrees Awarded Actual 1957 [a]	Actual 1967 [a]	Projected 1977 [b]
Anthropology	77	357	1,200
Economics and agricultural economics	849	2,147	5,100
Geography	182	463	1,200
History	1,256	4,621	14,600
Political science	535	1,775	4,900
Psychology and educational psychology	1,095	3,772	11,700
Sociology and rural sociology	515	1,193	3,300
Other social science	1,287	4,397	15,300 [c]
Total:			
Behavioral and social sciences	5,796	18,725	57,400 [d]
All fields of study [e]	61,955	157,892	373,200 [f]
Behavioral and social sciences (percent of all fields of study)	9%	12%	15%

[a] Actual values obtained from the Office of Education.
[b] For projection method, see Appendix D.
[c] The computed difference between the projected total and the sum obtained by projecting individual fields.
[d] Detail may not add to total because of rounding.
[e] All fields of study in total U.S. degree-granting institutions.
[f] Projected from Office of Education reports of actual degrees, 1958 to 1967, by methods used in projecting behavioral and social science degrees.

TABLE 9-4 EMPLOYMENT OF ECONOMISTS, PSYCHOLOGISTS, SOCIOLOGISTS, AND POLITICAL SCIENTISTS HOLDING MA OR PHD AS HIGHEST DEGREE, 1968

Types of Employer[a]	Economists		Psychologists		Sociologists		Political Scientists	
	MA	PhD	MA	PhD	MA	PhD	MA	PhD
Educational institutions	46%	76%	54%	60%	76%	88%	71%	87%
Federal government	17	8	5	7	5	3	9	5
State and local governments	5	4	14	6	6	1	5	2
Military	2	([b])	1	1	1	([b])	4	1
Nonprofit organizations	5	4	12	10	7	5	5	3
Business and industry	22	7	9	7	3	1	4	1
Self-employed	2	1	4	8	1	1	1	1
Other employers	1	([b])	1	1	1	1	1	([b])
Total	100%	100%	100%	100%	100%	100%	100%	100%
N =	4,021	6,008	7,499	14,370	2,104	3,272	1,730	2,951

[a] Excludes "Not employed" and "No report."
[b] Less than 1 percent.
Source: National Science Foundation, American Science Manpower, 1968, Appendix Table A-5 (in press).
Note: The National Register, from which these data come, is an incomplete and somewhat unrepresentative sample, but gives some impression of patterns of employment.

TABLE 9-5 DOCTORAL DEGREES ACTUALLY AWARDED IN 1957 AND 1967 AND PROJECTED FOR 1977, BY FIELD OF STUDY

Field	Degrees Awarded		Projected 1977 [b]
	Actual		
	1957 [a]	1967 [a]	
Anthropology	49	136	300
Economics and agricultural economics	313	680	1,700
Geography	47	79	100
History	314	655	1,600
Political science	156	390	900
Psychology and educational psychology	550	1,393	3,300
Sociology and rural sociology	134	327	600
Other social science	114	255	600 [c]
Total:			
Behavioral and social sciences	1,677	3,915	8,900 [d]
All fields of study [e]	8,756	20,621	51,300 [f]
Behavioral and social sciences (percent of all fields of study)	19.2%	19.0%	17.3%

[a] Actual values obtained from the Office of Education.
[b] For projection method, see Appendix D.
[c] The computed difference between the projected total and the sum obtained by projecting individual fields.
[d] Detail may not add to total because of rounding.
[e] All fields of study in total U.S. degree-granting institutions.
[f] Projected from Office of Education reports of actual degrees, 1958 to 1967, by methods used in projecting behavioral and social science degrees. The slight reduction in percent of total results in part from the very rapid increase of the doctorates in engineering.

146

Recommendations). Again, estimates for the future are reported on
the basis of trends from the past, on the assumption that similar conditions will prevail. Alternate projections are given in Appendix D.

Additional estimates of future doctorate production are available
from the questionnaire survey of department chairmen who were
asked to estimate the number of PhD's their departments would be
producing in 1972 and in 1977. For these purposes, the PhD-producing departments in each of six fields of study (anthropology, economics, history, political science, psychology, and sociology) were
classified into two groups, the *large* departments in terms of PhD
production (19 to 25 departments, depending on the size of the
field), and the *other* PhD producers, representing the remaining
departments in the field.* While the percentage of PhD's produced
within the large departments varies somewhat from field to field, the
large departments as a whole, representing 24 percent of the departments surveyed in these six fields, produced 50 percent of the PhD's
in 1967. The estimates of future PhD production by department
chairmen are given in Table 9-6. The data are helpful in making a
choice among the projections shown in Appendix D. It is quite clear
that many of the "large" producers of PhD's are exercising restraint
(detecting a limit to their resources) against an increase as rapid as
they have experienced over the past few years; they expect an increase
below the general trend between 1967 and 1972, and well below that
between 1972 and 1977. It is the "other" departments, many of them
newly entering into PhD production, who have or expect to have
facilities to expand rapidly. The total prediction of 10,609 doctoral
degrees in all behavioral and social science fields in 1977 (Table 9-6)
is 19 percent above the projection of 8,900 doctoral degrees from
trend data (Table 9-5).† Overall, department chairmen do not
expect the rate of growth predicted from the five years between 1962
and 1967 to continue at that rate. These department chairmen
cannot, of course, take into account newly formed departments, but
the rate at which new departments turn out PhD's is very slow during
their first five years or so; therefore, although new departments have
to be reckoned with, they will not make very large differences in the
few years considered.

---

*See Table A-3 in Appendix B for a listing of *large* departments in each field.
†An alternative projection, based on fitting a quadratic equation to the last 10
years of known degree production, projected a total of 11,000 doctorates for 1977.
See Appendix D, page 307.

TABLE 9-6 DOCTORAL DEGREES AWARDED IN 1967 AND ESTIMATED BY DEPARTMENT CHAIRMEN FOR 1972 AND 1977: BY FIELD AND BY SIZE OF DEPARTMENT FOR SIX FIELDS[a]

Field	Departments[b]	Doctoral Degrees					
		Awarded 1967		Estimated 1972		Estimated 1977	
		Total	Mean/Department	Total	Mean/Department	Total	Mean/Department
Anthropology							
Large	19	129	6.8	228	12.0	282	14.9
Other	32	24	0.8	175	5.5	284	8.9
Economics							
Large	23	386	16.8	500	21.7	567	24.7
Other	71	216	3.1	568	8.0	833	11.7
History							
Large	21	391	18.6	483	23.0	531	25.3
Other	85	341	4.0	811	9.5	1,242	14.6
Political science							
Large	25	275	10.9	354	14.5	427	17.1
Other	66	215	3.3	510	7.7	780	11.8
Psychology							
Large	21	379	18.1	521	24.8	629	29.9
Other	99	758	7.7	1,475	14.9	2,106	21.3

Sociology							
Large	23	181	7.9	290	12.6	386	16.8
Other	56	178	3.2	441	7.9	660	11.8
Totals, six fields							
Large	132	1,741	13.2	2,376	18.0	2,822	21.4
Other	409	1,732	4.2	3,980	9.7	5,905	14.4
Total	541	3,473	6.4	6,356	11.7	8,727	16.1
Agricultural economics	31	125	4.0	260	8.4	386	12.5
Educational psychology	38	263	6.9	502	13.2	717	18.9
Geography	45	89	2.0	265	5.9	427	9.5
Linguistics	31	76	2.4	184	5.9	270	8.7
Rural sociology	7	28	4.0	58	8.3	82	11.7
All behavioral and social sciences	693	4,054[c]	5.8	7,625	11.0	10,609	15.3

[a]All figures have been adjusted to correct for failure of some departments to report.
[b]Not all departments granted the PhD in 1967, but all granted at least one PhD between 1960 and 1966.
[c]Estimated total based on responding departments; actual total (from Office of Education) is 3,915.
Source: Departmental Questionnaire.

TABLE 9-7 RELATIVE GROWTH IN DEGREE PRODUCTION BY FIELD OF SCHOLARSHIP, ACTUAL DEGREES 1957 TO 1967; PROJECTED 1967 TO 1977

Field	Bachelor's Degrees		Master's Degrees		Doctorates	
	1967 as Percent of 1957 Actual	1977 as Percent of 1967 Projected	1967 as Percent of 1957 Actual	1977 as Percent of 1967 Projected	1967 as Percent of 1957 Actual	1977 as Percent of 1967 Projected
Behavioral and social sciences	253%	185%	323%	206%	233%	182%
Biological sciences	148	146	215	148	196	185
Physical and mathematical sciences	213	223	304	246	225	205
Engineering	116	112	265	254	439	322
Education	157	159	177	107	220	164
Arts and humanities	208	201	269	199	236	191

Source: Computed from Table A-14 in Appendix E. The projections for 1977 are based on Office of Education figures, which differ somewhat from those made by the survey staff.

GROWTH OF DEGREE PRODUCTION RELATIVE TO OTHER FIELDS

The growth in degree production in all fields of scholarship has been very rapid since 1957, and it is pertinent to compare the behavioral and social sciences with other fields in greater detail than in the earlier tables. By expressing the growth over a 10-year period as a percent of the degrees granted at the end of that period with the degrees granted at the beginning, a comparative figure can be obtained that corrects for the different initial sizes of the fields. This comparison for degrees in 1967 as a percentage of degrees in 1957, and for projected degrees in 1977 as a percentage of degrees in 1967, is given in Table 9-7. Bachelor's and master's production in the behavioral and social sciences showed the greatest growth of any of the fields between 1957 and 1967. Growth in doctoral production was third among the fields listed, far behind engineering but comparable with most of the other fields.

POSTDOCTORAL TRAINING

Increasing numbers of scientists in all fields seek a year or more of research training beyond the PhD degree. This pattern, however, is not established in the behavioral and social sciences (except to a limited extent in anthropology and psychology). For example, in the biological sciences, 27 percent of the PhD recipients between 1964 and 1967 went on with postdoctoral fellowships; in the physical sciences and engineering, 16 percent; the corresponding figure for social sciences generally (other than anthropology and psychology) is 3 percent; in psychology, 13 percent went on with postdoctoral fellowships; and in anthropology, 5 percent.*

The postdoctoral years can have a number of purposes in rounding out the training of the new PhD. He may want to improve his grasp of a special field that is more advanced in another institution where there is better equipment and where more up-to-date techniques can be acquired. Or he may seek to expand his interests into another discipline, as in the case of a developmental psychologist who needs to know more about linguistics to improve his understanding of the

---

*Data from *Doctorate Recipients from United States Universities, 1958–1966*, NAS Pub. 1489 (Washington, D.C.: National Academy of Sciences, 1967), Table 19.

TABLE 9-8 UNFILLED FACULTY POSITIONS IN PHD-GRANTING DEPARTMENTS, BY SIZE OF DEPARTMENT, AUTUMN 1967

Field	Number of Depts.ᵃ	Full-Time-Equivalent Faculty		Unfilled Positions		Ratio (3)/(1)
		Number (1)	Mean (2)	Number (3)	Mean (4)	
Anthropology						
Large	16	293	18.3	14	0.9	0.05
Other	28	286	10.2	24	0.9	0.08
Economics						
Large	19	674	35.5	34	1.8	0.05
Other	63	1,019	16.2	54	0.9	0.05
History						
Large	19	748	39.4	27	1.5	0.04
Other	73	1,533	21.0	56	0.8	0.04
Political science						
Large	20	572	28.6	29	1.5	0.05
Other	53	853	16.1	43	0.8	0.05
Psychology						
Large	19	657	34.6	36	1.9	0.06
Other	87	1,594	18.3	92	1.1	0.06
Sociology						
Large	20	480	24.0	30	1.5	0.05
Other	47	699	14.9	57	1.3	0.11
Geography						
All	37	374	10.1	44	1.3	0.13

ᵃNot corrected for missing replies.
Source: Departmental Questionnaire.

152

development of language in the child. In other cases, he may need to improve his command of research tools; for example, a political scientist may need more work in computer science, or a sociologist or historian may need more statistics. He may require some specific professional experience, such as a staff post in a mental hospital or a year in an anthropological field station. He may wish to serve an internship in a government agency or in some other nonacademic setting. The ends a postdoctoral year can serve are as many as the specializations covered by doctoral training; in some fields, of which anthropology is a good example, work abroad is very important, not only for strengthening language competency, but also for developing more intimate acquaintance with a society of special interest to the investigator.

The growth of postdoctoral training has crept up on the universities so that, although a professor may often be pleased to have someone from another university doing postdoctoral work with him, the university may be unable to provide space, equipment, library access, and the like. Without these, the opportunity for the postdoctoral fellow to have a satisfactory working relationship with his faculty colleagues is dim. It is likely that postdoctoral training will increase. Universities should begin to equip themselves for this eventuality.*

FUTURE FACULTY SUPPLY AND DEMAND

One of the principal obstacles to the more rapid expansion of the behavioral sciences both within and outside the universities has been shortage of professional personnel qualified for the instructional and research positions that are currently available. Department chairmen whom we surveyed reported that in 1967 they had substantial numbers of unfilled faculty positions at the beginning of the academic year. In most of the disciplines, unfilled positions constituted 5 or 6 percent of the full-time-equivalent faculty (see Table 9-8); but for geography and sociology, the percentage was higher. Further analysis shows a greater number of vacancies in those departments of anthropology and sociology that are not among the largest producers of PhD's. The existence of such unfilled positions, especially in departments anticipating the greater expansions in PhD output,

*See *The Invisible University: A Study of Postdoctoral Education in the United States*, NAS Pub. 1730 (Washington, D.C.: National Academy of Sciences, 1969).

gives rise to questions about the attainability of departmental goals. The shortages are doubtless even greater in the four-year colleges not included in our questionnaire survey.

Academic labor shortages at the 5 to 6 percent level probably ought not to occasion much alarm unless they are prolonged over a number of years. Most departments accommodate to a one- or two-person deficit in faculty by internal adjustments of workload. A longer term adaptation that is hidden from view in our data is the hiring of faculty with less than optimal qualifications—for example, a teacher who has not completed his PhD—when fully qualified personnel are not available. There is reason to believe, from studies of academic manpower, that this practice has been fairly common in the last decade.

These same studies suggest, however, that the supply and demand may come closer to equilibrium in the 1970's. Forecasts of demand suggest that although the percentage of teaching faculty members with doctorates in social sciences and psychology will reach a low of about 60 percent by 1970, there will be a sharp rise to from 72 to 75 percent by 1975, and a still further rise by 1980.*

Geography, currently a shortage field, seems likely to become even more so by 1974. The same is true for sociology, while history will be barely able to meet the demand for faculty in four-year colleges and universities. The outlook is brighter for anthropology and political science; both of these fields should be able to provide PhD staff for academic institutions and still be able to contribute to nonacademic research and service enterprises in the social sciences. Only economics and psychology are expected to make PhD's available to meet the demands from the nonacademic sectors at rates higher than present ones.

*John K. Folger, Helen S. Astin, and Alan E. Bayer, *Human Resources and Higher Education: Staff Report of the Commission on Human Resources and Advanced Education* (New York: Russell Sage Foundation, 1969), Ch. 3.

10
DEPARTMENTS
IN PHD-GRANTING
UNIVERSITIES

The typical American university is a collection of departments organized into schools or colleges. The college of arts and sciences is responsible for most of the teaching in the standard scholarly disciplines: the humanities and the physical, biological, and social sciences, both undergraduate and graduate. Around this college are a number of professional schools, such as schools of agriculture, business, education, engineering, law, medicine, public administration, theology, and social work. Some universities have only a few of these, while others have more than those named.

In addition to the college of arts and sciences and the professional schools, another set of institutions, devoted primarily to research, has mushroomed in our major universities: a variety of institutes (or laboratories or centers) commonly outside the administrative structure of the departments or of the professional schools. These three types of structure—the departments, the professional schools, and the institutes—share very nearly equally in the total amounts spent on organized behavioral and social science research in PhD-granting universities (Table 10-1).* Each of these types will be considered in turn—the departments in this chapter, the professional schools in Chapter 11, and the institutes in Chapter 12—as they bear on the work of the behavioral and social sciences within these universities.

---

*Research as reported in the tables that follow is separately budgeted research, commonly designated "organized research." It does not include the proportion of normal faculty salaries that permits the faculty members to engage in research without having a special budget.

TABLE 10-1 FUNDS EXPENDED FOR ORGANIZED BEHAVIORAL AND SOCIAL SCIENCE RESEARCH THROUGH DEPARTMENTS, PROFESSIONAL SCHOOLS, AND INSTITUTES, 1967

Research Unit Receiving Funds	Number in Sample	Sources of Funds (in thousands of dollars)			Total Behavioral and Social Science Research	Percent of Total Expenditures
		General University Sources	Federal Grants, Contracts	Other (including private foundations)		
Departments	693	$12,365	$ 52,539	$12,497	$ 77,401[a]	34
Professional schools	447	10,815	44,853	13,625	69,293[a]	31
Institutes	406	15,417	45,152	18,652	79,221[b]	35
Total		$38,597	$142,544	$44,774	$225,915	100

[a]See Appendix B for correction factors for failure to respond.
[b]Corrected for nonresponse only for institutes known to have behavioral and social science personnel or expenditures; that is, 406 were responding and eligible among the 893 institutes listed.
Source: Administrative Questionnaire, Professional School Questionnaire, and Institute Questionnaire.

THE DEPARTMENTS SURVEYED

Departments were included in the survey if they had granted at least one PhD between 1960 and 1966. The departments in six fields (anthropology, economics, history, political science, psychology, and sociology) were subdivided for purposes of our analysis into "large" departments—those producing the most PhD's— and "other" departments; there are between 19 and 25 departments in the first group, depending on the field. These large departments, as noted earlier (Table 9-6), produced 50 percent of the PhD's in these six fields. Departments in the other fields surveyed (agricultural economics, educational psychology, geography, linguistics, and rural sociology) were too few in number to justify classifying them in this way.* The number of departments included and the sizes of their full-time faculties are given in Table 10-2. In much of the discussion that follows, requirements such as money and space will be computed per full-time-equivalent faculty member in the department; because of the difficulty of separating the costs specifically for PhD research and training, a per-PhD cost might be spuriously high for a department that was turning out only an occasional PhD. The numbers of PhD's per department were given by field and size in Table 9-6.

THE COSTS OF A CONTEMPORARY SOCIAL SCIENCE DEPARTMENT

The annual cost figures for academic staff, other professional and nonprofessional staff, and the annual costs of equipment and supplies for a contemporary social science department are given in Tables 10-3 and 10-4. The mean costs per faculty member are not strikingly different between large and small departments, although (except for political science) the costs are consistently higher per man in the large departments.

The departmental expenditures for teaching and research (both undergraduate and graduate), as reported by department chairmen, are given in Table 10-5. Nondepartmental costs, such as libraries and student aid not administered by the departments and organized

*Although we have panel reports also in statistics, mathematics and computation, and psychiatry, their departmental matters are not included in our departmental survey.

TABLE 10-2 PHD-GRANTING DEPARTMENTS IN UNIVERSITIES, 1967: THEIR NUMBERS, AND FULL-TIME-EQUIVALENT FACULTY, BY FIELD AND SIZE OF DEPARTMENT[a]

Field and Size of Department	Number of Departments	Number of Full-Time-Equivalent Faculty	
		Total	Mean per Department
Anthropology			
Large	19	348	18.3
Other	32	326	10.2
Total	51	674	13.2
Economics			
Large	23	817	35.5
Other	71	1,136	16.2
Total	94	1,953	20.7
History			
Large	21	827	39.4
Other	85	1,785	21.0
Total	106	2,612	24.8
Political science			
Large	25	715	28.6
Other	66	1,063	16.1
Total	91	1,778	19.5

Psychology			
Large	21	727	34.6
Other	99	1,812	18.3
Total	120	2,539	21.2
Sociology			
Large	23	552	24.0
Other	56	834	14.9
Total	79	1,386	17.6
Totals, six fields			
Large	132	3,986	30.2
Other	409	6,956	17.0
Total	541	10,942	20.2
Agricultural economics			
Total	31	742	23.2
Educational psychology			
Total	38	585	15.4
Geography			
Total	45	455	10.1
Linguistics			
Total	31	314	9.8
Rural sociology			
Total	7	49	7.0
All behavioral and social sciences			
Total	693	13,087	19.0

[a] All figures have been adjusted for departments in the sample failing to reply. See Appendix B for method.
Source: Departmental Questionnaire.

TABLE 10-3 DEPARTMENTAL EXPENDITURES FOR PERSONNEL, EQUIPMENT, AND SUPPLIES PER FULL-TIME-EQUIVALENT (FTE) FACULTY MEMBER, 1967, BY SIZE OF DEPARTMENT, MEANS FOR SIX FIELDS[a]

	Large Departments (N = 132)	Other Departments (N = 409)	Mean, All PhD-Granting Departments (N = 541)
Salaries, academic staff per FTE faculty member	$12,410	$11,390	$11,640
Other professional personnel per FTE faculty member	3,330	2,820	2,940
Other nonprofessional personnel per FTE faculty member	1,910	1,330	1,470
Total costs for all personnel per FTE faculty member:			
Salaries	17,650	15,540	16,050
Fringe benefits	1,520	1,170	1,260
Total	$19,170	$16,710	$17,310
Equipment and supplies per FTE faculty member	$ 1,620	$ 1,380	$ 1,440
Total annual personnel and equipment and supply costs per FTE faculty member	$20,790	$18,090	$18,750

[a]The six disciplines included are anthropology, economics, history, political science, psychology, and sociology. For their separate costs, see Table 10-4.

Source: Departmental Questionnaire.

research outside the departmental budgets, are not included. Because of the different bookkeeping practices of universities, some gross discrepancies in totals appear when estimates are made from different sources; therefore, the figures in Table 10-5 are useful mostly for comparisons between departments. The departments are largely from the same universities, so that differences in accounting practices should affect the various disciplines in similar ways.

As shown in Table 10-1, the university administrations reported $65 million going to departments from government and other sources for research, but, as shown in Table 10-5, the departmental chairmen reported only $52 million going to the department from "other sources" (including government) in the same year. The discrepancy may be attributable in part to indirect costs that the department might not report (because it does not expend them), whereas the central administration receives them from grants in the name of the discipline; it might also be that research grants to members of the department are counted by the central administration as belonging to the discipline, even when the department chairman does not administer them. Unless university bookkeeping practices become more uniform, surveys of research financing will be subject to these large margins of error. If the administration figure is taken as the correct one, the departmental chairmen may be underestimating their expenditures from sources outside the university by 20 percent.

The direct costs for teaching (at both undergraduate and graduate levels) and for research administered through the departments total $248 million, as reported by the chairmen of the departments surveyed. The proportion reported as coming from general university sources is 81 percent in public universities and 74 percent in private universities, or 79 percent overall. University support ranges from a high of 97 percent for history to a low of 64 percent for psychology, reflecting both the amount of undergraduate teaching (almost entirely supported from university funds) and the availability of other sources of support for graduate instruction and research in some of the disciplines.

LIBRARIES

Libraries represent a major cost not covered in departmental costs, but essential to scholarly functioning. A check of the shelves in a few major university libraries led to an estimate that 40 percent of the holdings are books and journals in the behavioral and

TABLE 10-4 DEPARTMENTAL EXPENDITURES FOR PERSONNEL, EQUIPMENT, AND SUPPLIES PER FULL-TIME-EQUIVALENT (FTE) FACULTY MEMBER, 1967, BY SIZE OF DEPARTMENT, MEAN FOR SIX FIELDS

Departments	Large Departments		Other Departments		All PhD-Granting Departments	
	Mean Number of FTE Faculty per Department	Mean Cost per FTE Faculty Member	Mean Number of FTE Faculty per Department	Mean Cost per FTE Faculty Member	Mean Number of FTE Faculty per Department	Mean Cost per FTE Faculty Member
Anthropology	18.3	$19,237	10.2	$18,190	13.2	$18,580
Economics	35.5	22,450	16.2	17,520	20.7	18,720
History	39.4	17,110	21.0	14,600	24.8	15,230
Political science	28.6	16,220	16.1	16,540	19.5	16,450
Psychology	34.6	29,970	18.3	22,760	21.2	24,020
Sociology	24.0	20,330	14.9	17,680	17.6	18,450
Mean, six behavioral and social sciences	30.2	$20,790	17.0	$18,090	20.2	$18,750

Source: Departmental Questionnaire.

social sciences. Some 44 percent of the departments surveyed have some kind of departmental library, but this is often a modest reading-room that does not replace the central library. The operating cost for the 70 university libraries comprising the Association of Research Libraries for 1966–1967 was $150 million, including the costs of acquisition.* Thus we may assign, as an approximation, $60 million in library costs per year to the support of social science training and research at these 70 universities alone, exclusive of the costs of the already existing collections and buildings that hold them. Library collections are a national resource and should be maintained as such, but the costs are mounting too rapidly for private institutions, without assistance, to keep their collections complete and available. The behavioral and social sciences share this problem with all fields of scholarship.†

COMPUTERS AND COMPUTATION CENTERS

Our survey revealed how nearly universal the use of computers has become. Central computation centers were reported by 97 percent of the PhD-granting universities surveyed. Upwards of 90 percent of the economics, geography, sociology, and psychology department chairmen stated that some of their staff members used these facilities in their work. And 83 percent of the chairmen of all surveyed departments reported that some of their staff used computers either on- or off-campus. Even among history departments, which have become acquainted with computer possibilities more recently, 40 percent have one or more staff members making use of computers. Many departments have their own high-speed computers (in addition to terminals connecting them to computation centers): 20 percent of the psychology departments, 8 percent of the economics departments, and 6 percent of departments in all disciplines together.

A special inquiry was directed to the computation centers in the universities included in the survey. They were asked to supply

*Total expenditures for libraries by all institutions of higher education in 1965–1966 equaled $347.6 million. [Paul F. Mertins, *Financial Statistics of Institutions of Higher Education: Current Fund Revenues and Expenditures, 1965–66*, OE 52010-66 (Washington, D.C.: U.S. Office of Education, 1969).] If 40 percent of that total is assigned to behavioral and social science, the figure is $139 million.
†The report of the Carnegie Commission on Higher Education, *Quality and Equality: New Levels of Federal Responsibility for Higher Education* (New York: McGraw-Hill Book Company, December 1968), p. 42, recommends that federal library support under the higher education law be increased from $25 million in 1968 to $50 million in 1970–1971 and to $100 million by 1976.

TABLE 10-5 DEPARTMENT EXPENDITURES BY FIELD, 1967 (in thousands of dollars)

	Number of Departments	General University Sources [a]	Other Sources [b]	Total	General University Sources (percent of total)
Anthropology	51	$ 10,030	$ 2,600	$ 12,630	79
Economics	94	30,890	6,160	37,050	83
Agricultural economics	31	11,150	4,400	15,550	72
Geography	45	8,390	1,140	9,530	88
History	106	37,130	1,290	38,420	97
Linguistics	31	4,010	1,140	5,150	78
Political science	91	24,230	2,770	27,000	90
Psychology	120	41,690	23,540	65,230	64
Educational psychology	38	7,350	3,060	10,410	71
Sociology	79	19,940	6,090	26,030	77
Rural sociology	7	910	320	1,230	74
Total:	—				
Public	440	$142,290	$33,770	$176,060	81
Private	253	53,430	18,740	72,170	74
Total, all PhD-granting	693	$195,720	$52,510	$248,230	79

[a] As assigned to departmental budgets.
[b] Government, private gifts, foundations, as assigned to departments.
Source: Departmental Questionnaire.

164

information on the amount of computer time used by the departments, and the cost per hour for use in sponsored research. The results are given in Table 10-6. The total annual cost, estimated from the computation center questionnaire, comes to $4 million—a figure that is doubtlessly an underestimate because not all computer use is charged to using departments. Institutes and research centers were reported to use another $2.7-million worth of computer time. If we estimate approximately equal use by professional schools, the grand total is about $9.4 million per year for computer services to behavioral and social sciences through computation centers, omitting costs of other computer facilities available on campus and costs for computation done outside university facilities.

SPACE NEEDS

The current space occupied by the large departments and by the others producing PhD's is shown in Table 10-7. The figures do not include space such as lecture and seminar rooms shared with other departments. In most cases departments have enough space for an office for the staff member plus a moderate amount of space for graduate students and office workers. Psychology rather strikingly departs from these somewhat modest norms for space, as do anthropology, geography, and sociology to a lesser extent. Departments of economics, history, linguistics, and political science occupy quite moderate amounts of space.

Growth in faculty and in research creates demands for new space (Table 10-8). The total space hoped for depends primarily on expected increases in staff, but allows for some additional space per staff member as a reflection of more research obligations per full-time academic staff member.

The money required to supply this increased space would be substantial. Assuming a cost of $55 per square foot, the 5 million square feet that departments need in the next five years would cost $275 million; the added 3 million square feet required in the succeeding five years would cost another $165 million. Thus, funds for new space would average at least $44 million per year during the next decade.

EQUIPMENT NEEDS

Equipment requirements, like space requirements, show a tendency in the behavioral and social sciences to become laboratory-

TABLE 10-6 COMPUTER COSTS THROUGH THE COMPUTATION CENTER BY DEPARTMENT AND TYPE OF COMPUTER, FY 1967[a]

Discipline	Number of Departments	Cost for Computer Service per Department[b]				Total per Department	Total per Discipline
		Class A	Class B	Class C	Class D		
Anthropology	51	$ 180	$ 650	$ 210	$ 10	$ 1,050	$ 53,000
Economics	94	990	3,760	2,890	420	8,050	757,000
Agricultural economics	31	4,770	7,730	5,390	700	18,590	577,000
History	106	15	170	90	10	285	30,000
Political science	91	1,360	2,150	1,490	350	5,350	486,000
Psychology	120	1,330	4,740	1,580	1,640	9,290	1,114,000
Educational psychology	38	560	730	380	660	2,330	88,000
Sociology	79	1,590	3,260	2,830	770	8,450	666,000
Rural sociology	7	90	740	2,460	330	3,620	25,000
Geography	45	180	1,970	930	440	3,510	158,000
Linguistics	31	370	2,160	5	150	2,680	83,000
All departments	693	$ 990	$2,710	$1,600	$ 580	$ 5,880	$4,072,000[c]

[a]These costs are probably underestimated due to university accounting practices for computer time and due to the availability of computational facilities other than through the central computer facility on the campus, as well as off-campus.

[b]Computer service is usually reported in time. The computers of Class A (Very-High-Speed) were reported to cost about $300 per hour, those of Class B (High-Speed) about $165 per hour, those of Class C (Moderate-Speed) about $115 per hour, and those of Class D (Low-Speed) about $32 per hour. These are charges to those who conduct sponsored research, as reported by the computer centers in the universities surveyed.

[c]Detail may not add to total because of rounding.
Source: Computation Center Questionnaire.

oriented and data-based. The dollar values of present and needed equipment, expressed as a mean per department, are given in Table 10-9. The most striking figure is for psychology, in which an average large PhD-producing department already has an inventory (at replacement costs), of nearly $450,000 worth of apparatus and special equipment (such as animal quarters), and even those that produce fewer PhD's average $170,000 in equipment per department. The equipment inventories of other fields are much more modest, with anthropology and sociology again higher than the others because of their laboratories. A striking point is that the history and political science departments that are not now the major PhD producers appear to be looking forward to more equipment per department in the decade ahead than are the established major departments. The matter is, however, complex. The data show that large departments rated "good" or "adequate" (rather than "distinguished" or "strong")* in history and political science have the smallest amounts of equipment, and ask for the least in the future. Those departments seem to be retaining the older traditions of scholarship, in contrast with both the more distinguished departments and the newer ones now increasing their PhD production.

FUNDS FOR DEPARTMENTAL RESEARCH

Department chairmen were asked about their expectations of additional research funds for the future, in view of the expansion in PhD production, new faculty, and the enlargement of research activities of the departments (Table 10-10). They had behind them the experience of a five-year period, 1962 to 1967, in which federal funds for research had come in increasing amounts, averaging 256 percent over the five years (reaching even a tenfold increase for the educational psychologists due to increased funds for educational research generally).

A research program requires continuity. Once equipment has been acquired and the ancillary personnel employed to facilitate its use, professional research workers can greatly increase their research output, but only at an increased annual cost in salaries, materials, and other services connected with carrying research to its completion.

---

*According to Allan M. Cartter, *An Assessment of Quality in Graduate Education* (Washington, D.C.: American Council on Education, 1966).

TABLE 10-7 DEPARTMENTAL SPACE, FY 1967: MEAN SQUARE FEET PER DEPARTMENT AND PER FULL-TIME-EQUIVALENT FACULTY MEMBER, BY FIELD

Field	Number of Departments[a]	Space Occupied: Mean Square Feet per Department	Number of Faculty (full-time-equivalent)	Space Occupied: Mean Square Feet per Faculty Member
Anthropology				
Large	16	16,863	18.3	921
Other	27	6,993	10.2	686
Economics				
Large	19	13,926	35.5	392
Other	54	3,887	16.2	240
History				
Large	18	8,933	39.4	227
Other	72	4,999	21.0	238
			16.1	271
Political science				
Large	19	7,489	28.6	262
Other	53	4,362		

Psychology			
Large	18	43,644	34.6	1,263
Other	87	22,643	18.3	1,237
Sociology			
Large	19	12,753	24.0	531
Other	46	5,137	14.9	345
Mean, six disciplines[b]			
Large	109	17,113	30.3	565
Other	339	9,448	17.0	556
Total	448	11,313	20.3	557

[a]The numbers refer to actual departments reporting on space; not to the number in the universe of PhD-granting departments.

[b]Five of our reporting disciplines were too few in number to classify by large and small producers. Their space per faculty member was as follows: agricultural economics, 393 square feet; educational psychology, 587 square feet; rural sociology, 429 square feet; geography, 763 square feet; and linguistics, 270 square feet.

Source: Departmental Questionnaire.

TABLE 10-8 DEPARTMENTAL SPACE PRESENTLY USED AND PROJECTED NEW SPACE REQUIREMENTS OF PHD-GRANTING BEHAVIORAL AND SOCIAL SCIENCE DEPARTMENTS[a]

	FY 1967 (actual)	FY 1972 (projected)		FY 1977 (projected)	
		Amount	Percent of FY 1967	Amount	Percent of FY 1972
Space occupied	7 million ft²	12 million ft²	171	15 million ft²	125
Total capital investment, $55 per square foot	$385 million	$660 million	171	$825 million	125
Faculty, full-time-equivalent	13,087	18,191	139	22,379	123
Space per faculty member	535 ft²	660 ft²	123	670 ft²	102

[a]Includes disciplines not represented in Table 10-7. Corrected for missing replies.
Source: Departmental Questionnaire.

Department chairmen, having seen the tooling-up and expansion of the preceding five years at an annual increase of approximately 20 percent a year, considered a similar increase desirable for the next five years (1967 to 1972). By then, they expected some slowing of the rate of increase and believed they could meet their needs with a rate of increase on the order of 10 percent per year from 1972 to 1977. The slower rate later on is conditional upon the maintenance of the higher rate until the research enterprise is better established, particularly in the newer departments. In addition, it does not take into account the desires of the even newer PhD-granting departments that have been or will be established after our survey was conducted. Feared more than a slowing-down of support is a cutback, even temporary, which may destroy a research structure or break up a research team that it has taken years to build.

The growth trends forecast by the department chairmen reflect some combination of deliberate planning to prepare for the increased use of the behavioral and social sciences in the future and of response to the pressures of a larger population of young people wanting higher education at all levels through the doctorate and into post-doctoral training. Growth in these fields may not, in the short run, follow precisely the course these data suggest; nevertheless, these data provide as firm a basis as we have for realistic long-range planning.

The estimates by department chairmen must not be taken as standing for the total university commitment to research in the behavioral and social sciences. First, there are hidden costs, such as those resulting from reduced teaching loads. In addition, the department chairmen do not report all that the university administrators assign to their disciplines (see page 161), and the professional schools and institutes also have to be taken into account (cf. Table 10-1).

TABLE 10-9 RESEARCH EQUIPMENT: PRESENT VALUE AND FUTURE NEEDS, BY FIELD AND SIZE OF DEPARTMENT[a]

Field	Number of Departments	Present in 1967 (mean per department)	Needed New in Next 5 Years (mean per department)	Needed New in Next 10 Years (mean per department)
Anthropology				
Large	19	$ 74,730	$ 33,000	$ 63,000
Other	32	23,000	24,000	46,000
Economics				
Large	23	13,820	10,000	23,000
Other	71	14,630	12,000	25,000
History				
Large	21	2,350	1,000	2,000
Other	85	2,810	7,000	14,000
Political science				
Large	25	4,000	8,000	11,000
Other	66	6,850	15,000	31,000

Psychology				
Large	21	448,120	197,000	372,000
Other	99	172,940	149,000	270,000
Sociology				
Large	23	31,050	59,000	130,000
Other	56	15,880	31,000	60,000
Total equipment in inventory and needed, six disciplines				
Large	132	$12 million	$ 7 million	$13 million
Other	409	20 million	20 million	37 million
Total	541	$32 million	$27 million	$50 million

[a] Corrected for missing replies.
Source: Departmental Questionnaire.

TABLE 10-10 DEPARTMENTAL FUNDS FOR ORGANIZED RESEARCH FROM NONUNIVERSITY SOURCES, ACTUAL FUNDS FOR 1962 AND 1967, ESTIMATED FOR 1972 AND 1977 (in thousands of dollars)

Department	Number of Departments	FY 1962 Amount [a]	FY 1967 [b]		FY 1972 (estimated) [c]		FY 1977 (estimated) [c]	
			Amount	Percent of 1962	Amount	Percent of 1967	Amount	Percent of 1972
Anthropology	51	$ 1,009	$ 2,600	258%	$ 10,000	380%	$ 13,000	130%
Economics	94	1,897	6,160	325	15,000	240	23,000	150
Agricultural economics	31	3,110	4,400	141	14,000	320	19,000	140
Geography	45	438	1,140	260	4,000	350	6,000	150
History	106	513	1,290	251	4,000	310	7,000	175
Linguistics	31	569	1,140	200	4,000	350	5,000	125
Political science	91	748	2,770	370	8,000	290	13,000	160
Psychology	120	9,157	23,540	257	54,000	230	79,000	150
Educational psychology	38	294	3,060	1,041	8,000	260	12,000	150
Sociology	79	2,607	6,090	234	20,000	330	31,000	150
Rural sociology	7	175	320	183	1,500	470	2,000	130
Total	693	$20,518	$52,510	256%	$142,500	270%	$210,000	150%

[a] Derived from administration report of Federal Grants and Contracts for Research, for 1962, as ratio of such grants for 1967. Corrected for missing replies.

[b] From Departmental Questionnaire report of nonuniversity sources. See Table 10-5.

[c] From Departmental Questionnaire, needed funds for research.

11
THE BEHAVIORAL AND SOCIAL SCIENCES IN PROFESSIONAL SCHOOLS

We now turn our attention to the professional schools, which, as we said in Chapter 10, surround the colleges of arts and sciences on traditional university campuses.

THE EMPLOYMENT OF SOCIAL SCIENTISTS IN PROFESSIONAL SCHOOLS

In the autumn of 1966, approximately 5,000 behavioral and social scientists were employed in teaching or research capacities at 447 professional schools in the PhD-granting universities we surveyed. The survey was limited to professional schools of business, education, law, medicine, public health, public administration, and social work. Not represented were a number of other professional schools, such as communications and journalism, criminology, architecture, dentistry, engineering, librarianship, and nursing. Our survey totals are low because these schools, and professional schools not affiliated with PhD-granting universities, were omitted. Thus, for instance, many schools of education in colleges and universities that offer only bachelor's and master's degrees are excluded.

As Table 11-1 shows, the largest employers of behavioral scientists were medical schools. Psychiatrists predominated there, although the psychologists totaled about half as many as the psychiatrists, and sociologists were included in appreciable numbers. The second largest employers were schools of business, employing primarily economists but also psychologists and political scientists (in that order). Schools of education employ a substantial number of behavioral scientists,

TABLE 11-1 BEHAVIORAL AND SOCIAL SCIENTISTS IN SELECTED PROFESSIONAL SCHOOLS: FULL-TIME-EQUIVALENTS, AUTUMN 1966[a]

Discipline	Business	Business and Public Administration	Education	Law	Medicine	Public Health	Public Administration	Social Work	All Professional Schools Number	Percent
Anthropology	3%	0%	(b)%	0%	1%	6%	0%	6%	73	2%
Economics	73	57	(b)	29	0	5	17	3	1,038	22
Geography	(b)	0	1	0	0	0	1	0	12	(b)
History	1	0	2	3	(b)	0	1	1	35	1
Linguistics	(b)	0	1	0	(b)	0	0	0	10	(b)
Political science	8	43	(b)	35	0	11	45	6	312	7
Psychiatry	(b)	0	0	12	62	8	0	4	1,149	25
Psychology	10	0	94	0	30	35	1	20	1,586	34
Sociology	4	0	2	21	7	35	36	60	419	9
Total	100%	100%	100%	100%	100%	100%	100%	100%		100%

Behavioral scientists, total number of[a]	1,220	141	882	41	1,813	187	247	103	4,634
Schools represented, total number of	100	7	105	82	69	13	14	57	447
Mean, behavioral scientists per school	12.2	20.1	8.4	0.5	26.3	14.4	17.6	1.8	10.4
Behavioral scientists as percent of faculty[c]	31%	29%	22%	5%	14%	13%	83%	16%	19%

[a] All schools in sample; corrected for those not replying.
[b] Less than 0.5%.
[c] Percent of faculty for those reporting one or more behavioral and social scientists on the faculty.

Source: Professional School Questionnaire.

mostly educational psychologists. In some schools the professional staffs are very largely social scientists, as is the case in the schools of public administration. Overall, behavioral and social scientists make up 19 percent of the faculties in the professional schools that have one or more social scientists on their staffs.

The professional schools that employ the largest numbers of social scientists also spend the most research funds in the social sciences (Table 11-2). Thus, schools of business, education, and medicine together account for 84 percent of the social science personnel and 74 percent of the reported research expenditures for social science in professional schools. The patterns of research support differ from school to school, with education, medicine, public health, and social work receiving over half of their research support from the federal government; the rest receive the major portion from the universities themselves or from such sources as private foundations.

PROFESSIONAL SCHOOLS IN WHICH SOCIAL SCIENCE RESEARCH IS BETTER ESTABLISHED: BUSINESS, EDUCATION, AND MEDICINE

According to Table 11-1, over 4,000 behavioral and social scientists are employed in schools of business, schools of education, and schools of medicine; they spend from $7.5 million (business) to $33 million (medicine) annually for behavioral and social science research (Table 11-2). Thus, taken together, they represent a substantial part of the behavioral science research endeavor.

Business

The social scientists on teaching and research faculties in schools of business are chiefly economists, psychologists, and political scientists, with a scattering of anthropologists, geographers, historians, linguists, and psychiatrists.

In general, the psychologically and sociologically trained staff members have tended to be concerned with problems of management and organization (including the training of managers in human relations, leadership, and allied skills), as well as with research on the organization of productive work, supervision, incentives, and similar facets of industrial and service operations. Psychology and sociology make contributions also to the study of markets and marketing, advertising, personnel selection and management, and related topics.

On the whole, however, economics has had the most important influence on schools of business. Not only is a general understanding of money and banking, foreign trade, and industrial economics useful to the future businessman, but he is currently enlightened by economic concepts, including linear programming, game theory, and a range of microeconomic analytic ideas.

The future of the behavioral and social sciences in business schools is bright, but the assimilation of a wide variety of research specialists is not easy. The character of the school of business changes as social scientists from many fields are absorbed into its organization; conversely, the social scientists themselves undergo changes of interest as they become involved in professional settings.

One characteristic of the research commonly pursued in business schools is that it is closely in touch with the "clients" who make use of its products. Thus, management, or marketing, or labor relations are usually studied in the practical setting of specific businesses or industries. This direct attack on problems of the real world shapes the research in a way that makes it different from that done in the disciplinary departments.

Education

Because knowledge of individual differences and of the learning process is so fundamental in problems of schooling, it is not surprising that psychology and education have long been associated. Educational psychology is a required course for those seeking teaching certificates in virtually every state. In the United States today, approximately 3,000 PhD's identify themselves as educational psychologists.

There was a vigorous new thrust in education in the late 1960's. The 89th Congress (1965–1966) appropriated more money for education than the sum total appropriated by all previous Congresses. In 1965 alone, 25 major bills and a score of minor ones were enacted, creating a significant impact on education. Most sweeping of such recent acts are the Elementary and Secondary Education Act, the Higher Education Act, and amendments to the National Defense Education Act of 1968.

The rapid expansion of research and development in education immediately following this new legislation resulted in the formation of nine educational research and development centers at universities and 20 regional laboratories (later reduced to 15). These facilities temporarily placed severe strains upon available competent research

TABLE 11-2. EXPENDITURES FOR BEHAVIORAL AND SOCIAL SCIENCE RESEARCH IN SELECTED PROFESSIONAL SCHOOLS, 1967[a]

Source of Research Funds	Business	Business and Public Administration	Education	Law[b]	Medicine[c]	Public Health	Public Administration	Social Work[b]	Total Professional Schools Thousands of Dollars	Percent
General university sources	33%	70%	16%	20%	11%	2%	31%	12%	$10,815	15%
Federal grants and contracts	29	29	75	31	76	86	32	67	44,853	65
Other sources (includes foundations)	38	1	9	49	13	12	37	21	13,625	20
Total	100%	100%	100%	100%	100%	100%	100%	100%		100%
Total, in thousands of dollars	$7,477	$513	$10,291	$6,365	$33,465	$3,186	$1,982	$6,014	$69,293	

Number of schools represented	100	7	105	82	69	13	14	57	N = 447
Mean, research expenditure per school, in thousands of dollars	$75	$73	$98	$78	$485	$245	$142	$106	$155

[a] All schools in sample; estimates corrected for those not replying. Behavioral and social science research was defined as research carried on by persons whose highest degrees were in one of the social science fields, as in Table 11-1.

[b] Includes all reported research expenditures, owing to uncertainty about defining behavioral and social science research in law and social work schools.

[c] Medical school percentages from survey, but research total estimated as 8 percent of total research expenditures (based on information from the National Institutes of Health and the National Institute of Mental Health).

Source: Professional School Questionnaire.

workers in education and the behavioral sciences. Doctoral-level educational research training programs have been funded by federal grants in a number of universities to increase the number of competent specialists, but the supply still falls considerably short of the demand.

Besides psychology, sociology has been somewhat involved in professional schools of education, but the number of educational sociologists is relatively small. The educational sociologists have been interested in macrosystem studies, the dynamics of classroom interaction, and the effects of social environment (especially social class) on achievement in high school and on educational ambition. There was a reawakening of sociological interest in the educational process during the 1950's and 1960's, as evidenced by a remarkable growth of sociological literature on this subject.

The few anthropologists, economists, geographers, historians, linguists, political scientists, and sociologists shown to be employed by schools of education (in Table 11-1) may signify a developing interest in research over a larger spectrum. At the same time, considerable research on education is being conducted in departments of anthropology, economics, history, and sociology outside the professional schools of education. Adequate funding of research in education has been in effect only a few years, and an upsurge can be anticipated not only in the quantity and quality of research, but in its range as well.

Medicine

The behavioral and social sciences have a significant role in the contemporary medical school. The disciplines that have been most involved (in addition to psychiatry, which is based in the medical school as a clinical science) are psychology, social work, sociology, and anthropology (in that order).

Behavioral and social scientists in medical schools (including many nonpsychiatrists) have been attached to departments of psychiatry, not only because of their interests in personality assessment, psychotherapy, and research related to these processes, but also because of their interests in family problems and social pathology in the community. The growing interests of psychiatry in behavioral biology have also attracted biologically oriented behavioral scientists. As behavioral and social scientists become more prominently employed in medical schools, they gradually affect their curricula and organization. One manifestation of this is the appearance of departments of behavioral science in several medical schools. There is, however, incomplete integration of the behavioral sciences into the medical school curriculum; more exploration of new patterns is desirable.

A study of faculty in medical schools* showed that of all the behavioral scientists on the staffs (excluding psychiatrists), 71 percent were in departments of psychiatry, 6 percent in pediatrics, 5 percent in preventive medicine, and 18 percent scattered through other departments. Of the psychologists with PhD degrees in medical schools, half identify themselves as specializing in clinical, developmental, or personality psychology, and 20 percent in experimental psychology.

Anthropologists have studied the acceptability of health, sanitary, and medical measures, both curative and preventive, especially in nonwestern societies and in lower-class segments of western societies. Together with sociologists, anthropologists have been attentive to research on the delivery of medical services and the organization of such services, particularly in communities at large, including hospital organization and its effects on patient care. Sociologists also have looked carefully at the role of the physician and other health professionals, and have studied the social contexts of disease.

The domain of biomedical research extends far beyond the core concern with the biological determinants of disease and health; further progress requires a fuller understanding of the social, intellectual, emotional, and economic factors that influence well-being. Questions concerning growth and development, biological determinants of biological systems, social pathology, the design of health-care systems, and the organization and financing of the delivery of health services fall within the joint domain of the behavioral and biomedical sciences. More effective application of the behavioral sciences should also contribute to a better understanding of the social and economic health systems and of changing attitudes toward the health of society and of individuals.

The established tradition of research in both basic medical science and clinical medicine was reinforced by substantial government funds provided since World War II, and social scientists in medical schools benefit from this research atmosphere. The total amount available for research in the behavioral and social sciences in medical schools in 1966–1967 from the National Institute of Mental Health and the National Institutes of Health alone amounted to $22.1 million, repre-

*Carol E. Steinhart, *Behavioral Scientists in Medical Schools*, National Institutes of Health, Division of Research Grants, May 1967. (Mimeographed)

senting 8 percent of the total $276.5 million going to medical schools for all research from these sources during that year.

These brief introductions to the social scientists located within schools of business, education, and medicine indicate that those trained in these disciplines can work effectively in settings in which there is emphasis on solving problems that arise not from the interest of the investigator alone, but from the demands of the real world— the world of business, education, and health.

SCHOOLS OF LAW AND SCHOOLS OF SOCIAL WORK

We turn now to two other professional schools, quite different in character, for which the social sciences have strong relevance. Neither, however, has yet found a large place for social science research.

Law

As a profession, law is concerned, of course, with human relationships, and one might logically expect to find behavioral sciences treated as basic disciplines for the preparation of lawyers. Yet, for reasons that lie in the history of the legal profession and of university disciplines, law schools do not employ social scientists to any great extent, nor are they deeply involved in what is ordinarily considered social science research.

There is not in most law schools a distinctly organized, methodologically sophisticated, technically developed pattern of inquiry into scientific problems bearing on the substance of the profession. Many activities of lawyers resemble research, both in subject matter and in intellectual quality. Yet many of these activities are not classified as research by lawyers themselves.

Although a few law schools are moving boldly into research, thus setting the pattern for others, the distribution of research is still very uneven. Only 19 of the 68 law schools that responded to our survey reported any behavioral and social scientists on their staffs. Only 14 of these 19 reported any research expenditures within the behavioral or social sciences. The four with the largest amounts of total research accounted for $1.8 million of the $2.4 million expended for total research by these 14 schools (Figure 11-1).

The small size of the research effort arises in part from the way

THOUSANDS OF DOLLARS

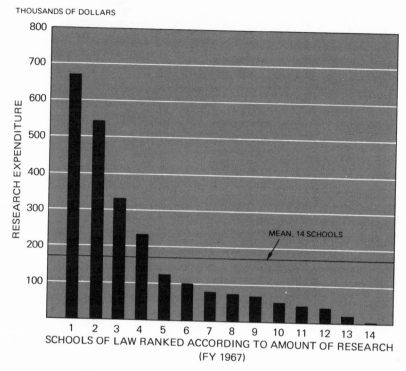

FIGURE 11-1 CONCENTRATION OF RESEARCH IN A FEW LAW SCHOOLS.

No effort has been made to separate behavioral and social science research from total identifiable research expenditures. All law schools reporting identifiable research. [Source: Professional School Questionnaire.]

in which law schools are organized, the way in which faculty are selected, how faculty personnel spend their time, and the kinds of published scholarship traditional within the legal profession. Because legal researchers at a growing number of law schools have expressed a desire to engage more actively in social science research, ways should be found to facilitate this. More manpower is needed (to release time for faculty research and to bring new research skills to the faculty) and for commensurate funds, space, and facilities. These call for cooperation of both law schools and funding agencies.

There are numerous possible research topics. One list includes such diverse topics as the effects of news media publicity on the administration of criminal justice; the economic impact of laws compensating victims of crimes; the attitudes of lower-class citizens toward lawyers and courts; the possibility of providing quantitative definitions of legal rules, such as "reasonable doubt" and "preponderance of the evidence"; and a whole range of studies in recidivism and rehabilitation of criminals. Substantial Ford Foundation grants have been made to several law schools in recent years to establish centers for the study of criminal justice. The recently authorized National Institute of Law Enforcement and Criminal Justice in the Justice Department will also have a large research component.

Perhaps the most essential first step is to broaden the disciplinary base of faculty and relax teaching schedules. Just as medical schools now employ a great many nonmedical personnel, law schools should be employing many more nonlawyers than they now do; in fact, their plans, as reported in the survey, show that they hope to do so. The burdensome teaching of large classes by senior staff members, who spend many hours reading and grading papers, is surely no more inevitable in law schools than in other units in the university. But law schools will not be able to move toward more empirical research without help; therefore, funding agencies should be prepared to encourage behavioral and social science research in law schools. Evidence clearly suggests that many law schools are now ready for these next steps—as they have not been ready in the past—and that they need encouragement. We, therefore, offer a recommendation in this direction.

RECOMMENDATION: DESIGNATED FUNDS FOR LAW SCHOOLS

The Committee recommends, in view of the expressed wishes of a growing number of law schools to engage in more behavioral and social science research, that National Science Foundation funds be earmarked for this purpose, with special grants to law schools to facilitate organized social science research.

In the next few years there will doubtless be changes in the relationship between law and other disciplines, to their mutual advantage. Lawyers are deeply concerned with conflict resolution, as their daily task is to try to adjust conflicts between adversaries. The analysis of conflict by social scientists could be strengthened and given greater cogency by close collaboration with those who have been accustomed to taking responsibility for the negotiation of conflict.

Social Work

In the first half of this century, as social work moved farther away from sociology, it veered toward psychiatry, with heavy emphasis on the individual caseworker and the one-to-one relationship with the client. A shift has occurred, however, putting the "social" back in social work practice and putting greater emphasis on social planning and social administration.

The professional structure of schools of social work today is a broad one. In addition to social workers themselves, the full-time faculties include sociologists, psychologists, anthropologists, political scientists, and economists, with the first two disciplines predominating (Table 11-1).

The school of social work, like the law school, has tended to stay rather close to its professional task. The total of 103 full-time social scientists (other than the social workers themselves) employed among the 57 schools allows less than two per school. Half of those schools reporting indicated no behavioral or social science research for 1966–1967. Other schools, more active in research, reported their total research expenditures for that year (including social science) to be only $6.0 million. Altogether, schools of social work average $106,000 per school for total research.

Schools of social work have no difficulty in finding outlets for their research services, or sources of funds to carry on the research; a few schools are engaged in substantial amounts of research (Figure 11-2). For example, one school spent approximately $800,000 on research during fiscal year 1967; most of this money came from the federal government. Its research programs during the year included a longitudinal study of 600 children entering foster care, a project concerned with surveying and evaluating service programs for youth in low-income areas, a survey of the use of nonprofessional personnel in 185 mental health programs, a study of 75 persons participating in VISTA (Volunteers in Service to America) following training at this school, a study of cognitive development in children, and other smaller research projects.

The standard master's degree program of schools of social work has been directed so strongly toward professional service that the doctoral programs built upon it have not led to much research. Because of the failure of most of the schools to take advantage of their research opportunities (with the conspicuous exception of a few as noted), it appears that some revolutionary effort at change—

THOUSANDS OF DOLLARS

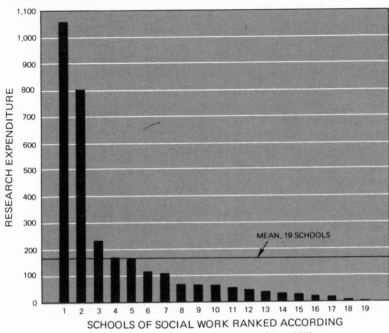

FIGURE 11-2 **CONCENTRATION OF RESEARCH IN A FEW SCHOOLS OF SOCIAL WORK.**

All schools of social work reporting identifiable research expenditures. [Source: Professional School Questionnaire.]

comparable to the change that came about in the medical schools following the Flexner report—may be called for.

We believe that both sociology and social work should play important roles in applied social research. There is room for both the academic department and the professional school in this broad area, just as there is a place for both the economics department and the school of business. Unless sociology departments and the schools of social work gear themselves for larger applied research tasks, others will undertake the work required.*

We do not make the same recommendation for the school of social work that we do for the law school, because funds are already ear-

---

*These others are not only social scientists, but engineers, for example, who have already begun to work on community problems.

marked for the areas in which social work schools should be competent. If some of these schools have trouble competing for the available funds, it is because they have failed to enlist research personnel who know how to plan and carry out the difficult research that needs doing. Thus, if they are to make themselves eligible for the support they want, it behooves those schools of social work not now engaged in research to upgrade their own research potential.

OTHER PROFESSIONAL SCHOOLS AND THEIR SOCIAL SCIENCE COMPONENTS

Three other professional areas call for some notice: communication and journalism, engineering, and architecture.*

Communication and Journalism

Because communication is a basic social process, every discipline concerned with human behavior must pay it some attention; thus, substantial numbers of studies we think of as constituting communication research have been done as part of psychology, sociology, anthropology, political science, or economics. Up until the last 15 years, the typical pattern was for scholars from these disciplines to work on communication research problems for a time and then to return to fields of research more central to their own disciplines.

Research centers and related doctoral programs have been established to provide some of the elements that communication research typically lacked—continuity and multidisciplinary approaches. Increasingly it was apparent that some of the important current problems were communication problems and that to study them adequately required the methods and insights of more than one discipline. Thus, the chief communication centers have been, from the beginning, places where social and behavioral science have been practiced and taught.

The major topics with which this new field deals are the mass media, the consumers of mass culture, the communication process, mediated teaching (including the efficient use of television, films, and programmed instruction), communication in economic and social

---

*These three were not included in our survey. Three others (business and public administration, public administration, and public health) were included in the survey, but data analysis was confined to that presented in Tables 11-1 and 11-2.

development, and advance information systems. With a charter as broad as that, there are great opportunities for contributing, not only to the advancement of knowledge, but also to education and social change.

Engineering

Just as the interests of economists touch our lives at many points, so do the interests of engineers. We have not surveyed the employment of social scientists in schools of engineering. We would not expect to find many there, although some interactions between engineering and social science are becoming increasingly evident. The advance of technology has profound influences on society, and the end of the Industrial Revolution is not yet in sight. The changes that technology brings can no longer be left to chance, but must be brought under social control with the cooperation of both physical and social scientists.* Thus, for example, problems of transportation, urban planning, waste disposal, pollution control, and depletion of natural resources call for concerted action of engineers and others.

What are the beginnings of such cooperation? Two may be mentioned. One, sometimes called systems analysis, is often undertaken jointly by engineers and economists. Another, commonly called human factors research, has a branch concerned with man–machine relationships in the design and operation of modern instruments, in which psychologists and engineers work closely together. These collaborative arrangements are beginning in the universities but are more advanced outside the university.

Architecture

Behavioral and social science research has a large role to play in relation to architecture. If form is to follow function, then architects must work closely with social scientists, whether the problem is the design of a single-family dwelling or an entire complex of workplaces, dwellings, and recreational spaces—the planned community. What are the impacts of various spatial arrangements on

---

*See U.S. House of Representatives Committee on Science and Astronautics, *Technology: Processes of Assessment and Choice*, Report of the National Academy of Sciences, July 1969.

human behavior and feelings of well-being? How can human needs be best served within reasonable economic boundaries? What flows of people and things are essential for modern man in urban settings? Psychologists, sociologists, historians, economists, geographers, anthropologists, and political scientists—the whole range of social and behavioral scientists—have much to contribute to the training and future needs of architects. There is clearly an important opportunity for greater communication and interaction among these groups.

THE FUTURE OF THE BEHAVIORAL AND SOCIAL SCIENCES IN THE PROFESSIONAL SCHOOLS

We asked the professional schools to indicate their plans for the future in the employment of behavioral and social scientists. The professional schools had the same optimistic expectations of increasing staff and funds as did the disciplinary departments.

The professional schools have two powerful advantages over the disciplinary departments in encouraging applied social research and development. One advantage is that the recipients of professional education are trained to be activists—agents of change. The physician does not simply study health and illness; he fosters one and attacks the other. As agents of change and action, professionals are accustomed to trying to influence others to alter their behavior. Professionals are educated to take constructive, inventive, action-oriented stances in relation to problems, rather than passive, analytic postures. The second advantage is that the training of professionals is oriented toward the delivery of services—toward the needs of whatever client system the professional deals with, rather than toward the internally generated needs of the investigator. This close connection with client needs tends to orient research toward practical problems and inventive solutions and, also, provides a ready-made relationship between practitioner and client that facilitates giving advice and help under customary and legal protections.

Although these advantages of the professional school as bases for applied and problem-oriented research are real, they are offset, to some extent, by the mission-orientation of the various professions. That is, some kinds of major social research bearing on policy and planning do not fall clearly within the concepts of business, education, law, medicine, public administration, or social work. Still, there are abundant opportunities within the professional schools to adapt social science research to problems within their purview, and the many moves in this direction are highly desirable.

Although the Committee believes that the professional schools should be encouraged to involve more behavioral scientists in both their research and teaching and should receive support from appropriate federal agencies for so doing, we do not offer specific recommendations. To do so in sufficient detail would require a more careful assessment than we are prepared to make of the differences between those professional schools that have moved farthest in involving behavioral and social scientists, those that have held back, and those that although wishing to move, have not been able to make administrative adjustments or to acquire the necessary resources. The matter is complex enough that merely urging the employment of more social scientists or teaching more courses in the social sciences is not sufficient to its solution. The fundamental requirement is that each professional school consider how these disciplines bear on its purposes and then include behavioral and social scientists to fulfill those purposes.

12
INSTITUTES AND UNIVERSITY ORGANIZATION FOR RESEARCH ON SOCIAL PROBLEMS

Although there is a close relationship, in principle, between basic research and applied and developmental work, basic research tends to receive more attention from behavioral scientists in universities. Many academic scientists value the prestige that their contributions to basic research and theory give them in the eyes of their peers more than whatever rewards might be obtained from clients who would find their work useful. It is no wonder that university scientists prefer the kind of research that is satisfying in itself (because it is self-initiated and free of restraints) and leads not only to scientific knowledge, but also to respect and status tendered by those whose judgments they value most. It is no wonder, either, that their value systems are passed on to their students. Thus, much of the applied work in disciplinary departments is done by those who for one reason or another do not compete for the highest prizes of their disciplines.

Faculty members of professional schools have a different sort of commitment to their own areas of research, and, as indicated in the preceding chapter, are likely to direct their applied work to the interests of external clients or the mission of the professional schools.

The circumstances of the disciplinary departments and of the professional schools are such, therefore, that some kinds of applied research are unlikely to be undertaken at a high level within these organizational structures. However, the interest within universities in problem-centered research has led to the development of a third kind of research organization. This is the research laboratory, center, or institute, often outside any department or professional school. These take multiple forms, as we shall see, and use a variety of names. For convenience we shall call them all institutes.

193

TABLE 12-1 BEHAVIORAL AND SOCIAL SCIENTISTS IN DEPARTMENTS, PROFESSIONAL SCHOOLS, AND INSTITUTES, AUTUMN 1966 (FULL-TIME-EQUIVALENTS)

Behavioral Specialty	All Professionals in the Discipline			Total	
	Departments	Professional Schools[a]	Institutes[a]	Percent	Number of Persons
Anthropology	76%	8%	16%	100%	891
Economics	66	25	9	100	4,080
Geography	91	2	7	100	501
History	94	1	5	100	2,782
Linguistics	78	3	19	100	401
Political science	74	13	13	100	2,414
Psychology	59	30	11	100	5,306
Sociology	67	20	13	100	2,123
Average all specialties	71	19	10	100	
Total professional workers, number of	13,087	3,485	1,926		18,498

[a] Excluding psychiatry personnel.
Source: Departmental Questionnaire, Professional School Questionnaire, and Institute Questionnaire; corrected for missing replies.

THE INSTITUTE AS A SUPPLEMENT TO
DEPARTMENTS AND PROFESSIONAL SCHOOLS

The institutes appear in many varieties and in profusion at universities. They arise for several reasons, including administrative convenience, but some, at least, are directly and specifically concerned with current social problems. At the universities we surveyed, we recorded a number of institutes of which 406 were separately budgeted and were involved in behavioral and social science research. The full-time-equivalent professional employees of these institutes account, overall, for about 10 percent of the behavioral and social scientists in these universities (Table 12-1).*

The proportion of research funds expended through institutes, which, as shown in Table 10-1, amounts to about 35 percent, is greater than the proportion of research personnel. The apparent imbalance here can be explained only conjecturally. It seems likely that applied research is more expensive than basic research, and that team efforts— which are often extruded from departments into institutes for administrative reasons—are more costly than the work of individual scholars. Where there are survey operations (as in institutes of sociology and political science), field parties in distant locales (anthropology), extensive and/or costly equipment (anthropology and psychology), the costs of research are likely to be high. Table 12-1 supports our interpretation, showing that these four fields provide a majority of all behavioral and social science research personnel in the institutes surveyed.

To find out what proportion of the institutes are multidisciplinary or social-problem oriented, they were classified topically, as shown in Table 12-2. About half fit the multidisciplinary or social-problem class; the rest fall primarily within the province of one discipline or the narrower concerns of a professional school. But, among the multidisciplinary institutes are a substantial number of training centers for area studies. They are generally not oriented toward social-problem research but toward developing expertise on a particular part of the globe. For the most part they concentrate on the language, culture, history, social structure, and institutions of a region or an area.

In short, at least two thirds of the research and service institutes in major universities are not primarily concerned with applied social

*The research expenditures in departments, professional schools, and institutes have already been presented in Table 10-1.

TABLE 12-2 TOPICAL CLASSIFICATION OF UNIVERSITY INSTITUTES DOING RESEARCH IN THE BEHAVIORAL AND SOCIAL SCIENCES, 1966–1967

	Number	Percent
A. Primarily multidisciplinary social-problem-oriented		
Area studies (Latin America, Far East, and so forth)	56	14%
Urban and regional studies	31	8
International relations, foreign policy, and political development of new nations	24	6
General social science (including ten Survey Research Centers and other supportive facilities)	23	6
Man and natural resources	18	4
Industrial relations, labor and management	17	4
Impact of science and technology on society	11	3
Population studies	10	2
Law, criminology, delinquency	7	2
Poverty and disadvantaged groups	5	1
Total, Group A	202	50%

B. Primarily in the province of one discipline or the narrower concerns of
a professional school

Anthropology, mythology, folklore	36	9%
Learning and instruction	32	8
Economics, econometrics, general business	32	8
State and local government, public administration	31	8
Human development and individual differences	22	5
Counseling (mental health, rehabilitation)	20	5
Interpersonal relations, group dynamics, communication	13	3
Animal psychology, experimental psychology (other than learning)	9	2
Language and linguistics	9	2
Total, Group B	204	50%
Total, all institutes	406	100%

Source: Institute Questionnaire.

TABLE 12-3 BEHAVIORAL AND SOCIAL SCIENCE RESEARCH: EXPENDITURES IN SINGLE-DISCIPLINE AND MULTIPLE-DISCIPLINE INSTITUTES IN FISCAL YEAR 1967

	Behavioral and Social Science Research Expenditures (in thousands of dollars)					
	Single-Discipline Institutes (N = 167)		Multiple-Discipline Institutes (N = 239)		All Institutes (N = 406)	
General university sources	$ 4,524	29%	$10,893	17%	$15,417	19%
Federal grants and contracts	7,620	48	37,532	59	45,152	57
Other sources (including foundations)	3,566	23	15,086	24	18,652	24
Total	$15,710	100%	$63,511	100%	$79,221	100%
Mean per institute	$ 94		$ 266		$ 195	

Source: Institute Questionnaire.

research or development, but, rather, they work to extend and continue the traditional academic work of the disciplinary departments or they draw upon the resources of two or more disciplines in the pursuit of primarily academic objectives.

If we classify the institutes, not by title but by the professional personnel employed, we find that among the 406 institutes there are 167 whose research staffs come entirely from one discipline. These 167 institutes are largely departmental adjuncts or split-off laboratories. The remaining 239 are multidisciplinary. The multidisciplinary institutes not only spend more research money in total, but also they tend to have somewhat larger research budgets per institute (Table 12-3). They also tend to draw more heavily upon federal funds in support of their research.

The Limitations of the Institute Organization in Universities

Certain limitations of departments and present professional schools have led to the proliferation of institutes, but the question remains of whether the institutes have managed to solve the problems left to them by the departments and the professional schools. The institutes' successes in some cases lie in their very willingness to attack problems that others have neglected in their research: urban problems, poverty, delinquency, conservation of resources, and the impact of technology on society. Some institutes have succeeded in meeting their objectives, in maintaining stability in operations, in attracting high-level staff; others, however, have floundered because of instability of budgets, inability to hold scholars of high level, and the tendency for research to diverge from the announced objectives of the institutes.

A part of the difficulty lies in the characteristically small size of most institutes and in their dependence on one or more academic departments to provide the framework for the behavioral scientists' work. Most institutes draw upon departmentally based faculty for part-time staff, who are pulled two ways: toward the institute's purposes and toward the academic role of the department. Most institutes do not control the training of the students who work in them, and, indeed, few even organize courses. With rare exceptions, the students are academic stepchildren.

These limitations make it unlikely that the institutes provide a sufficient counterforce to the restraints on applied research in departments and professional schools. The difficulties common to many institutes are the following:

1. The institute generally does not control tenured faculty positions. Unless it does, the positions will be determined by departments having objectives such as maintaining a "balanced" array of subfields of the discipline, an objective that is usually in conflict with the task of the institute.

Departmental appointments accentuate the motivational drift back toward the department among faculty personnel who divide their time between department and institute. Furthermore, the institute may need types of professionals who are not in demand in any of the conventional departments, and who, if they must come on temporary appointments, become second-class citizens in the university community.

2. The institute does not have resources in "hard money." If the institute has to sustain itself by grants and contracts, its staff must spend a great deal of time in writing proposals and in negotiating them; it is tempted to move in directions "where the money is," which may not be where its research objectives do or should lie.

3. The institute does not control the training of its own graduate students, even of those who do their dissertations within the institute. As long as the graduate student has to meet departmental requirements, he is less likely to pursue a truly innovative, multidisciplinary training program appropriate to the objectives of the institute; he may be forced to cast his dissertation in a familiar departmental mold even though he uses the resources of the institute.

Thus, while institutes are a partial aid to widening the scope of research and training in the university, they operate under significant handicaps. We are led, therefore, to suggest a new form of organization for training and research in the behavioral and social sciences within the university.

PROPOSAL FOR A NEW FORM OF ORGANIZATION: A GRADUATE SCHOOL OF APPLIED BEHAVIORAL SCIENCE

There can be little doubt that the behavioral and social sciences will become better basic sciences if their methods and findings are repeatedly and continuously tested for relevance to actual social behavior. An academically sound and organizationally firm base is needed for the development of behavioral and social science that is applicable to the large problems of society. The attack on such problems should not wait for crises to call attention to social pathology but should be on a continuing and long-range basis, with full attention given also to the rich theoretical contributions that can be made. Through research on genuine social problems, social scientists can improve the substance of their fields according to their own aspirations, while also serving society.

We believe that an effective organizational structure for problem-oriented social science research must be multidisciplinary, including both individuals with training in more than one discipline and specialists from various disciplines committed to working on common research problems. The work must be applied not only in the narrow sense of doing the bidding of a client who has a problem to be solved, but also in the broad sense of being pertinent to the persisting critical issues of the real world. Furthermore, its status in the university must be such that potential scientists of the highest caliber can be recruited, trained, and retained.

We propose a Graduate School of Applied Behavioral Science as a means of meeting these requirements.

RECOMMENDATION: A GRADUATE SCHOOL OF APPLIED BEHAVIORAL SCIENCE

The Committee recommends that universities consider the establishment of broadly based training and research programs in the form of a Graduate School of Applied Behavioral Science (or some local equivalent) under administrative arrangements that lie outside the established disciplines. Such training and research should be multidisciplinary (going beyond the behavioral and social sciences as necessary), and the school should accept responsibility for contributing through its research both to a basic understanding of human relationships and behavior and to the solution of persistent social problems.

The establishment of a new school in the university structure should be undertaken only after the most careful consideration and should not be undertaken at all if other means would be as efficacious. We are convinced that the location of the behavioral and social sciences within the specialized departments of the arts and sciences colleges of our universities militates against the development of the potential of these sciences as contributors to the solution of social problems. The whole tradition of specialist scholar–teacher–student relationships works against concern for the arts of practice and also against large-scale multidisciplinary research and instruction. The experience of the recent past attests to these incompatibilities. It would be easy to collect many illustrations of how alien applied or professional sciences are within the arts and sciences faculties of universities. There are always a few exceptions, but the estrangement of applied research from the departments tends to be greatest in those universities where the departments are strongest, and thus tends to degrade applied work in the very settings where it might best gain prestige.

Although we refer to the new instrumentality as a school, other organizational arrangements might serve similar ends. One such possibility exists in the established professional schools. For example, a school of business that wishes to broaden itself into a general school of administration and policy planning might conceivably assume many of the functions of the new school, and other existing professional schools could take on other functions. Another possibility is to consolidate existing institutes as the core of a research center in the behavioral and social sciences, with greater stability than the separate institutes now possess. The Institute for Social Research at the University of Michigan, for example, has achieved a good deal of stability over the years and represents a consolidation of three centers with differing functions: the Survey Research Center, the Research Center for Group Dynamics, and the Center for Research on the Utilization of Scientific Knowledge. Except for its dependence on the departments of the arts college for instructional and degree programs, it comes close to our proposed Graduate School of Applied Behavioral Science. We do not wish to prejudge the variety of administrative arrangements that might be developed; however, in recommending a Graduate School of Applied Behavioral Science, we hope to have made clear (1) that we are dissatisfied with the limitations of the present departmental and professional school structure and (2) that some inventiveness, beyond the proliferation of specialized institutes, is necessary to make behavioral and social science research more substantial and more effective in contributing both to the solution of social problems and to the training of those who do this kind of research.

There are perhaps a dozen different ways in which present limitations might be overcome and universities could better organize themselves toward the ends we have in mind. We are more interested in the goals than in the organizational patterns, but we make an explicit proposal to be as clear as possible about what it is that we hope to see achieved.

The Program

The program is not very well suggested by the expression "applied behavioral science," except that this expression calls attention to the intent to be unabashedly concerned with making behavioral and social science research bear directly on issues of public policy and social problems. It would probably *not* be concerned to any large extent with many of the familiar problems of applied behavioral science, such as personnel selection and training, research on advertising and selling, plant location, or other such matters in which benefits are largely to the advantage of particular clients already served by the professional schools rather than to the society at large. Instead, the program might include research on the administration of law enforcement and the delivery of justice, on the provision of medical services, or on the management of welfare schemes and educational institutions. The applications intended are at the level of social issues, policy, and planning.

The expression "applied behavioral science" is also somewhat misleading as it suggests a sharp distinction between basic and applied research—a distinction that we do not accept (Chapter 4). Many problems of a basic nature can be worked on best in a school of the kind proposed—such as the development of appropriate social indicators and the extent to which they can be made aggregative. A large number of methodological problems could appropriately be studied—such as linear, nonlinear, and dynamic programming, mathematical modeling, computer simulation, and multivariate data analysis—but always in the context of their potential relevance to social problems, although they need not relate directly to them.

The school should help correct the impression that behavioral science is a "soft" science by applying "hard" behavioral and social science methods to social research. The collaboration of scientists other than behavioral scientists, facilitated by such a school, should enrich the variety of methods and skills that can be used. Just as the quantitative methods used should be the most advanced and most precise that are available, so too theory construction should go on at a high level. Thus, a statistic on the increase in the number of policemen, no matter how well assessed, is not a measure of how well crime is being controlled; data gathered without concern for theory may be either useless or misleading.

Existing models can, of course, be applied in new ways, even while new models are being invented. Familiar methods of linear programming could be applied to the optimal allocation of resources in poverty areas, sociometric methods could be used for detecting leadership roles in various subcultures, and multidimensional scaling could be used to compare the valuational systems of different groups of people. In other words, a team of workers gathered together in a new school would find the state of the art sufficiently advanced for them to move into their tasks promptly and with confidence in useful outcomes.

The problems of society are manifold, and presumably each school would select some few focal areas in which to do its major research, while covering other areas in its instructional program. Its methodological work might cover a wider range than its topical research. In developing relationships to clients it would not be limited by any *a priori* commitments, such as those of an agricultural school, a business school, or a medical school. Because of this freedom to choose, it could work on emerging problems that belong to no particular professional school, such as the conservation of resources, intergroup conflict, the human effects of transportation systems, social mobility, or the use of leisure. Probably many of the clients would come from government, where the increases in scope of governmental activities have led to the creation of agencies, or smaller units within agencies, concerned with most of the problems that society faces. Many of these units now have no place to turn for workers trained specifically in areas pertinent to their missions. The new schools not only could train such needed professionals, but also could provide a mechanism by which additional training could be arranged for those already at work in such units. By having some professional workers on leave from the government spending a year in the school, the visitor as well as the regular students would profit.

Specifications

What kind of organizational structure would such a school have? We shall try to be as specific as possible, realizing fully that ours is not and cannot be a design necessarily suitable to any particular campus. Nevertheless, clarity will be gained by referring to it as an actual entity to be created and we would characterize it as follows:

1. The Graduate School of Applied Behavioral Science would be organized much like other professional schools, with a full-time faculty, a guaranteed budget, and degree programs. It would grant the usual advanced degrees of the social science departments, especially the doctoral degree (PhD). The PhD degree signifies a scientific orientation in contrast to a professional one—professional in the narrower sense of a service profession.

We emphasize the importance of a full-time core faculty and a separate budget. The faculty should be chosen according to criteria related to the objectives of the school and must not be subject to veto by the discipline-oriented departments, whose considerations of balance and specialization may be inappropriate in this setting. Furthermore, there must be room for needed faculty members who do not represent any of the existing departments in the university in which the school is located. There will, of course, also be places for part-time faculty from other parts of the university; one advantage of the university setting is the availability of scientists with diverse competencies. We believe that it would be a serious mistake, however, to rely too heavily on joint and part-time appointments, in view of possible conflicts of interest with the disciplinary departments.

A degree program is desirable to attract scholars while they are young and to train people for the many posts in community, state, and nation calling for individuals trained as these will be trained. The aim of the degree program should not be academic in the sense of training primarily for placement in the academic world; the program can be truly intellectual without being narrowly academic. At present, an able scholar tends to make his name within his discipline before turning to the more applied or policy-oriented concerns of his specialty. If he turns to the new work without multidisciplinary experience, he may find himself meeting obstacles to communication with the clients he serves or even with the colleagues with whom he collaborates. If he has relevant experiences early in his career, as will be possible in the new school, he is likely to be more useful in such cooperative problem-solving. Radical innovations in the training program can permit students and faculty more time for working together on significant research tasks.

2. The new school should not establish subunits paralleling those of the disciplinary departments in the regular arts and sciences faculty. If departmentalization is needed, it should be along functional lines, cutting across the disciplines, or along social problem lines. There might be a program focused on man–environment relations, organizational change, the city, or methodological problems, such as modeling, simulation, or information flow. The disciplinary departments of the university would continue, essentially as they are now, *outside* the new schoool. As the school would not have a traditional disciplinary organization, there would not be duplication of structures or competition, although one might expect to find political scientists or economists, for example, in both places.

3. Topical research units, similar to those of some of the current institutes, such as urban centers or institutes for the study of the development of new nations, might be incorporated and, conceivably, might become the nuclei for department surrogates. However, provisions should be made for terminating programs lacking in vitality, so that they would not be built indissolubly into the structure.

4. Affiliations with responsible agencies outside the university should be established for purposes of both research and training. Equivalents of internships or apprenticeships could be provided in organizations where actual problem-solving, social innovation, policy planning, and program implementation or evaluation go on. Faculty members might serve tours of duty in operating agencies, and corresponding provisions could be made for staff of operating agencies to serve as visiting professors or scholars in residence at the new school. Functional integration with one or more client systems (as in the medical research–medical-care coupling) is one of the surest ways of maintaining vitality and contemporaneity.

We wish to be as realistic as possible about the new school that is being proposed. Hard work will be required to bring it into being in any given university, and further intense efforts will be needed to make it succeed. The school (or its equivalent) will commit scarce university resources, and, even though it lies outside the departments, some of its resources may have to come from existing departments and schools. Great care will be required in recruiting able students motivated for public service and also capable of the necessary scientific detachment to work as scientists on research projects and in the associated areas of development and innovation.

Undergraduates of today would quickly knock on the doors of the new school. We believe that the school might well offer some courses to undergraduates, but that it should not offer a bachelor's degree until it is well established, at which time the question of including such an undergraduate major might again be raised. The history of other professional schools dealing with social problems—such as social work schools, which have devoted their energies to the training of professional or technical workers rather than scientists—does not encourage following their model in establishing this new school.

Instructive Precedents

Recently, several universities have inaugurated programs having much of the flavor of those implied by our recommendation, but in no case fully embodying what we are proposing.

One example is the Doctoral Program in the Policy Sciences at the State University of New York at Buffalo. This program, initiated in September 1968, is under the Faculty of Social Sciences and Administration, an organization resembling somewhat the school that we are proposing, except that it includes the disciplinary departments in the behavioral and social sciences, together with the professional schools of social welfare and business administration. The program faculty is responsible for setting the degree requirements and serves essentially as a degree-granting department; for example, it offers a minor within the program for departmental majors, just as it asks for departmental minors from those majoring in the program. The core faculty is small, consisting of the program director and six to eight members who hold at least half-time appointments in the program; much of the teaching responsibility is carried by the regular faculty of Social Science and Administration. Here, then, we have a local arrangement, capitalizing on the fact that the arts and sciences faculty and professional school faculties in related areas are now one. The program features, among other things, internships selected in line with the plans of degree candidates, in such sites as hospitals, mayors' offices, poverty programs, legislators' offices, federal departments, and public schools.

A second example is the Public Policy Research Organization (PPRO), an agency of the state-wide University of California system, administered from the Irvine campus. Established in 1966, it began full operation with the appointment of a director in 1967. The objectives are announced as follows:

. . . to foster the initiation, conduct, and utilization of research and analysis on problems of public policy by: (1) establishing major continuing research programs on the basis of their relevance to current and future problems, (2) performing such policy studies for governmental and other agencies as will enhance the basic policy research programs, and (3) participating in the development of training programs in the field of policy research and analysis.

The areas in which PPRO expects to develop major research programs are educational organization, urban and regional planning, and coordination of public services. These are the types of programs sometimes found in professional schools, and sometimes in institutes. The possible desirability of instituting a degree program is recognized.

Yale University, building upon an earlier experience with the Institute of Human Relations, announced an Institute of Social Science, approved in 1968 and soon to become operative. In supporting its applied purposes, President Kingman Brewster asserted:

> . . . It is obvious that the social sciences are taking their place alongside medicine and law as resources for constructive human and social action. Practical problems can be just as intellectually rigorous, just as challenging to intellectual ingenuity as the solving of more theoretical puzzles or the search for more abstract truth. Clinical teaching and research need not genuflect before the pure medical scientist. Action oriented legal scholarship and teaching can be at least as rigorous and stimulating as the model building of the "pure" social scientist.*

The Yale arrangements differ from both the Buffalo and the Irvine illustrations. The governing board will be drawn from the faculty of arts and sciences and the learned professions; staff members will normally have joint appointments approved by the departments. The degree programs, at least for the present, will rest with the departments. The institute will be organized into "Centers" instead of departments, originally a Center for Urban Studies, a Center for Educational Studies, and a Center for the Study of Management, all of which draw upon existing institutes at Yale. Despite the more general title, the institute is clearly applied in its orientation, although not narrowly vocational or service-oriented.

At Pennsylvania State University a College of Human Development has been created and organized in five divisions: Man-Environment Relations, Community Development, Biological Health, Individual and Family Studies, and Human Development. The faculty are drawn from psychology, sociology, political science, and economics and, also, from architecture, law, practical police work, medicine, public health, biochemistry, nutrition, and public administration. No degrees beyond

*Kingman Brewster, Jr., "The Report of the President" (New Haven, Conn.: Yale University, 1968), p. 28.

the master's are offered as yet, but there are plans for doctoral programs and there are active vocationally oriented bachelor's programs in public health planning and in law enforcement and the administration of justice. Although somewhat different from the school we envisage, this divisional structure clearly does not follow conventional disciplinary lines.

We believe that these developments at Buffalo, Irvine, New Haven, and University Park are responsive to a need felt within universities for new forms of organization, and they encourage us to support the recommendation as we have stated it.

Some of the characteristics looked for in the proposed school are also found in the Woodrow Wilson School of Public Affairs at Princeton and in the John F. Kennedy School of Government at Harvard; both schools are now involved in programs of training for the PhD. Several schools of business now have research programs ranging widely beyond business and industry. Thus, what we are proposing is not entirely new and untried. The existing programs find no difficulty in placing those who complete their training, so that the academician's fear that employment opportunities will be limited to the economist, psychologist, sociologist, or other behavioral scientist with a standard disciplinary label proves to be unfounded.

Creating a Professional Identity

Several steps can be taken toward creating a new identity for the PhD recipient of the new school.

The first step is by way of identification with the faculty. If care is taken to select regular faculty members from those fully committed to intellectually rigorous, action-oriented, policy-related, problem-solving research—men who themselves have prestige because of their accomplishments in action as well as research—a base will be provided until such time as a new profession emerges.

Two additional institutional steps can be recommended toward the establishment of a new professional identity: (1) the creation of a Society for Applied Behavioral Science and (2) the establishment of more journals as outlets for the research reports from Graduate Schools of Applied Behavioral Science. The products of the schools would then "belong" in the new society, and the society and the journals would, in turn, "belong" to them. The initiative in these matters would come from the schools themselves; our Committee in noting these steps is not itself proposing a new society or a new journal.

If several Graduate Schools of Applied Behavioral Science were in the planning stage at once (as they may very well be) it would behoove their proponents to join together to establish a society and a journal in their early planning. We do not propose to specify the details, but the journal should publish mainly data-based reports (and not become merely a collection of essays) to represent the nature of the new schools. The meetings of the new society should be genuinely scientific, with programs not only data-based but multidisciplinary and problem-oriented, to emphasize the uniqueness of the new schools. Thus, the students in and graduates of the new Graduate Schools of Applied Behavioral Science would come to identify themselves with others who share their common objectives.

13
BEHAVIORAL AND SOCIAL SCIENCE RESEARCH OUTSIDE THE UNIVERSITY

The problems of a rapidly changing society are found in the field, the factory, and the marketplace; responsibilities for social decisions and policies are shared by citizens, workers, managers, and elected and appointed officials. The issues with which social science deals originate in real life; thus, one of the demands on social scientists is that their research be done there, and have its impact there, in the communities in which people interact, communicate, cooperate, and come into conflict. We have been concerned that universities organize their research so as to provide a climate for research pertinent to the genuine social problems as they arise in their "natural settings." But the university is not the only center of research, and we will now examine social science outside the universities, in both governmental and nongovernmental agencies.

OPPORTUNITIES FOR SOCIAL SCIENCES BEYOND ACADEMIC BOUNDARIES

There are many expressions of concern that behavioral and social science knowledge is not better used than it is by management in industry or by policy-makers in government. The managers and policy-makers charge that social scientists do not answer their questions; the social scientists reply that they are asked to give advice only in times of crisis, are not given appropriate assignments, or are not listened to in those areas in which they are best equipped to be of service.

The problem of effective use of the social sciences is complex.

Scientific information must be collected, stored, and retrieved in response to particular situations. Management must be educated about the functions and methodology of applied social science research and about the interpretation of social science data. Behavioral and social scientists must be educated about the problems confronting business and government. Furthermore, the appropriate roles of the manager and the scientist must be defined. In any case, it is evident that fruitful cooperation between the manager or policy-maker and the social scientist depends on mutual respect and a clear understanding of the terms of their collaboration. The possibilities of such understanding are greatest where scientist and manager work together. For many purposes this opportunity is best provided in the corporation office or within an agency of government.

Behavioral and social scientists are finding many opportunities to work in these settings. Unfortunately, the data on behavioral and social science research outside the university are fragmentary, for at least two reasons. First, there are problems of definition. It is often difficult to distinguish between the social and behavioral science component and other components of an activity. In the development of computer-assisted instruction, for example, a behavioral scientist may work with a computer specialist, a content (subject matter) specialist, a teacher, and an electronics technician. How should the activity be classified: as research in behavioral science, as educational development, as engineering, or as something else? Second is the problem of sampling. While much of engineering research and development is done in large firms with special research budgets, much social science research goes on in small units, in a private hospital, a local market research firm, or an urban planning commission. These reasons have thus far prevented the National Science Foundation from including the behavioral and social sciences in its surveys of research in industry. It is hoped that this lack will be remedied in the near future.

BEHAVIORAL SCIENCE IN GOVERNMENT

Government's requirements for information of the kind that social scientists are expected to provide are increasing steadily, and governments at all levels—local, state, and national—are large employers of social scientists. These scientists are engaged in a wide variety of activities, including basic and applied research; the development of new methods and systems of handling public problems; the introduction, testing, and administration of new approaches in operational programs; the collection of general-purpose social science data, such as the population census; and the formulation of policy.

The Federal Government

The federal government is the largest supporter of behavioral and social science research. It is also one of the largest employers of social scientists, second only to the universities in employment of recent recipients of the PhD. Social scientists are to be found at all levels of civil service, in the Cabinet, and in the Executive Office of the President. Those who are not personally engaged in research but who are top managers or policy planners, because of their background in the relevant fields of scholarship, are in a position to identify needs for research in the social sciences (and, where appropriate, related natural sciences), to bring practitioners and researchers together, to interpret research results for practical needs, and to innovate through executive programs and legislative proposals.

Economists are the most widely deployed and most numerous social scientists within the government, accounting for 40 percent of the total number (Table 13-1). Psychologists are next, 22 percent, followed by a general category of social scientists, 15 percent. The Department of Defense employs the largest number of behavioral and social scientists, with the Veterans Administration and the Departments of Agriculture and Labor following; each of these accounts for 10 percent or more of the total.

The federal government expended for its intramural basic and applied research in behavioral and social sciences an estimated $77 million in fiscal year 1967.* Any such estimates necessarily contain a degree of arbitrariness because the routine aspects of massive social science data-gathering activities, like similar aspects of natural science data-gathering, are not classified as research under the general conventions governing statistical surveys of research and development, although the data so gathered are often used in social science research. If

---

*The estimate was made by the survey staff from available data and is incorporated in other tables (see Table SR-1, Summary and Recommendations). An independent estimate, eliminating some aspects of psychology, came to $75 million. (U.S. House Committee on Government Operations, *The Use of Social Research in Federal Domestic Programs*, A Staff Study for the Subcommittee on Research and Technical Programs, 90th Cong., 1st sess., 1967, Pt. I, p. 21.)

TABLE 13-1   PROFESSIONAL SCIENTIFIC AND TECHNICAL PERSONNEL
IN THE FEDERAL GOVERNMENT, BY OCCUPATIONAL GROUP, OCTOBER
1966

Occupational Group	Personnel, All Agencies	
	Number	Percent
Anthropology	122	1.5%
Economics	3,337	39.7
Geography	150	1.8
History	529	6.3
Psychology	1,879	22.3
Social science (other; includes sociology)	1,223	14.5
Foreign agricultural affairs	110	1.3
Manpower research analysis	33	0.4
Operations research	852	10.1
Urban planning	173	2.1
Total		
Behavioral and social scientists	8,408	100.0%
All scientific personnel	71,672	
Behavioral and social scientists (percent of all scientific personnel)	11.7%	

Source: National Science Foundation, "Scientific and Technical Personnel in the
Federal Government, 1966," *Reviews of Data on Science Resources*, NSF 68-16,
1968, pp. 14–16.

$118.3 million (Table 7-1) for these closely allied general-purpose
social data-gathering activities is combined with the $77 million for
research, the total for intramural social science research and data
collection for 1967 would be $195.3 million.

The intramural research activities of the various agencies are too
diverse to summarize briefly. The National Institute of Mental Health
has a heavy intramural research commitment (some $20 million per
year), of which a substantial portion is behavioral and social science
(chiefly but not exclusively psychology and sociology), covering a
wide spectrum.

The Department of Defense supported behavioral and social science
research and development to the extent of $34 million in fiscal year
1966, of which intramural research and development amounted to
$8 million, or about 24 percent, the rest going to universities and
other nongovernmental research agencies.* The intramural research

*Data from statement by Dr. Donald M. MacArthur, in U.S. Senate Committee
on Government Operations, *National Foundation for Social Sciences*, Hearings
before the Subcommittee on Government Research, 90th Cong., 1st sess., 1967,
Pt. I, pp. 233–234.

is classified as human performance, manpower selection and training, and human factors engineering. Research support by the Department of Defense to agencies outside the government includes two other broad areas: cultural and social factors and policy-planning studies.

The creation of new agencies whose missions involve social amelioration accounts in part for new demands on social and behavioral scientists, and this growth is likely to continue at an accelerated rate. The Civil Service Commission estimates an increase in the federal employment of social scientists of 18.4 percent between 1967 and 1971, as compared with a 7.8 percent increase in the total federal employment and 9.9 percent in the professional scientific category.*

This expansion is likely to occur in a multitude of other areas, as is recognized in the following statement from the Special Analysis of the 1969 budget:

> The application of these criteria [for research on problems of national concern] is clearly evident in the scope and size of research and development related to national defense, space exploration, atomic energy, and public health. But it is also reflected in newer areas of federal concern such as education of the disadvantaged, poverty, transportation, urban development, and crime prevention where research and development programs are coming into existence or increasing significantly in scale.

Our discussion to this point has focused on social science research within the federal government.

There is a group of social scientists, difficult to identify professionally and even harder to count, who are employed in the government as managers and administrators or in various policy-making positions.

Some 1966 data available for psychologists employed in the U.S. Public Health Service show that 41 percent are employed as researchers, 43 percent in various forms of administration, and the remaining 16 percent in clinical practice and other tasks.† Data for 170 sociologists employed by the federal government in 1960 showed them performing three major functions: research, program management, and consultation, with research predominating.‡

---

*U.S. Civil Service Commission, *Federal Workforce Outlook, Fiscal Years 1968–1971*, March 1968, pp. 12 and 16.
†Sidney H. Newman and Marie Ali, "How Psychologists Are Utilized in the United States Public Health Service," *American Psychologist*, 23, February 1968, 139–141.
‡Naham Z. Medalia and Ward S. Mason, "Position and Prospect of Sociologists in Federal Employment," *American Sociological Review*, 28, April 1963, 280–287.

State and Local Governments

State and local governments, like the federal government, are turning their attention to urgent social needs. Thus, in addition to their traditional interest in health, natural resources, and highways, the states are sponsoring and conducting research on problems of pollution, crime, education, and poverty. This is reflected in considerable expenditures for social science research and development as shown in Table 13-2. Thirty-six state governments reported ex-expenditures in these fields; whereas 35 reported expenditures for agricultural sciences and 33 for both medical and biological sciences.*

There were 565 social scientists reported as engaged in research in state agencies as of January 1964, or 15 percent of the total of 3,886 social scientists employed by the states. The distribution by field of science is shown in Table 13-3. The largest proportion of state social science employees is in health and welfare, with a heavy concentration of psychologists, and in highways and public works, largely economists, while agriculture and conservation account for a sizable number in several fields. These areas account for three quarters of all the social scientists employed by state agencies; the rest are scattered throughout other agencies.

Many agencies of government at the local level—schools, hospitals, jails, planning bodies—employ behavioral and social scientists in research as well as in service capacities. In 1967 their research and development expenditures totaled $9.6 million.†

NONGOVERNMENTAL AND NONACADEMIC OPPORTUNITIES FOR RESEARCH

To gain more concrete information on what behavioral and social scientists do outside the university and the government, we undertook a small survey in the Boston area. This is a pilot study; therefore, not much can be made of it as a quantitative indication

---

*National Science Foundation, *R&D Activities in State Government Agencies, Fiscal Years 1964 and 1965*, NSF 67-16, 1967. These statistics do not include state support of research and development activities at state universities and colleges, for example, agricultural experiment stations.

† National Science Foundation, *R&D Activities of Local Governments, Fiscal Years 1966 and 1967*, NSF 69-14, 1969. The social sciences represented 33 percent of the R&D budget.

TABLE 13-2 STATE AGENCY EXPENDITURES FOR RESEARCH AND DE-
VELOPMENT BY FIELD OF SCIENCE, 1965 (in thousands of dollars)

	1965	
	Amount	Percent
Psychology		
Basic	$ 1,607	
Applied	910	
Development	959	
	$ 3,476	4
Social science		
Basic	$ 1,156	
Applied	4,632	
Development	7,447	
	13,235	15
Other fields of science		
Basic	$27,588	
Applied	33,522	
Development	10,065	
	71,175	81
Total, all fields of science	$87,886	100

Source: National Science Foundation, R&D Activities in State Government
Agencies, Fiscal Years 1964 and 1965, NSF 67-16, 1967, p. 23, 25, 27.

of what social scientists do in communities in general, but it does
indicate to some extent the diversity of the things they do. The basis
for sampling was all the economists and psychologists with addresses
in the Boston area and who were on the membership lists of the
American Economic Association and the American Psychological
Association. Both organizations include members with the master's
degree as well as those with the doctorate. These lists included 566
economists and 760 psychologists. For this area (in which the academic concentration is high), 19 percent of the economists and 37
percent of the psychologists fit the nonacademic, nongovernmental
classification. These were then sampled on a random basis and (after
finding that a few had moved without leaving addresses or were not
available on three telephone calls) a final sample of 21 economists
and 46 psychologists resulted.

We found that just under half were involved in research appro-

TABLE 13-3   SOCIAL SCIENTISTS IN STATE GOVERNMENTS, JANUARY 1964

	Number Employed	Percent	Number Engaged in Research	Percent
Economists	692	18	218	39
Sociologists and anthropologists	202	5	85	15
Other social scientists	495	13	74	13
Clinical psychologists	1,978	50	140	25
Social psychologists	147	4	23	4
Other psychologists	372	10	25	4
Total				
Behavioral and social scientists	3,886	100	565	100
All scientists	16,686		2,866	
Behavioral and social scientists				
(percentage of all scientists)	23		20	

Source: U.S. Department of Labor, Bureau of Labor Statistics, *Employment of Scientific, Professional, and Technical Personnel in State Governments, January 1964,* Bulletin #1557, 1967, p. 7.

priate to their training; most of the others were doing some sort of professional consulting that draws on their training but could not be classified as research. A few were performing administrative activities that made no special call upon their training.

We were also interested in what kinds of topics would occupy the nonacademic researchers. The interviewers uncovered 31 research projects engaged in by economists and 64 by the psychologists. A classification of these appears in Table 13-4.

Business and Industry

As indicated earlier, the National Science Foundation survey of research in industry does not include the social sciences, so an accurate estimate of the amount of such research there is not possible. We attempted an estimate of the aggregate of expenditures for research and development in industry and arrived at $289 million contributed by industry to its own behavioral and social science research and development in 1967.* Industry also receives approxi-

*See Appendix C, page 295.

TABLE 13-4   RESEARCH BY NONACADEMIC ECONOMISTS AND
PSYCHOLOGISTS IN THE BOSTON AREA, SUMMER 1968

Project Classification	Number of Projects
By economists	
Analysis and forecasting of economic conditions	4
Microeconomics: Analysis and forecasting for individual products and markets	9
Labor and manpower economics	8
Systems analysis and operations research	8
Personnel problems	2
Total, economics projects	31
By psychologists	
Human factors and man–machine interaction	12
Social psychology and organizational behavior	10
Clinical and counseling	20
Systems analysis	3
Physiological psychology	15
Test batteries and other technological development	6
Total, psychology projects	64

Source: Boston Area Survey.

mately $30 million per year from the federal government for this purpose. The total (for the year 1966–1967) of $319 million would mean some 10,600 social scientists in industry engaged in research and development, if each required a budgetary allowance averaging $30,000 largely for his own salary and some clerical and secretarial assistance. The personnel total, as an approximation, is supported by data from the National Science Foundation's Register of Scientific Personnel, which is known to underestimate those in the private sector of the economy. It shows 17 percent of the reporting economists and psychologists in 1966 to be employed in business and industry; this percentage would account for 8,500 members among the 50,000 who belong to the professional associations of these two fields. Considering the nonmembers and those from other disciplines and the underrepresentation of applied scientists in the Register, a figure of roughly 10,600 professionals employed in business and industry is plausible. The estimates of expenditures per research social scientist are supported by the data of Table 13-5, which show a mean expenditure in nonprofit institutions of $29,750 per scientist engaged in research and development.

TABLE 13-5 SOCIAL SCIENCE IN INDEPENDENT NONPROFIT INSTITUTIONS, 1966: EMPLOYMENT AND RESEARCH AND DEVELOPMENT EXPENDITURES[a]

	Total of Social Scientists (full-time-equivalent)		Engaged in R&D		Current Expenditures for intramural R&D (in thousands of dollars)	
	Number	Percent	Number	Percent	Amount	Percent
Economists	840		823		$ 30,213	
Sociologists	154		150		4,856	
Political scientists	235		235		6,822	
Psychologists	1,354		907		16,670	
Other social scientists	802		734		26,208	
Total social scientists	3,385	18.2	2,849	17.0	$ 84,769	14.8
Other scientists	15,257	82.8	13,855	83.0	489,273	85.2
All scientists	18,642	100	16,704	100	$574,042	100

[a]Total number of institutions with a science program reporting is 546 (excludes data for nonprofit hospitals, voluntary health agencies, professional and technical societies and academies of science, and private philanthropic foundations).
Source: National Science Foundation, *Scientific Activities of Nonprofit Institutions, 1966* (in press).

Much of this research in industry (presumably the 90 percent on which industry expends its own funds) is for its own purposes, which include economic planning, business forecasting, market research, consumer studies, personnel and management research, human-performance studies, and man–machine interactions. The Columbia Broadcasting System reported, in 1968 testimony to the President's Commission on the Causes and Prevention of Violence, that it annually spends $400,000 on social research. Early in 1969, the National Broadcasting System announced a 5-year, $500,000 study of influences (including television) bearing upon violent activities engaged in by members of the younger generation.

Research Institutes

A number of well-established nonuniversity and nongovernmental research institutes serve both government and industry through grants and contracts and carry out a certain amount of research on their own initiative. These include the nonprofit institutes and those organized like other businesses to show a profit on their operations. Nonprofit institutes of this kind include familiar ones with long histories, such as the National Bureau of Economic Research, the Brookings Institution, and the Educational Testing Service. Many came into being after World War II—the RAND Corporation, the System Development Corporation, the Battelle Memorial Institute, the Stanford Research Institute, and many others.

In January 1967, 18 percent of all scientists and engineers engaged in research and development in independent nonprofit institutions were social scientists. Social science research expenditures accounted for 15 percent of their total research and development performance in 1966. The data are summarized in Table 13-5. During the period 1964–1966 the number of social scientists engaged in research and development in these institutes increased 34 percent, and research and development expenditures in the social sciences increased by 65 percent.

Executives in some of the largest of these institutes have indicated that an increasing part of their growth is in aspects of science that fit within the behavioral and social sciences. These include, among others, studies related to the brain and central nervous system, population dynamics, information processing and control, natural resources control and planning, education, law enforcement, urban systems planning, systems economy research, and manpower planning.

The growth of economics, systems sciences, and management sciences can be indicated by the data from the Stanford Research Institute, a nonprofit institute founded by but essentially independent of Stanford University. In 1962 352 professionals were employed in economics and management sciences, including 47 PhD's; 5 years later, in 1967, there were 906 in this work, of whom 100 were PhD's. The PhD's in economics and management science represented 16 percent of the 293 PhD's employed in 1962 and 24 percent of the PhD's in all fields in 1967 (other fields included life sciences, physical sciences, and engineering). Behavioral scientists are employed in other parts of the institute, but the economics and management sciences areas serve to indicate the trend toward increasing emphasis on the social sciences. If even 10 percent of the institute's 1967 research budget of $56 million is allocated to the behavioral and social sciences, this represents a sizable investment in such research, and similar investments are being made in many other institutes across the country.

The RAND Corporation's recent decision to expand its non-defense-related research and analyses will also mean more social science expenditure and a greater demand for qualified social scientists.

Many research organizations, incorporated like other businesses and earning money for their stockholders, serve purposes similar to those of the nonprofit research institute. A leading example is the Arthur D. Little Company. Others conduct research related to more general industrial or commercial purposes. George Gallup's American Institute of Public Opinion provides a commercial service, widely purchased by newspapers, that includes a market research service to private customers.

We have no data on which to base any firm assertions about the quality of research done in nonprofit research centers as compared with profit research centers; both must meet acceptable standards to hold clients who are sufficiently critical to distinguish between good and bad research.

PREFERRED PATTERNS FOR RESEARCH ORGANIZATIONS

We examined various research institutes within the university in Chapter 12, and concluded that they served useful purposes, although they are somewhat limited by the pull of the disciplinary departments away from research directed to the solution of social problems. This pull is likely to be felt less in nonprofit institutes outside the universities. Some believe that problem-solving research can be conducted better there than in the university, for the nonprofit institutes may be more likely to follow research through to its ultimate application. We have already indicated (in Chapter 8) that we believe classified research belongs more properly there than in teaching centers; however, there are other advantages, such as the ease of gathering task forces of workers of varied experience, the possibility of setting up field stations away from the university location, and the chance for exclusive attention by the researcher to the task, without concern for such ancillary tasks as the training of graduate students. Furthermore, a closer collaboration between researcher and client in the whole process favors greater acceptance of the results than when there is too much separation between the producer of the research and its consumer.

Several proposals for the establishment of high-level institutes have been made by other committees interested in the behavioral and social sciences. One proposal is for a center to be located in Washington: a national institute for advanced research and public policy.* The Report of the Special Commission on the Social Sciences of the National Science Board† proposes that a number of social problem research institutes be established by universities and other organizations. These institutes would be characterized by interdisciplinary professional staffs that will concentrate their efforts on particular social-problem areas. The institutes would work closely with, responding to the needs of, the client-sponsor, thus ensuring a flow of persons between the institute and the user agencies. A third possibility, of course, is the strengthening of institutes within the universities themselves. We believe that if graduate schools of applied behavioral science are established within universities, some of the difficulties of discipline orientation will be overcome, and the university-based centers will not face their earlier difficulties in becoming more truly problem-solving.

*The Behavioral Sciences and the Federal Government, NAS Pub. 1680 (Washington, D.C.: National Academy of Sciences, 1968).
†National Science Board–National Science Foundation, Knowledge Into Action: Increasing the Nation's Use of the Social Sciences, Report of the Special Commission on the Social Sciences, NSB 69-3, 1969.

We approve the development of institutes of various kinds, including those operated as profit-making business enterprises. No evidence has come to us that there are unique advantages of one over the other. Imagination, initiative, resourcefulness, and courage are where you find them and cannot be defined by the structure of institutions, relative to either their affiliations or their size. The ultimate criterion is the usefulness of the product in the solution of pressing problems.

14
FEDERAL SUPPORT
OF RESEARCH
IN THE
BEHAVIORAL AND
SOCIAL SCIENCES

The major role of the federal government in supporting research requires no documentation. In this chapter, we examine the history and nature of federal support of research in the behavioral and social sciences over the past decade and make proposals regarding the future.

THE GROWTH OF FEDERAL SUPPORT RELATIVE TO OTHER AREAS OF SCIENCE

During the 10-year period of fiscal 1958 through fiscal 1967, the behavioral and social sciences* have received a small but increasing fraction of the federal funds designated for basic and applied research (Table 14-1). The percent of total obligations rose from 3.7 percent in 1958 to 5.6 percent in 1967, reflecting the increasing concern of government (and research institutions generally) with social problems. In view of the general increase in funds over the years, the growth is more rapid than these percentage figures imply; comparison of the actual sums available to the behavioral and social sciences for 1958, $40 million, and for 1967, $297 million, reveals a more than seven-fold increase during that 10-year period (not correcting for the inflation in the value of the dollar). Two disciplines, economics and psychology, have been particularly well supported financially, while others have not fared so well.

---

*In federal reports, the fields are designated as psychological and social sciences. Included are anthropology, economics, geography, political science, biological and social psychology, sociology, the history and philosophy of science, and some aspects of history and linguistics.

225

TABLE 14-1 FEDERAL OBLIGATIONS FOR RESEARCH, BY FIELD OF SCIENCE, FISCAL YEARS 1958–1968 (in millions of dollars)

Fiscal Year	Total Amount	Field of Science			Psychological and Social Sciences	
		Life Sciences, Amount	Physical, Engineering Sciences, Amount	Other (Residual), Amount	Amount	Percent of Total
1958	$1,079	$ 342	$ 698	$ (a)	$ 40	3.7
1959	1,403	417	897	33	55	3.9
1960	1,941	511	1,323	33	73	3.8
1961	2,620	629	1,764	132	96	3.7
1962	3,273	810	2,152	190	120	3.7
1963	4,041	922	2,871	97	152	3.8
1964	4,464	1,045	3,145	77	197	4.4
1965	4,854	1,167	3,386	70	230	4.7
1966	5,271	1,301	3,630	74	266	5.0
1967	5,273	1,451	3,429	95	297	5.6
1968 [b]	5,406	1,586	3,418	82	321	5.9

[a] Not available.
[b] Estimated.

Source: National Science Foundation, *Federal Funds for Research, Development, and Other Scientific Activities, Fiscal Years 1967, 1968, 1969*, Vol. 17, NSF 68-27, 1968, p. 230.

It is difficult to determine the level of federal funding that will be required in the next decade. The complex factors that determine the rate of growth in a particular field of science, including the requirements of the government for the output of that field, make any fixed claims for particular disciplines sound like special pleading. The growth of universities, the improvement in precision of social science research methods, the enlistment of more manpower into these fields, and the growing concern for solving social problems, all interact to require a continued rate of growth not too different from that recently attained.

In estimating requirements, we wish to make an important and essential distinction. A projection on the basis of present trends is necessarily a conservative one and essentially amounts to an assertion that the social sciences of the future will be about as they are today, except for population growth, increases in degree production, and increases in faculty requirements. Yet we have made such a projection, which we call *projected normal growth*. Beyond this is another estimate, one that allows for quantum jumps as new programs are undertaken. We shall attempt to summarize these needs as *projected new programs*, involving a new scale of data-gathering, the preparation of social indicators, and the establishment of new types of schools and institutes not now in existence.

Projected Normal Growth

Requirements for research staffs in universities and colleges, government, and nonprofit and industrial establishments suggest a growth rate in personnel of about 7 to 8 percent a year over the coming decade; if costs per person remained stable, there would be a corresponding increase in funds for personnel. However, it is assumed that an annual increase in cost per person of an additional 5 percent is to be expected. Thus, we arrive at an estimated minimum growth rate of about 12 percent a year.

At such a rate, there would be little chance for new facilities, and existing ones would have trouble maintaining themselves, were support to fall below this minimum level. It would be false economy to fall below this level and cause the disbandment of research teams that have been gradually assembled and trained to work together over the years. These teams include technical workers and caretakers whose value to the research team has steadily increased because of what they have learned at work; to disrupt such a task force for

TABLE 14-2 ESTIMATED FEDERAL FUNDS FOR THE BEHAVIORAL AND SOCIAL SCIENCES AT UNIVERSITIES AND COLLEGES, ASSUMING ALTERNATE RATES OF NORMAL GROWTH (in millions of dollars)

Category	1967 Base	1972 (estimated)		1977 (estimated)	
		At 12 Percent per Annum	At 18 Percent per Annum	At 12 Percent per Annum	At 18 Percent per Annum
Basic and applied research	$143 [a]	$252	$327	$445	$ 749
Construction	51 [b]	90	117	159	267
Student aid	75 [c]	132	172	233	393
Institutional and departmental support	24 [b]	42	55	75	126
Total	$293	$516	$671	$912	$1,535

[a] Estimated from survey (see Table 10-1).
[b] Construction and institutional support estimated as 10 percent of totals to colleges and universities. See U.S. Department of Health, Education, and Welfare, *Toward a Long-Range Plan for Federal Support for Higher Education*, January 1969, Table 4a, pp. 47–51.
[c] Estimated from data in U.S. Office of Education, *The Academic and Financial Status of Graduate Students, Spring 1965*, OE-54042, 1967, Table 17, p. 30.

even a few months could mean many months of rebuilding before the efficiency of the operation could be restored when funds again became available.

We have suggested a minimum rate, in view of the stringency of government funds at the time of this report. But we also suggest a more realistic rate of growth (more nearly comparable to that of the preceding 5 years), for the time when funds for science research may again become more sufficient to the needs: this suggested rate is 18 percent per year. Depending on the duration of the present stringency, deficits that build up will have to be made up; therefore, this growth rate (below the 20 percent growth per year experienced earlier) is classified as "normal growth" and does not take into account the major increments that new programs may call for.

The annual growth of 20 percent during the last decade represented growth not only in universities, but also in intramural research in government and in the nonprofit research centers and industrial establishments. Therefore, our recommendation for the support of the behavioral and social sciences is across the board.

RECOMMENDATION: RATE OF FEDERAL FUNDING FOR NORMAL RESEARCH SUPPORT

The Committee recommends an annual increase in funds available from the federal government for support of basic and applied research in the behavioral and social sciences of between 12 and 18 percent to sustain the normal growth of the research enterprise over the next decade.

What is the meaning, in dollars, of this projected normal growth in the support of universities and colleges? In 1967 the federal government contributed $293 million to the behavioral and social science enterprise in colleges and universities (Table 14-2). This includes $143 million for research and an additional $150 million for the construction of facilities, for institutional and departmental support, and for aid to students. The table shows that the cost, based on the two growth rates, will be between $900 million and $1.5 billion in 1977.

The support of basic and applied research in universities and colleges represented about half the total federal obligations for research in the behavioral and social sciences in 1967; the rest went to intramural research within the government and to industrial, nonprofit, and other research centers. On the assumption that comparable

TABLE 14-3 ESTIMATED FEDERAL FUNDS FOR BASIC AND APPLIED RESEARCH IN THE BEHAVIORAL AND SOCIAL SCIENCES, ASSUMING ALTERNATE RATES OF NORMAL GROWTH (in millions of dollars)

	1967 Base	1972[a]		1977[a]	
		At 12 Percent per Annum	At 18 Percent per Annum	At 12 Percent per Annum	At 18 Percent per Annum
Nonuniversity					
Government intramural	$ 77	$136	$176	$239	$ 403
Industrial, nonprofit and so forth	77	136	176	239	403
Total, nonuniversity	$154	$272	$352	$478	$ 806
Universities	143	252	327	445	749
Grand total, basic and applied research in behavioral and social sciences	$297	$524	$679	$923	$1,555

[a] Estimated.
Source: Table SR-1 (Summary and Recommendations) for base.

growth in the various sectors is needed, projections of total basic and applied research funds on the same basis as for universities are presented in Table 14-3.

The total amount of support required from the federal government for research in all sectors and for the related activities of universities and colleges in the social science fields in 1977 (combining the totals for universities in Table 14-2 with the nonuniversity totals of Table 14-3) is estimated at between $1.39 billion for the lower growth rate and $2.34 billion for the higher rate.

Projected New Programs

The recommendations in preceding chapters call for some overall accounting. Although these estimates are imperfect, we have attempted to suggest the orders of magnitudes involved by citing the costs of comparable existing enterprises. Our estimates show that the recommended projects will add substantially to the total obligations for behavioral and social science research and development, perhaps close to $100 million per year. The costs for projected new programs are itemized in Table 14-4.

In Table 14-4 for each new venture we identify a related kind of activity that is already going on, which can serve as a reference base for approximate costs. Thus, we believe that the newly proposed National Privacy Commission will have activities analogous to those of the present Office of Statistical Standards or the Advisory Commission on Intergovernmental Affairs and have, therefore, set its costs as similar to the costs of those agencies. The central system of coordinated data within the new National Data System is estimated to cost about what is now assigned to the Analysis and Publication of General Purpose Data on Social Phenomena. The sustaining sums required for survey research centers are based on the experiences of existing survey centers; the costs of surveys that will be needed for the improvement of social indicators are based on Census and other agency costs of surveys now conducted largely for economic purposes. The annual social report is equated in cost with the cost of the Council of Economic Advisers, because the existing Council is able to derive most of its information from existing data. Similar logic is followed in finding a parallel between data storage in archives and the current operating costs of the National Archives; costs for Graduate Schools of Applied Behavioral Science are assigned on the basis of Office of Education Research and Development Centers (with

TABLE 14-4 ESTIMATED ANNUAL COSTS FOR PROJECTED NEW PROGRAMS

Program	Estimated Annual Cost When Operative	1968 Reference Costs[a]	
National data system			
Commission on Privacy	$ 500,000	Office of Statistical Standards	$ 597,000
		Advisory Commission on Intergovernmental Affairs	510,000
Central system without new data	20,000,000	Analysis and publication of general purpose social data on social phenomena[b]	19,630,000
Social indicators (central staff without special surveys)	1,500,000	Office of Science and Technology	1,212,000
Survey research centers, national and regional			
Sustaining support	2,500,000	National Opinion Research Center[c]	200,000
		Survey Research Center[c]	500,000
Newly initiated surveys	25,000,000	Agricultural Statistical Reporting Service	14,200,000
		Special Census on Population and Housing	17,637,000
		Bureau of Labor Statistics, Manpower and Employment	8,452,000
		Prices and Cost of Living Index	3,203,000
		National Health Statistics	7,871,000

Annual social report (privately developed)	750,000
Nongovernmental storage and retrieval of research data (including libraries, data archives, and historical archives)	20,000,000
Graduate Schools of Applied Behavioral Science (10 at $2,100,000)[d]	21,000,000
Estimated total costs, projected new programs when operative	$91,250,000

Council of Economic Advisers	858,000
National Archives	17,961,000
USOE–funded R&D Centers[e]	(each) 1,000,000
Bureau of Applied Social Research, Columbia University[f]	1,000,000

[a] Unless otherwise noted reference costs are from Bureau of the Budget, *The Budget of the United States Government, Fiscal Year 1970,* Appendix, 1969.

[b] National Science Foundation, *Federal Funds for Research, Development, and Other Scientific Activities: Fiscal Years 1967, 1968, and 1969, 17,* NSF 68-27, 1968, p. 257.

[c] Need for sustaining support to maintain continuity of research program estimated by organizations cited.

[d] Costs of Graduate Schools of Applied Behavioral Science estimated as follows:

R&D Budget	$1,000,000
Instructional budget, including aid to graduate and postdoctoral students	1,000,000
Space Costs	100,000
Total	$2,100,000

[e] *Journal of Research and Development in Education, 1,* Summer 1968.

[f] From the organization cited.

an additional amount allowed for instructional costs in a graduate school).

It should be noted that these amounts make no allowance for the costs of relatively independent institutes as recommended by two other reporting bodies. The national institute for advanced research in public policy, as recommended by an earlier committee,* would probably cost about $5 million per year, after its buildings and facilities were established, if we judge from the annual costs of the Brookings Institution ($5 million) or the American Institutes for Research ($5 million). The specifications as to size of operation are not entirely clear: Resources for the Future, for example, operates on an annual budget of $1.8 million. Another committee† has proposed as many as 25 institutes, starting with a few institutes at an initial budget of $10 million and moving eventually to the total of 25 at about $50 million annually. Because these are not included in our recommended sum in Table 14-4, the required total might be half again as large if every recommendation of the other committees were financed along with those of this Committee.

FEDERAL AGENCIES SUPPORTING RESEARCH IN THE BEHAVIORAL AND SOCIAL SCIENCES

Many agencies contribute to the support of research both intramurally and extramurally. Some details are available for the total federal support for anthropology, economics, psychology, and sociology for the fiscal year 1967; the remaining social sciences, including educational research of a nonpsychological nature, are grouped together, as summarized in Table 14-5. Psychology is the major beneficiary of support by the Department of Health, Education, and Welfare (chiefly through the National Institute of Mental Health, the Office of Education, and the National Institutes of Health); economics is the major beneficiary of other agencies. Anthropology, supported on a smaller scale, receives its major contribution from the National Science Foundation. Sociology receives research money

---

*The Behavioral Sciences and the Federal Government, NAS Pub. 1860 (Washington, D.C.: National Academy of Sciences, 1968).
†National Science Board–National Science Foundation, Knowledge Into Action: Increasing the Nation's Use of the Social Sciences, Report of the Special Commission on the Social Sciences, NSB 69-3, 1969.

from a wide range of agencies. If we remove the contribution of the Office of Education from the "other social sciences" in Table 14-5, on the ground that it represents research on education *per se* rather than disciplinary research, we have a total of $46 million remaining for contributions to geography, history, linguistics, political science, and social welfare. The amounts allocated to geography, history, linguistics, and political science are limited *in toto*, as indeed they were found to be at the level of support of university research (cf. Chapter 10).

The large number of agencies that support research in the behavioral and social sciences illustrates a principle that is deeply embedded in the American political system, sometimes described as the principle of "pluralistic support." This means, in this context, that many agencies support research that fits within a common classification (for example, economics or psychology), despite differences in emphasis related to the missions of the different agencies. The practice of reporting research by discipline leads to the appearance of far greater overlap and duplication than actually exists; research on commodity markets supported by the Department of Agriculture and on wage structure by the Department of Labor are both properly called "economics," for example, although they are concerned with different topics. Although some danger of overlap and inefficiency exists, such overlap provides for some checks and balances that are productive. Also, of course, the research that an agency itself sponsors is likely to come more strongly to the attention of the policy-makers within that agency. Thus, the doctoral dissertations and other research projects supported by the Manpower Administration of the Department of Labor under the Manpower Development and Training Act are listed in its publications in a manner that calls them to the attention of those who are concerned with research bearing on manpower training.*

From the point of view of the individual researcher who seeks funding for his research endeavors, there is some advantage in having more than one place to turn, whether it be separate agencies within the government or separate foundations outside it. This is true particularly for innovative and unorthodox approaches to research for which it may be difficult to get a sympathetic hearing. Multiple sources produce greater stability in the research enterprise and protect

---

*For example, see the series U.S. Department of Labor, Manpower Administration, *Manpower Research Projects*, published annually.

TABLE 14-5 FEDERAL OBLIGATIONS FOR RESEARCH BY AGENCY AND FIELD OF SOCIAL SCIENCE, FY 1967 (in thousands of dollars)

Agency (in order of overall social science support)	Anthropology	Economics	Psychology	Sociology	Other Social Science	Total, Social Science
National Institute of Mental Health	$ 2,359	—	$ 31,791	$15,819	—	$ 49,969
Office of Education	—	—	20,671		$25,860	46,531
Social and Rehabilitation Service	—	—	2,363	(ª)	21,713 ª	24,081
National Institutes of Health	18	—	12,709	1,615	1,313	15,655
Other, Department of Health, Education, and Welfare	—	—	112	227	3,527	3,866
Total, Department of Health, Education, and Welfare	$ 2,377	—	$ 67,651	$17,661 ª	$52,413 ª	$140,102
Department of Defense	618	1,034	23,438	1,983	5,277	32,350
Department of Agriculture	143	28,517	—	895	205	29,760
National Science Foundation	4,152	4,832	8,040	3,219	3,857	24,100
Office of Economic Opportunity	—	8,700	—	10,106	—	18,806
Department of Labor	—	8,644	—	—	—	8,644
Other agencies	3,923	17,865	8,913	2,529	9,737	42,967
Total	$11,213	$69,592	$108,042 ᵇ	$36,393 ª	$71,489 ª	$296,729

ª Corrected for an error in the source publication, in which Social and Rehabilitation Service obligations of $13,656,000 are incorrectly listed under "Sociology" instead of under "Other Social Science."
ᵇ The total for psychology is divided into $47,837,000 for its more biological researches and $60,205,000 for its more social researches.
Source: National Science Foundation, Federal Funds for Research, Development, and Other Scientific Activities: Fiscal Years 1967, 1968, 1969, Vol. 17, NSF 68-27, 1968, p. 146.

it from sudden and arbitrary changes in agency policies for research support. We endorse the principle of pluralistic support for behavioral and social science research through many federal agencies and recommend that this dispersion of support be continued.

In general, the Committee is pleased with the dispersion of support through those agencies presently supporting research. Major support now comes from the Department of Health, Education, and Welfare (especially, the National Institute of Mental Health, the National Institutes of Health, and the Office of Education), the National Science Foundation, the Department of Defense, and the Department of Agriculture. Except for a certain sensitivity in some disciplines concerning support by the Department of Defense, no special problems have arisen. We have earlier indicated some cautions with respect to classified research (cf. Chapter 8), and the problems of overseas research also present some potential difficulties (cf. Chapter 16). We recognize, however, that the national defense is a necessary part of governmental activity, that behavioral and social science research is an essential ingredient, and that much of the research supported by the Department of Defense has clearly been beneficial to the advancement of the behavioral and social sciences and the interests of society, especially in areas such as human factors, man–machine interrelations, job and team training, and economic measurement.

Many of the mission-oriented agencies have found it to their advantage to support basic as well as applied research and to assist graduate education and special training. The Veterans Administration has played an important role in the education of clinical psychologists and the Office of Naval Research in advancing basic research in social and physiological psychology, geography, and mathematical economics. The National Institute of Mental Health (both when it was a component of the National Institutes of Health and now as a separate agency) has been especially skillful in blending support of basic research and education in behavioral science with its mission —the advancement of mental health. Perceiving the relevance of fundamental work in such fields as psychophysiology, psychopharmacology, and developmental psychology, the National Institute of Mental Health has not hesitated to work in those fields—as well as in such fields as cultural anthropology, sociology of the family, and medical sociology, which, at first sight, seem somewhat distant from the mental health mission; however, experience with the venturesome projects has often shown that relevant research emerges from even apparently distant starting points. The training of graduate students in basic behavioral science has also added to the supply of specialists capable of working on such applied, problem-oriented programs as the various "centers" that the National Institute of Mental Health has formed to study suicide prevention, alcoholism, crime and delinquency, narcotics and drug abuse, and community mental health.

The National Institutes of Health, although mission-oriented, also support basic research in the behavioral and social sciences, especially through the National Institute of Child Health and Human Development (which covers the life-span from infancy through old age), the National Institute of General Medical Sciences, and the National Institute of Neurological Diseases and Stroke.

We note our satisfaction with these supporting agencies, but in line with the principle of pluralistic support, we welcome an increase in behavioral and social science research support, both intramurally and extramurally, in other mission-oriented agencies.

RECOMMENDATION: AGENCIES NOW SUPPORTING LITTLE BEHAVIORAL AND SOCIAL SCIENCE RESEARCH

The Committee recommends that agencies, now little involved in behavioral and social science research but with missions to which such research is relevant, expand their support of basic and applied research in the behavioral and social sciences.

This recommendation applies to agencies with responsibility for domestic and foreign policy problems that are not now deeply involved in social science research (for example, the Departments of Commerce, Housing and Urban Development, Justice, Transportation, State, and the Federal Communications Commission). The recommendation is that they not only conduct intramural research, but also support extramural research bearing on their problems in both basic and applied areas.

THE SPECIAL ROLE OF THE NATIONAL SCIENCE FOUNDATION

The National Science Foundation, because its entire mission is the encouragement and support of science and scientific research, is of central interest to the scientific community in general.

The early legislation establishing the National Science Foundation included social sciences residually in the category of "other sciences." Thus, the social sciences made a rather slow start, although the Foundation gave them some support from the beginning and has paid increasing attention to their needs. It established a separate research division for the social sciences in 1960 and has included almost all these disciplines in its educational and institutional grants programs. In fiscal year 1968, it made grants for the social sciences totaling nearly $37 million: $15.7 million for research, $13.6 million for education, and $5.1 million in institutional block grants and development programs (the remainder being assigned to computer, international, and information activities, as well as to intramural purposes). The social sciences claimed 6 percent of the obligations for research grants and institutional support and 10 percent of the funds for science education. The institutional support programs for science-development purposes are the newest at the Foundation and are under-applied-for in behavioral science, probably because college and university administrators believe (rightly or wrongly) that they will fare better if they ask for funds in the physical or biological sciences. The administration of the National Science Foundation has declared its interest in the social sciences and its willingness to support them, however.

The original basis on which the National Science Foundation began to aid social science was development of these disciplines as scientific enterprises through grants for basic research. Recently a revision in the National Science Foundation Act not only specifically authorized the Foundation to encourage applied research, but also identified the social sciences explicitly as an area for Foundation effort. The Committee recognizes the importance of these legislative changes and has two recommendations related to them:

RECOMMENDATION: NATIONAL SCIENCE FOUNDATION SUPPORT FOR APPLIED RESEARCH

The Committee strongly supports the proposition that the National Science Foundation should vigorously exercise its newly broadened authority to support applied as well as basic research in all the social sciences, and that the Congress appropriate funds for this purpose.

RECOMMENDATION: NATIONAL SCIENCE FOUNDATION SUPPORT FOR RESEARCH ORIENTED TOWARD THE SOLVING OF SOCIAL PROBLEMS

The Committee recommends that the National Science Foundation prepare itself organizationally to give special impetus to multidisciplinary problem-solving research centering on the behavioral and social sciences in collaboration with scientists from other disciplines.

Both of the foregoing recommendations pose difficulties. There is some resistance within the scientific community itself to applied research, especially within the one agency that previously had no mission other than the support of basic research. We believe, however, that any effort to maintain a sharp distinction between basic and applied research is faulty and that to force this distinction by designating an agency to support only basic research is more likely to weaken than to strengthen the total scientific enterprise. We believe that the National Science Foundation can be trusted to continue its support of basic research (as indeed even mission-oriented agencies have done) and that its moving into applied work will permit it to consider all scientific research proposals on their merits. There may be some question about its supporting proposals that ought to be supported by other agencies, but the National Science Foundation can serve as a useful clearinghouse, as it already does for proposals in some fields in which agency interests overlap; for example, research with children.

We believe that the National Science Foundation should broaden its support of historical research explicitly related to the social sciences. Recognizing that this raises problems in defining the programs of support of the Foundation and the National Endowment for the Humanities, we urge the two agencies to negotiate clear lines of program interest.*

The organizational channels for applied research are not clear within the universities, especially for types of social problem-oriented research that may require, for example, architects and planners to

---

*The only projects within history now explicitly included within the National Science Foundation are those in the history of science. This field, while deserving of support, does not represent the behavioral science-oriented developments within history.

work along with those from many disciplines. But the National Science Foundation need not be constrained by the limitations of disciplinary organization within universities; it has, indeed, shown wide scope in some of its programs, such as the International Geophysical Year, radio astronomy, and weather modification. The same kind of imagination should be exercised in the social sciences. In addition to the ambiguities in relation to the organization of science in the universities, there are ambiguities in applied research because of the responsibilities assigned to various agencies of government, so that functional organization of National Science Foundation programs around urban development or labor utilization might run afoul of other agencies. Yet these problems are not insoluble; manpower research, for example, appears both within the Foundation and the Department of Labor. We think of such functional topics as migration, conservation of resources (including human resources), social change, and the social influence of technology as types of topics around which programs might be developed. The National Science Foundation may have to take a somewhat active role, setting aside funds for specific purposes and stimulating proposals in new directions. If Graduate Schools of Applied Behavioral Science develop, they would become a natural source of proposals for such funds.

The two previous recommendations bear on the discussions that have been going on in recent years over the desirability of a new national social science foundation. The bill to establish such a foundation would create an agency that bears a striking resemblance to the National Science Foundation, in that it would encourage the development of a basic social science along traditional disciplinary lines and free of the "mission-orientation" of other operating government agencies. Yet, the discussions of the bill have often stressed the intentions of its proponents to use social science innovatively in confronting the nation's social problems and to encourage the social sciences to probe for their root causes. We believe that our emphasis upon applied social research and problem-solving is consistent with these latter expressed intentions but not with the form of organization proposed in the bill. The issue of a separate foundation for the social sciences, however, remains. If the previous two recommendations are followed, we would not feel the need for a new agency. However, if for any reason it is not found feasible to carry them out, some alternative may have to be sought. We state this in the form of a stand-by or contingent recommendation.

RECOMMENDATION: POSSIBLE NEED FOR A NEW AGENCY

If for any reason the National Science Foundation is unable to fulfill the obligations implied in the two previous recommendations, the Congress should consider enacting legislation to create a separate and independent agency, organized along functional lines, to support basic and applied behavioral and social science research contributing to the solution of social problems.

Discipline-orientation exercises an inhibiting influence on appropriate research into significant social problems; thus encouragement should be given to research that is not organized along familiar disciplinary lines. This must not be construed to mean that we wish disciplinary research to be weakened or abandoned; quite the contrary. It is our conviction, however, that the behavioral and social sciences will come into better balance if discipline-oriented basic research is supplemented by added attention to responsible policy-oriented research.

THE MANNER IN WHICH FEDERAL FUNDS FOR RESEARCH ARE DISTRIBUTED TO THE UNIVERSITIES AND TO RESEARCH INSTITUTES

We have already indicated our general satisfaction with the various agencies' use of their research funds to support and encourage research with a maximum of freedom to the individual investigator to publish and take credit for his work (with the exception always of classified research, which has to be considered separately).

A number of funding methods are used: project grants, typically reviewed by panels of peers; various types of grants to departments and to institutions (or "block grants," as they are sometimes called); and various kinds of small grants. In addition, there are special–purpose grants and contracts, in which the agency supplying the funds tends to take more initiative in proposing a topic for research, though usually without stating the details.

While a number of suggestions arose in our Committee deliberations, the issue over methods of support of scientific research are general and not specific to the behavioral and social sciences. Therefore, we have chosen not to offer our comments in any detail; instead, we refer to the careful studies of the methods for allocating funds for higher education that have been made by others.*

The present arrangements for distributing research funds appear to work out reasonably well in channeling research funds to younger and older investigators, although in a recent study the department heads of 36 departments in economics, psychology, and sociology (among 167 heads of these departments replying) believed that their younger investigators were doing inadequate amounts of research, primarily because of lack of funds.†

An issue that arises as often as any other is that of long-term funding, of 5 years and beyond, to assure the continuity of research. The funding agencies commonly see the desirability of long-range funding, but tend to be limited by legislative policies over which they have no control. These policies should be modified because discontinuity leads to inefficiency and frustration in many kinds of research, especially in the longitudinal studies of individuals and organizations so important within the behavioral and social sciences.

While all sciences need continuity in research, the problem is particularly acute in the behavioral and social sciences for two reasons. First, change in both people and social institutions is often slow and subtle and can be studied only by following people and institutions over long periods of time. Second, in view of the undeveloped nature of some facets of the field, there is need for many exploratory studies that require time before definitive studies can be accomplished; if time is not allowed for both, research becomes fragmented and does not become conclusive. Hence, it is imperative that provisions be made for sustained support of promising research over a period of years.

*National Science Board–National Science Foundation, *Toward a Public Policy for Graduate Education in the Sciences,* NSB 69-1, 1969; National Science Board–National Science Foundation, *Graduate Education: Parameters for Public Policy,* NSB 69-2, 1969; U.S. Department of Health, Education, and Welfare, *Toward a Long-Range Plan for Federal Financial Support for Higher Education,* January 1969; Carnegie Commission on Higher Education, *Quality and Equality: New Levels of Federal Responsibility for Higher Education* (New York: McGraw-Hill Book Company, December 1968).

†National Science Foundation, *Support and Research Participation of Young and Senior Academic Staff, 1968,* NSF 68-31, 1968, pp. 17 and 19.

15
PRIVATE SUPPORT OF SOCIAL AND BEHAVIORAL SCIENCE RESEARCH

THE FOUNDATIONS

The philanthropic foundation has played an extremely important role in the development of the behavioral and social sciences, well out of proportion to its total investment in these fields of science, which we have estimated at $39 million, or 3 percent of the total support for social science in 1967 (Table 1-2).

The development of non-Western studies in American colleges and universities offers a case in point. Sizable grants from the Rockefeller Foundation, the Carnegie Corporation of New York, and later the Ford Foundation helped American scholars to internationalize curricula and broaden their research interests. Beginning in the mid-1940's, new scholars were trained both for academic life and for government service. Furthermore, the area study approach helped to pioneer the combination of academic disciplines in a multidisciplinary setting. More recently, the federal government has assumed responsibility for funding area studies, building on the firm base created with private support.*

The term "behavioral sciences" gained currency as a result of the designation of a program area so named in the Ford Foundation at the time of its establishment as a national philanthropic organization in 1950. Through its research and training grants, which totaled several million dollars before the program was terminated in 1957,

---

*See George M. Beckmann, "The Role of the Foundations in Non-Western Studies," In Warren Weaver, U.S. Philanthropic Foundations: Their History, Structure, Management, and Record (New York: Harper & Row, Publishers, 1967), pp. 395–409.

the foundation had a profound impact on the development of the basic sciences of individual behavior and human relations. Free funds were granted to individual scholars and to several major universities to support developments in the social sciences; other funds were provided to universities for self-surveys that produced evaluations of existing programs and uncovered opportunities in the social sciences. Support was then provided to make investment possible in the most strategic of these opportunities. Although these grants directly aided only a few universities, others on their own initiative conducted similar surveys and the effects were multiplied. The behavioral sciences program of the Ford Foundation also established the Center for Advanced Study in the Behavioral Sciences, later to become independent but with some endowment from the foundation. The foundation supported a large program in research in mental health before the National Institute of Mental Health had begun its dramatic enlargement.

The withdrawal of the Ford Foundation as one of the major sponsors of the behavioral sciences was a source of concern to those in the field particularly because the cancellation of the program came at a time when congressional committee attacks on foundations appeared to make them somewhat timid in sensitive areas. One of the major advantages of foundations is that they have the freedom to enter research areas that government finds relatively difficult to support; this advantage appeared to be threatened when a major foundation withdrew from areas in which it was deeply committed. This does not mean that the Ford Foundation has refused all support to the behavioral sciences by abandoning this division of its work. Its overseas and international programs have been very productive, and on a topical basis, it is assisting a number of social science fields domestically, such as urban renewal and crime research.

Since 1907, the Russell Sage Foundation has supported, through its own research and through grants, programs designed to improve the utilization of social science knowledge. In recent years, it has been in the forefront of the movement to develop social indicators. It has been instrumental in developing cooperative programs involving lawyers and social scientists. In addition, the foundation is actively engaged in a program aimed at assessing the social, ethical, and legal consequences of recent scientific advances in biology. Russell Sage is unusual among foundations in maintaining its own intramural staff for social science research.

Demography in the United States was developed in large measure through the generous support of private foundations. Prior to World War II, the Scripps Foundation for Research in Population Problems and the Milbank Memorial Fund played an important role in trying to understand the broader social and political implications of changes in the world's population. The first university-based program in demography was established at Princeton in 1936 by the Milbank fund and later was supported by the Rockefeller Foundation. The Population Council, established in 1952 with Rockefeller funds, brings together social scientists, biological scientists, and persons in technical assistance, working on the complex and interwoven problems of controlling the world's population.

The foregoing examples merely illustrate the many kinds of things foundations have done in relation to the behavioral and social sciences. The foundations themselves show concern over their ecological niche in the support of research now that federal support is on such a large scale. They have come up with several definitions of their roles. Some have chosen to encourage research in a particular discipline, notably the Wenner-Gren Foundation, which gave a great forward thrust to research in anthropology with its primary support of that field before the National Science Foundation and National Institute of Mental Health began increasing their support. Other foundations have favored local areas. For example, the Hogg Foundation, established by private endowments but with an administrative base at the University of Texas, is concerned with mental health, and its programs are limited largely to the State of Texas. It also serves as a consultant to smaller foundations in Texas, helping them to find appropriate roles for their efforts. Although the foundations, both large and small, generally have several major emphases at any given time, these tend to shift as new opportunities arise, or as other agencies (including the government) begin to take major responsibility for fields in which the foundations were operating.

Foundation trustees and executives continue to struggle with the problems of how each of the foundations can best meet its obligations. We have only a few guidelines to propose:

1. Often because of a philanthropist's interest in human welfare and the betterment of the conditions of life, foundations have commonly supported medicine and the social sciences. With the massive support of medical research now available from many sources, the opportunities in the social sciences remain major ones. Although foundations have been generous in this general area, they have

occasionally been unadventurous and have not given the leadership that might be expected of them.

2. The areas that most require foundation support in the behavioral and social sciences are those that are (a) sensitive areas (such as religion, politics, and personal practices), where political pressure might make it inadvisable or impossible for governmental agencies to operate, (b) areas that may involve critical assessment of governmental operations and programs, (c) international projects, where government support is under suspicion, and (d) very-high-risk areas, where both ideas and investigators are untried.

Even by these criteria, government-sponsored research has often been fully as daring and innovative as that supported by foundations. Foundations should be ready to move out in front, especially where daring and risk are involved.

Research is not the only function of foundation support, and local foundations often have the opportunity of supporting demonstration projects looking toward improvement of the quality of life, where research itself is but a small part of the project. Social science comes in through aid in planning and in monitoring the projects, so that some generalizations may emerge that will be useful elsewhere.

A private foundation can help to maintain the independence of the social sciences and can foster their critical and challenging role. The institutions of government themselves will benefit from a strong private presence in social science research. Some topics will always be neglected by government agencies, for various reasons, and the government will be too deeply involved in some others to be either an objective or a detached sponsor of research relating to them. The private foundations should expand their support of the social and behavioral sciences to maintain the healthy state of these disciplines, as well as to ensure that important areas of social research are not neglected for bureaucratic or political reasons.

The development of evaluation research on public programs is of particular importance. So, too, is the place of the private foundation in developing social indicators, a social report, and the Graduate Schools of Applied Behavioral Science, as recommended earlier in this report.

Private foundations have often played a special role in providing funds for pilot studies preparatory to the planning of more extensive investigations. If the pilot studies turn out well, applications are then prepared for more substantial funding either by foundations or by government agencies; if they do not turn out well, the larger program is either abandoned or redirected. This is a useful practice that may well be continued.

A related practice, one that runs into difficulties, is the support of more substantial programs for a few years, in the hope that they will then be taken over either by the universities themselves or by government supporting agencies. Such initial support, "seed money," helps a young venture to get on its feet, but it runs the risk that a venture well under way may be abruptly deprived of funds.

The experience of private foundations in international education shows some of the difficulties. After supporting foreign-area studies for more than a decade, the foundations might well have expected to be relieved of some of this responsibility when the International Education Act was authorized in 1966. But the Congress failed to provide funding for this act for 3 successive years, and expectations of a smooth transition—which would preserve and continue the programs devoted to training experts on various foreign areas—have been frustrated. In all, it would seem highly desirable for governmental and private sources of support to make a greater effort to coordinate their actions to avoid the worst features of cyclical "boom or bust" financing of social science.

The private foundations are to be encouraged to be increasingly venturesome in their support of social science research, particularly as the sciences become more involved in policy areas. The value of their funding for free and independent social science, though the amounts entailed may be small in comparison with the magnitude of government funding, cannot be overestimated.

THE LEARNED COUNCILS

In addition to the philanthropic foundations themselves, there is a class of private nonprofit organizations that include among their functions an intermediary role between fund-granting agencies (public as well as private) and research performers, especially at colleges and universities. Prototypical examples are the Social Science Research Council, the American Council of Learned Societies, the American Council on Education, and the National Research Council. The Brookings Institution, Resources for the Future, and the National Bureau of Economic Research have somewhat the same character, but they perform more intramural research than do the councils. The councils act as a source of both stimulation for needed research and better training for research; they also provide research grants and fellowships to individual scholars. In actually granting research funds, these councils depend largely or exclusively on short-term grants that they themselves receive from private foundations or public agencies, because they do not have substantial endowments of their own. The work of the councils is conducted through committees of scholars and scientists whose members are principally university-based and who give freely of their time and energy in guiding the programs. They have the respect and confidence of the research community, and they strive to advance research and education in relevant disciplines and topics. They are useful means of collaboration between sectors of the society built on broad and informed acquaintances with research scholars; they are informed about the changing frontiers of research, and possess mechanisms for bringing together resources and talent.

Because of their relatively weak long-term funding, however, the councils need both sustaining funds for administrative costs and venture capital for ideas that are too nascent to command project support.* These organizations can provide government with a type of capacity it cannot provide for itself, and are truly national resources. As such, they deserve the sympathetic interest and tangible assistance of both private foundations and government agencies to ensure their continued vitality.

*Alan Pifer, "The Nongovernmental Organization at Bay," *In Annual Report* (New York: Carnegie Corporation, 1966).

16
WORLDWIDE
DEVELOPMENT
OF
SOCIAL SCIENCES

The focus of this report has so far been on the behavioral and social sciences in the United States. This is appropriate to its purpose as a domestic document; but we need also to understand the importance that these sciences have for the rest of the world, and the importance of the rest of the world for these sciences. In both respects, U.S. scientists are deeply involved and their role is significant in cross-national research and in international collaborative work.

Behavioral and social scientists benefit from cross-national exposure. To a greater extent than the physical and biological sciences, the behavioral disciplines must study their subjects in a variety of contexts. Thus, they must have access to a variety of social systems and a broad range of cultural arrangements in order to test the generality of their propositions about human behavior and to avoid parochialism in their understanding of the dynamics of society. This requirement is a central concern of anthropologists who have taken on the task of documenting the entire range of human social adaptation to the totality of habitats. Political scientists increasingly concern themselves with comparative political development, and economists find much enlightenment in the study of economic systems that are quite different from our own—ranging from simple barter economies through very complex, industrialized systems that are centrally planned and controlled, as in some of the socialist countries.

The study of a country by a social scientist who is native to another is an ancient and honorable practice. When America itself was a new and underdeveloped nation, it excited the curiosity of European scholars. DeTocqueville's perceptive analysis of American democracy in the nineteenth century and the masterly and compendious *American Commonwealth* of Lord Bryce are but two examples. Though not always flattering, these analyses were nonetheless revelatory and instructive to us, as well as to the rest of the world; these scholarly studies were real contributions to international understanding.

In the last 50 years foreign social scientists' interest in the United States has lessened somewhat although it has not disappeared, as evidenced by Gunnar Myrdal's landmark analysis of our racial problems in the 1940's and by Brogan's study of American national character, which appeared somewhat later. American social scientists over the same period of time have steadily widened their comparative interests, especially in the developing world. Where local national capability in the behavioral sciences was weak, researchers from the United States usually had to do without local collaborators or had to find and train coworkers themselves. Partly as a result of these very efforts, but mostly through the development of international exchange programs for professors and graduate students from developing countries, the general situation has slowly begun to change nearly everywhere. In some countries that had little or no social scientific establishment at the end of World War II, there is now a substantial professional development that makes possible genuinely collaborative international research; some examples of this are discussed in the following paragraphs.

One elaborate study in progress involves political scientists of four countries studying citizen participation in political life. The research was jointly planned and is being conducted by scholars in Japan, India, Nigeria, and the United States. Because the instruments for data collection were carefully prepared to ensure comparability of response, it will be possible to make systematic comparisons of similarities and differences among the four nations and to test some general hypotheses concerning patterns of social and political change. Important training and field experience have been gained by graduate students in all the countries; this has helped to develop and strengthen a new cadre of scientific workers. Finally, the successful conclusion of this collaborative undertaking will provide a base for further joint undertakings in the future. For example, the American scholars have been asked by social scientists in a number of Eastern European countries to extend the study to that part of the world.

Along with the advantages of such collaborative undertakings, the considerable amounts of time and money necessary for research programs of this complexity must also be considered. The four-nation phase of the study referred to above will take 6 or 7 years, from the first planning meeting of the scholars to the completion of the data analysis and write-up. This has been estimated to be at least 1 year longer than a more traditionally organized study, where the Americans would have simply gone to the foreign countries and done the work. The participating researchers estimate that roughly one third of the project's cost can be attributed to the costs of the collaboration itself. It is hard to assign a dollar value to the collaboration, but it can be said with assurance that the study itself is better for it, in addition to the side benefits in training and experience for the collaborators.

Collaborative cross-national studies will have an important role in relation to various types of social comparisons. We are familiar with the interlocking of economic and monetary problems throughout the world, but we are finding that other problems—educational ones, for example—also have international aspects. An important international study of education is under way in which 12 nations around the world are participating. The first report published in 1967 on achievement in mathematics presented the results of a study of 133,000 students in the classrooms of 13,000 teachers in more than 5,300 schools in the 12 countries. Important benchmarks are provided for assessing the relative successes of the schools in the different nations as they attempt to teach mathematics. Great ingenuity was used in securing comparable tests translated into different languages and in solving many other problems connected with a survey on this scale. The same group of scholars is assessing the teaching of other subjects, such as reading, and French and English as foreign languages. These studies go well beyond mere data-gathering; but even as data-gathering enterprises, they help open up some of the possibilities that lie in international collaboration. Scientists of the 12 nations participate as equals in these investigations; the first report was prepared by a Swedish psychologist and educator.*

American psychologists, psychiatrists, and sociologists have cooperated with Danish and Swedish colleagues to improve the understanding of inheritance of schizophrenia. This collaboration, partially supported by the National Institute of Mental Health, is facilitated by the birth record data regularly collected and available for research in these countries.

Another example of an international multidisciplinary research

---

*Torsten Husén, ed., *International Study of Achievement in Mathematics* (New York: John Wiley & Sons, Inc., Publishers, 1967).

project is the Survey of Language Use and Language Teaching in Eastern Africa, supported by the Ford Foundation. Personnel are from British, American, and African universities, and the funds are channeled through American and African institutions. Members of the country teams include linguists, sociologists, anthropologists, and specialists in language education. The project makes provision for associated research under local sponsorship, as well as fellowships for Africans to attend universities in Africa, Great Britain, or the United States. So far the participation of Africans on the country teams has been very limited, a situation that, it is hoped, will be changed as the training aspects of this and related programs begin to be recognized. Data will be published in monograph-length country studies, and at least two of these will also appear in the national language of the country—Amharic for Ethiopia and Swahili for Tanzania.

Cooperation among social scientists from several countries has many advantages. Not the least of these is that it helps to remove cultural blindness, the taking-for-granted of what, to the investigator, has become customary.

For such a multinational program to be effective, the collaborators must be selectively interdependent. Some programs go wrong because people are brought together through impersonal, formal processes and find that they cannot work together constructively. The importance of informal international networks of social scientists is now being recognized.

PROBLEMS OF COLLABORATIVE RESEARCH

Not only are the social sciences developing almost everywhere in the world (albeit unevenly, as we have pointed out) but, concomitantly, social scientists in many developing nations have understandably become preoccupied with the application of social science to their own national concerns. Thus, although some new opportunities for research are opened, the interest of local scholars in collaborating on research that originates in the concerns of the U.S. scientist may diminish. In fact, in some of the developing countries, there has grown up a rather negative attitude toward research that is of interest to an alien investigator but that appears to have no direct relevance to national or local situations. Collaborative planning can avoid such negatives and can maximize the satisfactions derived by those involved in the research.

Collaborative research involves serious and widespread problems. They are more severe in some countries and in some disciplines than in others, but they should not be minimized. True collaboration in research requires social scientists in the foreign locales whose background and training qualify them and who are *actively and practically* interested in such collaboration. The economic and political contexts in which they live and make their careers have to be such as to make the collaboration professionally valuable, on balance, rather than detrimental. The social scientist from the United States must be prepared to give, as well as to get, collaboration and opportunity to satisfy interests.

The Committee believes that when field research is to be done abroad by American social scientists, on other than an individual basis, they should make every reasonable effort to collaborate with indigenous scholars in such a way that those scholars can enjoy the fullest possible participation in the research, appropriate recognition of this participation, and equal access to the resulting data. The Committee also believes that the U.S. social science community would gain much from collaborative field research by foreign scholars in the United States.

It is important in the current international atmosphere that American behavioral and social scientists make clear to their collaborators and hosts in other nations the nature of their sponsorship and the sources of their support. We agree with the position taken by an earlier committee that reviewed behavioral science in the federal government that "primary responsibility for government support for behavioral science research and training conducted in foreign countries by universities in the United States be placed in agencies and programs committed to basic research and research training. . . ."* Nevertheless, we do not believe that sponsorship should necessarily be limited to such agencies and programs. Mission-oriented agencies— such as the Agency for International Development, the Arms Control and Disarmament Agency, the Office of Naval Research, and the Peace Corps—have in the past supported research projects abroad in an unobjectionable manner. Funds from mission-oriented agencies should be for projects with legitimate scientific objectives and their results should be unclassified. An open and above-board approach by agencies and scholars of all countries would help greatly to establish international credibility.

*The Behavioral Sciences and the Federal Government, NAS Pub. 1680 (Washington, D.C.: National Academy of Sciences, 1968), Recommendation 5, p. 9.

The need for increased funding for the international activities of American universities, including research, has recently been documented.* The amount of money for the various international purposes of the universities from private and public sources has recently been decreasing. Federal funds for social and behavioral research on foreign areas and international affairs in 1968 were $6.4 million below the 1967 level of $40.6 million, a drop of 16 percent.†

The Committee believes that it is essential that the federal government counter this trend in recognition of the importance of international collaboration. We urge the Congress as a first step to provide the funds authorized under the International Education Act of 1966.

In suggesting that private and public sources in the United States provide more funds for international research, we also wish to suggest that international research should be financially, as well as intellectually, collaborative. While many countries of the world, and in particular the developing nations, are not able to invest very large sums in social research at this time, the principle of multinational funding of projects should be established.

INTERNATIONAL ARRANGEMENTS FOR STRENGTHENING THE BEHAVIORAL AND SOCIAL SCIENCES

To realize the ideal of fully shared responsibility in conducting research throughout the world, it is essential that social scientists understand each other, and have appropriate training to permit them to collaborate as equals.

The Organization for Comparative Social Research in Oslo, Norway, has had an important impact on the development of modern social science in Belgium, France, England, Germany, The Netherlands, Norway, and Sweden. Although funded initially by the Ford Foundation, it is not an American enterprise, although American scholars have participated. Political scientists, sociologists, psychologists, and others have taken part in jointly conceived programs of experimentation and survey research. A major product of the col-

---

*A Crisis of Dollars: The Funding Threat to International Affairs in U.S. Higher Education (New York: Education and World Affairs, 1968).
†"Federal Funding of Foreign Area Research: A Survey," FAR Horizons, 2, January 1969.

TABLE 16-1   EDUCATIONAL EXCHANGES WITH THE UNITED STATES IN THE BEHAVIORAL AND SOCIAL SCIENCES

	Foreign Students and Scholars in the U.S.		American Students and Scholars Abroad [a]	
	Students (1967–68)	Scholars (1967–68)	Students (1966–67)	Scholars (1967–68)
Africa	1,595	57	58	102
Europe	2,555	371	1,315	493
Far East	4,511	417	246	169
Latin America	2,983	69	585	185
Near and Mid-East	1,918	98	156	68
North America	2,230	64	481	13
Oceania	273	33	50	22
Total	16,065	1,109	2,891	1,052
Total, all fields	110,315	11,641	21,579	4,775

[a] These data are probably underestimates since they were collected from institutions abroad. Many American scholars and students overseas are doing independent or collaborative research, are not affiliated with foreign universities, and would not, therefore, be included.

Source: *Open Doors 1968* (New York: Institute of International Education, July 1968), Tables 3, 4, and 5.

laboration, in addition to its publications, has been the scientific preparation of social scientists who are now occupying positions of importance at universities and research institutes in Western Europe and who, in turn, are actively engaged in training new social scientists.

Another project, funded by the Ford Foundation, involved economists at the University of California in the development of economic training and research facilities at the University of Indonesia. Begun in the mid-1950's, the project has continued uninterrupted, despite the break in United States–Indonesian relations in the 1960's. Indonesian students have come to the United States for training and research under the auspices of the program. Joint research projects in Indonesia have trained additional students. In the beginning, American professors of economics organized and carried on the teaching program at the University of Indonesia, which is now fully in the hands of Indonesian scholars. As a result of these efforts, a first-rate faculty of economics has developed in Indonesia, which has in turn supplied many of the economic advisers now serving the top levels of the Indonesian government.

The international exchange of students and scholars for purposes of training and research represents one of the most important opportunities for developing an international social science. Through such programs—whether they be formal or informal, private or governmental—an international network of colleagues is developed. Opportunities for Americans to study and do research overseas are essential for the development of the social sciences; it is equally important that foreign students and established scholars have opportunities to study and do research in the United States. Table 16-1 suggests the magnitude of the exchange of persons in the behavioral and social sciences.

A large number of international and regional organizations of a nongovernmental nature foster communication in the behavioral and social sciences. These include, among others, the international associations in anthropology, demography, economics, sociology, statistics, psychology, mental health, and political science. The meetings of these associations, usually held at 2-year or 4-year intervals, have attracted increasingly large numbers of participants from many countries.

Besides these disciplinary groups, there are specialized and regional organizations. One of the most important is the Latin American Social Science Council, established in 1967, which now has 45 social science research institutes as members and a vigorous research program on social and economic development. A number of North American social scientists gave advice on its founding and the Council has received financial assistance from the Ford Foundation. There is also a hemispheral disciplinary association, the Interamerican Society of Psychology, which meets annually and has individual members from North, South, and Central American countries.

A somewhat different example is the European Association for Experimental Social Psychology, founded in 1965. This group grew out of an initiative of the Social Science Research Council (U.S.), which recognized the need for an organization to bring European research workers together for their mutual benefit. During the late 1940's and the 1950's, the burgeoning of experimental social psychology in the United States had attracted attention in Western Europe and stimulated a considerable international exchange of professors through whom American technique and research results were effectively exported; as it developed, European research became known in this country. But European work often was not as well diffused among Europeans, because professional lines of communication had been formed trans-Atlantically rather than internationally on the Continent. Recognizing this curious gap, the Social Science Research Council convened some meetings of social psychologists from Europe and the United States, and out of these discussions grew both the European Association and the council's own Transnational Social Psychology Committee whose membership is multinational. The committee and the Association have subsequently cosponsored programs for training European research workers and research conferences that included social psychologists from the nations of Eastern Europe. The committee has also begun collaborative efforts in Latin America.

Another kind of international collaborative effort is the Committee on Political and Social Science in Italy, cosponsored by the Social Science Research Council and the Adriano Olivetti Foundation. Organized at the request of the Italian partners, this binational body has undertaken to strengthen the graduate programs in social science at selected Italian universities through the establishment of training centers and other means. The fact that many of the Italian professors participating in the committee's ventures have themselves had some postgraduate education at universities in the United States has certainly contributed to the committee's success.

Another nongovernmental organization of potential importance for social science is the International Social Science Council. Through its bimonthly journal and other activities it is working toward the development of an international social science community. One of its most interesting experiments is the formation of the European Coordination Center for Research and Documentation in the Social Sciences. Established in 1963 in Vienna with financial assistance from UNESCO (United Nations Educational, Scientific, and Cultural Organization), it provides an institutional structure designed to facilitate international collaboration among research organizations in a large number of countries. The center has developed comparative cross-national research programs on such diverse topics as industrialization, delinquency, economic assistance and development, peace, social development, national planning, and the diffusion of innovations in rural communities.

There are a number of other international and intergovernmental programs, mostly affiliated with or offshoots of the United Nations, such as the World Health Organization or the International Labor Organization. Central for the behavioral and social sciences is UNESCO. The Department of Social Science of UNESCO is in a particularly strategic position to develop an international behavioral and social science. It works through a number of existing organizations, has assisted in the creation of new ones, and encourages organizations—such as the International Brain Research Organization (IBRO)—to strengthen their activities in the behavioral sciences. Unfortunately, despite a very large contribution from the United States to the total UNESCO budget, the Department of Social Science is starved for funds. A major effort must be made to strengthen the department's program by bringing its activities into the mainstream of development and innovation in the social and behavioral sciences and by assisting it to promote the application of social science knowledge to the problems confronting the world today.

It seems clear from the record that international collaboration can be an effective and acceptable way of encouraging the development of the behavioral and social sciences outside the United States while, at the same time, securing benefits to our domestic enterprises in these fields. The mode of collaboration is important and national sensitivities sometimes need special attention. It is often desirable to approach collaboration through organizations deliberately designed to promote it, especially for researchers who do not have established relationships with coprofessionals in countries where they wish to work. The Committee believes that organizations, binational or multinational, that have an interest in developing the international social science community should have increased support from both public and private funding agencies. Furthermore, such support should be made available for sustaining these organizations and their broad purposes on a continuing basis, rather than only on a project basis, because the cultivation of a truly international community is a slow and steady task. The desirability of continuing an organization's work should be judged on the basis of its total performance record, rather than on the estimated merit of a single proposed activity.

17
OUTLOOK FOR THE BEHAVIORAL AND SOCIAL SCIENCES

The rate of growth of the behavioral and social sciences will depend on the wisdom and foresight with which they are organized and funded, but whatever the temporary perturbations, these disciplines will continue to develop both as sciences in their own right and as aids in the handling of social problems.

THE EDUCATIONAL ROLE

As basic sciences of mankind and society, the behavioral disciplines will continue to be an important part of the education of young people. The record of the 1960's shows that college students in increasing numbers majored in social sciences and also that the number of degrees awarded in these subjects increased at a more rapid rate than in the physical sciences. One likely explanation of this trend is that, currently, the attention of young men and women is being drawn increasingly to the problems of society. They seek to understand why the cities of the nation are in trouble, why there is conflict between racial groups, what the implications of population growth are, and what might be the prospects of control of that growth. They are puzzled by the prevalence of violent crime and curious about the nature and causes of mental illness, suicide, homosexuality, drug addiction, and alcoholism. They want to understand economic development, international tensions, monetary crises, inflation, war, and revolution.

Most students are drawn to the social sciences because they want to understand the pathologies of society or its tenants. Some may even be attracted because they seek help in solving personal problems and in comprehending social disorders that have touched their own lives. When they get into their studies, they find that their instructors and textbooks are more concerned with explaining the "normal" processes of growth and functioning of individuals and institutions, in providing a background of understanding against which pathological events can be seen as departures from the normal, but departures that can be explained only by reference to it. Once this perspective is gained, the student is on his way to a scientific understanding of social phenomena. He learns that mental illness is a product of traumatic relationships between individuals—parent and child, husband and wife, worker and supervisor, and so forth—with perhaps a genetic component as well in some kinds of illness. But he comprehends the etiology better when he has studied patterns of normal development in children and knows something about the variability of individuals as they grow.

Because understanding of man and the social arrangements under which he lives is important to the general student, as well as to the specialist, the educational role of behavioral and social scientists goes well beyond the training of experts in the social science fields. The same may be said of the products of their basic researches. These are contributions to the cultural and intellectual life, regardless of their immediate utility.

THE COMPLEXITY OF SOCIAL PROBLEMS

There is a tendency for those who turn to the social sciences for answers to the problems of society to yearn for ready-made solutions to big problems. Students often start this way, but they soon become aware that there are no easy solutions, and they become more realistic about the contributions that behavioral science can make to improving the human condition. There is promise of significant contributions, but the answers cannot be hurried. An example, described in some detail, may help to make clear why this is so.

It seems reasonably clear that protein malnutrition in infancy and early childhood can lead to retarded mental, as well as physical, development. We ask the behavioral scientist (working with a nutritionist) to determine whether or not this is the case, and to suggest how best to see that deprived children get the protein they need. This all seems easy enough until we find out what is actually involved in developing the necessary scientific evidence.

There are now detailed field studies of this problem in several developing countries; and others are in progress. The details are far from clear, and the links of causation are not firmly established, because events associated with poverty and underprivilege, besides poor diet, can certainly affect intellectual growth. Some of these are parents' interactions with the infant, the availability of playthings that stimulate cognitive growth, and the richness or barrenness of preschool and early school environments. Infectious diseases and intestinal parasites, both characteristic of unsanitary and crowded environments, exacerbate the effects of malnutrition. Also, the genetic makeup of the parents and child cannot be neglected. It is not even clear just when the protein deficiency ceases to be critical, or to what extent an early deficiency can be made up later. When is early malnutrition permanently damaging to the mental apparatus, dooming the person to a limited capacity for understanding and performance? Is it reversible? Severely protein-malnourished children (who suffer from symptoms described as kwashiokor or marasmus) are demonstrably retarded on simple psychomotor tests even after full nutritional recovery has occurred. The degree of retardation in less severely malnourished cases is harder to evaluate.

Given this degree of uncertainty about the relation between malnutrition and mental development, the recommendations one might make about action to improve the situation are not clear. Certainly the obvious suggestion is to improve the diet of the children, especially its protein content. It would be hard to oppose such a humane move, yet it might not be the most important, expedient, or effective step. It might not even work unless ways are also found to reduce the burden of infectious diseases. If protein supplementation were provided by major gifts from outside the community or country where the undernourished children live, it would not affect the socio-political–economic matrix in which children become malnourished. This is not to deny the immediate and short-run benefits of treating "symptoms," but simply to assert that such treatment does not solve underlying problems.

A program to remedy underlying causes of malnutrition in infancy and early childhood must include a formidable catalogue of measures to overcome poverty, reduce the spread of infectious disease, improve the earning capacity of worker-parents, stimulate economic growth, extend the marketing of agricultural products (and possibly redistribute proprietorship in cultivation), and change dietary habits—to mention but a few. If that list of obstacles is discouraging, consider two further pertinent points. Experience with protein-supplementation programs has not been uniformly favorable. Not only is a powdered milk supplement of dubious value when it must be mixed with the contaminated water that is the only kind available to the villager, but also it may not even produce the physical effects desired. In one study in which a milk supplement was fed to children in a Central American village—children who were between 1 and 5 years of age and several years retarded compared with well-nourished children—there was no demonstrable growth improvement compared with children in a "control" village who received no supplement. The reasons were partly the heavy burden of infectious disease and the difficulty of obtaining regular participation in the supplementation programs.

Finally, it seems unlikely that improved diet alone could remove such deficiencies in intelligence, learning, and behavior as exist among the deprived populations of ill-fed areas. Poor diet and poverty go together with increased exposure and susceptibility to infections, with illiteracy and ignorance, with unskilled work and unemployment, and with unstimulating environments and unexciting companions. There is a distinct possibility that improvements in the educational and interpersonal environment would be equal to or of greater importance than improvements in the food intakes of many underprivileged and underfed populations.

The problem of malnutrition and intellectual development has been discussed at length because it illustrates certain points that must be kept in mind when we think about the social sciences and their possible contribution to resolution of social problems. First, "the" problem is really several problems inextricably woven together, hard to separate even analytically and virtually impossible to treat singly because of strong interaction effects. Second, even though animal experiments have shown the effects of dietary deficiency, the precise nature of the relation between diet and retardation is so poorly specified (how much protein deficiency causes how much retardation: how reversible is the mental loss?) that the optimum strategy for action is unclear. Third, an apparently purely "behavioral" problem incorporates aspects of biochemistry (the growth promoting value of diet supplements), of infectious disease (infections increase the severity of malnutrition and are more severe in malnourished individuals), of genetics (the possibility that intellectual capacity is heritably limited), of economic development, of political policy (education and land utilization), and even of international trade (the deplorable tendency of some manufacturers of starches that have no protein value to advertise them as if they were ideal baby food).

Finally, the example points to the slow and difficult nature of "solutions" to some of our social problems. Even though the behavioral sciences are on the edge of horizon–broadening discoveries, even though their methods of getting new knowledge are constantly improving, and even though the measures we have advocated for their improvement promise to accelerate their usefulness, it is plain that some social problems will be with us for a long time to come. That is partly because of their sheer massiveness and the amount of resources and power that will be necessary to effect changes; it is also because some features of the problems may be anchored in customs, beliefs, and attitudes that are primitive (in the sense of learned early) and may be retained for a generation, while others may be in the genes, where change is even slower.

The moral is not despair, but patience and renewed effort. Social scientists will have to make strenuous efforts and work collaboratively with those who manage educational institutions, government agencies, research organizations, and philanthropic foundations, as well as with the public at large.

THE INTEGRATION OF SOCIAL SCIENCE KNOWLEDGE

Social scientists themselves will have to do all they can to assure a sufficient supply of trained manpower to handle the increased responsibilities of the future. They must exercise their ingenuity in teaching and research to attract talented young people, to challenge their imagination and stimulate their ambition. Behavioral scientists must communicate their research findings with clarity, reflecting the excitement of work in these fields. They must defend freedom of inquiry and seek to build an intellectual structure in which many can work at varied tasks. They must prepare themselves for a vastly increased scale of research if they are to manage the enterprises we have suggested. For example, the task of developing social indicators and a social report will require not simply more and better manpower but adroitness in using many diverse skills and levels of training. Accurate data can be collected only if those at the head-counting and question-asking phase are diligent and knowledgeable, motivated to do their job well, and proud of it. The analysts at the next stage must depend on accurate raw data, because the sophistication that analysis requires is wasted if it is set to work upon "fiction." Finally, at the level of indicator building and validation, where talent for theoretical thinking and imagination are required, we must have a plentiful supply of the best talents. And all these people must work in harmony with each other and with large-scale computing machinery governed, again, by specialized talent. The problems of managing such an enterprise are not exceeded by those of space technology, or comprehensive medical care, or deep ocean exploration.

If social and behavioral scientists are to manage complicated and comprehensive attacks on social problems, they will have to learn how to improve the integration of their own diverse knowledge and technique. As these disciplines become more sophisticated, they will surely grow more specialized and more separate. The need for better means of communication, education, and utilization will grow apace. As knowledge becomes more fragmented, the challenge of applying various fragments—even knowing which ones to select— becomes greater. Social science generalists, intellectual "managers" who deal in the exchange of specialized information, will become more common than they are now, and their cultivation calls for an educational strategy other than specialized-discipline training.

Comparatively few social scientists now are practiced in organizing a work group, dividing up tasks, delegating most to subordinate specialists, and assembling pieces. Only a relative few have mastered the complexities of really large-scale research or have learned how to use nonscientists to handle some of the mechanical and financial problems of such investigations. These skills need improvement and perhaps could be taught more systematically than they are at present, when, for the most part, a graduate student apprentices himself to an individual investigator working on a one-man project of limited scope.

SOCIAL EXPERIMENTATION

In their attempts to contribute to the solution of social problems, prudent behavioral and social scientists will need to experiment with various action strategies, on a small scale, rather than prematurely settling on a single "solution." But for some members of the public at large, the very term "experiment" connotes a risky, untried action, undertaken in ignorance and possibly harmful to those who take part in it. In fact, of course, most actions the society takes to improve social conditions are untried, risky, and undertaken in at least partial ignorance of their effectiveness and of possible unanticipated undesirable outcomes. Is it not more prudent to try out such actions on a small scale, under conditions that allow the valid measurement of effect and the ruling out of accidental causes of success? Is it not more responsible to try out an idea, or a plan, on a small number of people, selected deliberately to provide a fair test of it than to launch a wholesale program? Is it not better to approach problem-solving with an inquiring, tentative, comparative frame of mind than to place all bets on a single strategy to which its proponents become inextricably committed? It often happens that almost all the variations in "treatment" that would be needed in a genuine experiment do, in fact, occur in the course of implementing a new social program. But, the variations occur so haphazardly and are so poorly "controlled" that nothing can be learned from them. Whatever "price" an experiment requires of those subject to it may be paid anyway, but without the return of any useful knowledge or results.

Just as several varieties of compensatory education programs are being tried out and compared, as well as several plans for providing income supplements to families in poverty, so it seems reasonable to experiment on a small scale with more than one variation in strategy in other areas.

In education, for example, it seems entirely likely that both machine technology and behavioral science discoveries will open up many new directions for instruction. If computer-assisted instruction is to find a proper place in elementary schools (or earlier), not only will there have to be considerable research on what can be most efficiently taught by computer, but also there will have to be changes in the traditional role and technique of the classroom teacher. Whether more or fewer teachers will be needed is not clear, nor what their level and type of training should be. An even greater change in teacher requirements will be required if the school age is lowered for children. If very young children regularly attend school, teachers will have to cope with very different kinds of learning and will have to know much more about early childhood development (physical, emotional, and social, as well as intellectual) than most now need. The opportunity for inventiveness in developing these new roles, in deciding what amount and kind of education the new breed of teacher must have, is equaled only by the need for experimentation under carefully controlled conditions.

THE PUBLIC INTEREST

If there is to be any substantial increase in social experimentation, the public must have a voice in what is permitted. This is not simply a matter of public acceptance of scientific methods of gaining information, but more importantly, of public participation in decisions that affect the utilization of scientific knowledge. This is true not only for the classical social problems such as poverty and crime. It may be even more important where the products of science and technology may stimulate fundamental changes in human affairs. We are likely to see many such problems in the future, of which two are sufficiently near at hand to be of genuine concern: drugs that affect personality and control of human genetics.

As a first instance, consider the probable widening, and more diverse, development of drugs that have predictable and limited psychological effects. These will present problems of regulation that are akin to the ones we now experience with the so-called tranquilizing drugs and narcotics. Tranquilizers arouse concern because—despite their desirable benefits to the mentally ill and their help and comfort to those who suffer borderline disturbance but are able to function adequately with their help—there is a good deal of suspicion that such drugs are being used in far greater amounts than these evident needs justify. Whether the "tranquilized" portion of the population includes some needlessly drug-dependent individuals, whether a psychological dependency (as distinct from a physiological one) develops and what its dynamics are, what the mental or emotional costs incurred as a result may be—all these questions and many more like them demand investigation. It would appear that physicians have been relatively permissive in prescribing such drugs, and the evidence suggests that many Americans already attempt to control their emotional states with drugs on a systematic and regular basis.

In time, it is likely that drugs with other, perhaps more specific, effects will be produced. Drugs that contract and expand awareness, so that pain and boredom are experienced only briefly while contentment dwells in consciousness, would present perhaps novel problems in regulation. Drugs that can affect particular motives and moods, can elevate and depress specific drive states, and can improve or disorganize specific sensory or cognitive functions are all possible in the psychopharmacology of the future. Totally apart from physiological side-effects, addictive properties and the like, drugs with properties such as these open new opportunities for human progress, yet pose gigantic problems of regulation and wise use. Would a memory-improving drug have altogether positive attributes, or might it be a more comfortable society if some things were forgotten more easily? If a cognition activator were very expensive to produce, should it be allowed to be used by those who can most readily afford it, or should society intervene to see that those who need it most get it? If it were not expensive but as available as aspirin, would the pressures of competitive society virtually force everyone to take the drug regularly so as not to be disadvantaged? Possibilities of this sort can be spun out endlessly, but they all emphasize the need for basic knowledge about social and psychological consequences of purposeful alteration of behavior through drugs, and the need for widespread and enlightened public discussion of drug use.

As a second instance, it is probable that some features of the genetic makeup of the human infant will be controllable in the near future. Suppose one controllable feature is the gender of the child. If parents could choose to have a boy or a girl, what would happen to the sex ratio which results, in nearly all human populations, in a slight but persistent surplus of females? Would the overall results of individual parents' choices suit society's long-run needs? Would it be desirable to consider social (legal?) controls on freedom of gender choice?

Clearly, in connection with the first of these three questions, behavioral science might be expected to make a contribution. Action relating to the second question would benefit from an appropriate admixture of demographic facts and projections, with open debate about the values implied by different gender distributions in future populations, and the dangers of extensive changes in sex ratios. The last of the three questions is clearly a matter on which citizens ought to debate, and the matter should not be settled on scientific grounds alone.

A large number of other questions arise in connection with genetic controls, the exploration of which demands collaboration between social scientists and members of the general public. Suppose aggressive behavior is genetically determined and can be genetically controlled. Would it be desirable to eliminate aggressiveness from human character? Competitiveness? Who is to control the use of "genetic surgery"? What gene pools are to be favored? What ones eliminated, if any? The list can be elaborated, but it is evident that not only complex but totally novel questions of goals and values must be involved in the problem-solving. The behavioral scientist's contribution to the discussion lies in answering questions of scientific fact, contributing to the formulation of alternatives in realistic and well-informed terms, and helping to anticipate the consequences of various possible actions.

A SENSE OF URGENCY

Basic science commonly moves at a leisurely pace, except at moments of breakthrough, when new discoveries spread like wild-fire. But the pace of applied research can be quickened when the necessity is great, and many advances are made under the pressures of war and crisis. The behavioral and social sciences, if they are to contribute effectively to the quality of life, may have to move more rapidly than is altogether congenial to the scientist.

Some social problems have been with us for a long time and are not going to disappear soon. But some of them have become so accentuated within a short time that there is a race between solution and disaster. International problems are the most severe in this respect; although the social sciences may be of help, the urgency for reduction of international tensions is so great, and the dangers of modern weapons so great, that the solution will have to be more political than scientific in the short run.

There are other kinds of urgent problems for which social science understanding is needed because there are no satisfactory methods of meeting them. Thus, population control was formerly effected by famine, disease, and war, but these "natural" controls are insufficient and unacceptable in the modern world, and other methods are needed. Recommending birth control without suggesting other changes may be as ineffectual as protein feeding programs alone seem to be. Pollution is an urgent problem because some of the effects, which can still be reversed, may not be reversible after a time—for example, for the sake of saving Lake Erie, Lake Tahoe, or the San Francisco Bay. Problems of dislocation and racial tension associated with the cities, with unequal employment opportunities, and inadequate education, have their urgent aspects, and traditional approaches seem increasingly unworkable. It is most often true that behavioral science can make a contribution to solving such problems by introducing fresh alternatives, by reconceptualizing the problems, by pointing to features of them that have been overlooked in traditional common-sense views of them. Social invention is not easier than any other kind and resistance to it may be stronger, but social innovation is always possible.

Many problems of human behavior are solvable only through political decisions and are aided only moderately by scientific knowledge. Many crises that arise in the relations between nations are of this kind. Even when the scientific basis of a solution is available, the skills of leadership, diplomacy, negotiation, and persuasion are needed to implement the effective use of the scientific knowledge. Even when scientific information carries weight in relation to a public problem, it will not all be provided by social scientists. Many social problems involve large components of physical science and technology, and some social difficulties can be ameliorated by applications of technology. Thus, for example, an improvement in urban transportation might ameliorate many of the social side-effects of inadequacies in existing systems: dissatisfactions in work owing to time spent in commuting; parent-child interactions disrupted by the late arrival of the father home from work; failures to enjoy cultural advantages provided by the city because of congestion, limitations on parking, and related difficulties. Although the solution to these problems is usually essentially technological (better transportation), economic and political decisions are, of course, involved.

CONSERVATIVE OR INNOVATIVE?

The social sciences tend to ally themselves with social innovation and social change, although they are not necessarily the instrumentalities of political revolutionaries. Social scientists generally think of social change as occurring best in an orderly fashion and within the framework of existing institutions, rather than by the destruction or overturning of social order. A good deal of attention is given, in social science, to how social order is generated and maintained, as well as to how it is changed. This emphasis on the study of normal social functions sometimes leads observers to consider the social sciences as inherently conservative and the handmaidens of establishments of various sorts. Social scientists, however, are most concerned with understanding processes in human society and in predicting the effects of change, whatever the sources of change may be. They are today perhaps less concerned with social management, with the design of social change, than many people think they should be. They may be more concerned in the future, when the development of these disciplines has moved further along.

In fact, however, the behavioral and social sciences are *potentially* some of the most revolutionary intellectual enterprises ever conceived by the mind of man. This is true basically because their findings call into question traditional assumptions about the nature of human nature, about the structure of society, and the unfolding of social processes. They challenge the inevitability of business cycles, the instructional and rehabilitative value of punishment, and the superiority of white skin. Psychology has already had a powerful impact on child-rearing and on adults' views of their own sexuality. Economics has shaken traditional faith in the unregulated market and weakened resistance to planned and directed economies.

The revolutions wrought and being wrought by the physical and biological sciences have proceeded typically by the introduction of new technology—gunpowder, steam engines, electricity, vaccines, birth-control pills, and genetic surgery. These technological developments have seemed to be only the results of new inventions when they were first introduced, and their powerful effects on the structure of society and the pattern of human behavior came almost unnoticed —certainly unheralded.

The behavioral and social sciences probably do not qualify for the technological model of a scientific revolution. Theirs, when it comes, will follow a different course, at least in the first stages. The broad application of their knowledge to human problems necessarily entails a change in our conception of ourselves and how we should live together, work and govern ourselves, teach and learn, and talk and listen. Instead of offering a piece of technology to fix a specific problem, the behavioral sciences may suggest ways for men to organize their relationships more satisfactorily and to improve the adaptive process itself. There can be no higher ambition for a science and none more humane.

APPENDIXES

APPENDIX A
CONTRIBUTORS TO THE WORK OF THE SURVEY COMMITTEE

MEMBERS OF THE PANELS

The chairmen and co-chairmen of the panels served on the Central Planning Committee, but the total membership of each panel participated in the preparation of the individual panel reports.

ANTHROPOLOGY

Allan H. Smith, Washington State University, *Chairman*
John L. Fischer, Tulane University, *Co-chairman*
Stephen T. Boggs, University of Hawaii
Elizabeth F. Colson, University of California, Berkeley
Eugene Giles, Harvard University
Dell H. Hymes, University of Pennsylvania
Douglas W. Schwartz, School of American Research, Sante Fe, N.M.
Sherwood L. Washburn, University of California, Berkeley

ECONOMICS

Carl Kaysen, Institute for Advanced Study, *Chairman*
Robert M. Solow, Massachusetts Institute of Technology, *Co-chairman*
Hollis B. Chenery, Harvard University
Arnold C. Harberger, University of Chicago
Dale W. Jorgenson, University of California, Berkeley
James N. Morgan, University of Michigan
Guy H. Orcutt, The Urban Institute
Joseph A. Pechman, Brookings Institution
Melvin W. Reder, Stanford University
Nancy Ruggles, National Bureau of Economic Research
Henri Theil, University of Chicago
James Tobin, Yale University

HISTORY

David S. Landes, Harvard University, Chairman
Charles Tilly, University of Michigan, Co-chairman
Paul J. Alexander, University of California, Berkeley
Howard F. Cline, Library of Congress
Sigmund Diamond, Columbia University
Samuel P. Hays, University of Pittsburgh
John Higham, University of Michigan*
Thomas C. Smith, Stanford University

POLITICAL SCIENCE

Heinz Eulau, Stanford University, Chairman
James G. March, University of California, Irvine, Co-chairman
David Easton, University of Chicago†
Harry Eckstein, Princeton University
Robert E. Lane, Yale University
Joseph LaPalombara, Yale University
Harvey C. Mansfield, Columbia University
Warren E. Miller, University of Michigan
Ithiel de Sola Pool, Massachusetts Institute of Technology
Austin Ranney, University of Wisconsin

PSYCHOLOGY

Kenneth E. Clark, University of Rochester, Chairman
George A. Miller, Rockefeller University, Co-chairman
Launor F. Carter, System Development Corporation
Wayne H. Holtzman, University of Texas
Neal E. Miller, Rockefeller University
Richard L. Solomon, University of Pennsylvania
Eliot Stellar, University of Pennsylvania
John Thibaut, University of North Carolina
Robert D. Wirt, University of Minnesota

SOCIOLOGY

Neil J. Smelser, University of California, Berkeley, Chairman
James A. Davis, Dartmouth College, Co-chairman
Hubert M. Blalock, University of North Carolina
Otis Dudley Duncan, University of Michigan
Seymour M. Lipset, Harvard University
Lloyd E. Ohlin, Harvard Law School
William H. Sewell, University of Wisconsin‡
Ralph H. Turner, University of California, Los Angeles
Stanley H. Udy, Jr., Yale University

*Served until July 1967.
†Served in planning stage only.
‡Served until August 1967.

GEOGRAPHY

Edward J. Taaffe, Ohio State University, *Chairman*
Ian Burton, University of Toronto
Norton S. Ginsburg, University of Chicago
Peter R. Gould, Pennsylvania State University
Fred Lukermann, University of Minnesota
Philip L. Wagner, University of California, Davis

LINGUISTICS

Charles A. Ferguson, Stanford University, *Chairman*
Joshua A. Fishman, Yeshiva University
Joseph H. Greenberg, Stanford University
Dell H. Hymes, University of Pennsylvania
Winfred P. Lehmann, University of Texas
George A. Miller, Rockefeller University

PSYCHIATRY

David A. Hamburg, Stanford University, *Chairman*
Douglas D. Bond, Case Western Reserve University
Leon Eisenberg, Massachusetts General Hospital
Roy R. Grinker, Michael Reese Hospital, Chicago
Frederick C. Redlich, Yale University
Melvin Sabshin, University of Illinois
Albert Stunkard, University of Pennsylvania

STATISTICS, MATHEMATICS, AND COMPUTATION

William H. Kruskal, University of Chicago, *Chairman*
John P. Gilbert, Harvard University
Leo Katz, Michigan State University
R. Duncan Luce, University of Pennsylvania
Alex Orden, University of Chicago
I. Richard Savage, Florida State University

THE COMMITTEE STAFF

RESEARCH ASSISTANTS

Kathryn McKean
Carl P. Swenson

SECRETARIES

Nancy Main Linsley, *Senior Secretary*
Line R. Rosen
Virginia L. Seymour

BOSTON AREA SURVEY

Robert T. Blakely, III
Marie Corcoran
Cyrus F. Gibson

OTHER INDIVIDUALS WHO CONTRIBUTED TO THE WORK OF THE SURVEY COMMITTEE

The following persons, not members of the committees of the survey, contributed helpfully by providing data, criticisms, or working papers used in connection with the overall report. Others who aided in the preparation of the panel reports are listed in those reports.

Harry Alpert, UNESCO
Kathryn S. Arnow, National Science Foundation
Albert D. Biderman, Bureau of Social Science Research
Frederick D. Boercker, National Research Council
Arthur H. Brayfield, American Psychological Association
Orville G. Brim, Jr., Russell Sage Foundation
Harvey Brooks, Harvard University
J. H. U. Brown, National Institutes of Health
R. K. Brunsvold, Stanford Research Institute
Marjorie O. Chandler, U.S. Office of Education
Alexander L. Clark, National Research Council
Preston S. Cutler, Center for Advanced Study in the Behavioral
    Sciences
Edward Z. Dager, National Science Foundation
Henry David, National Research Council
Richard Dershimer, American Educational Research Association
Theodore H. Drews, U.S. Office of Education
L. L. Ferguson, General Electric Company
Abbott L. Ferriss, Russell Sage Foundation
Charles Frantz, American Anthropological Association
Howard Freeman, Brandeis University
William A. Glaser, Columbia University
Mason Haire, Massachusetts Institute of Technology
Geoffrey C. Hazard, Jr., American Bar Foundation
Sterling B. Hendricks, U.S. Department of Agriculture
Howard H. Hines, National Science Foundation
Eleanor C. Isbell, Social Science Research Council
Eugene H. Jacobson, Michigan State University
Norman Kaplan, George Washington University
Dudley Kirk, Stanford University
Evron M. Kirkpatrick, American Political Science Association
Charles W. Laughton, University of Texas
John W. Lehman, American Statistical Association
Milton Levine, National Science Foundation
Gardner Lindzey, University of Texas
Richard T. Louttit, National Institute of Mental Health
Gene M. Lyons, Dartmouth College

Bayless Manning, Stanford University
Stephen A. McCarthy, Association of Research Libraries
Lloyd N. Morrisett, Carnegie Corporation of New York
Frederick Mosteller, Harvard University
Manning Nash, University of Chicago
J. Warren Nystrom, Association of American Geographers
Benjamin L. Olsen, National Science Foundation
Mancur Olson, University of Maryland
Harold Orlans, The Brookings Institution
Albert Rees, Princeton University
Herbert H. Rosenberg, National Institutes of Health
Maurice Rosenberg, Columbia University
Eli A. Rubinstein, National Institute of Mental Health
Melville Ruggles, Council of Library Resources
Wilbur Schramm, Stanford University
Joseph H. Schuster, National Science Foundation
Nevin S. Scrimshaw, Massachusetts Institute of Technology
Barton E. Sensenig, III, Bureau of Social Science Research
Laure M. Sharp, Bureau of Social Science Research
Elbridge Sibley, Social Science Research Council
Herbert A. Simon, Carnegie-Mellon University
Conrad Taeuber, U.S. Department of Commerce
Eric Trist, University of California, Los Angeles, and
    Tavistock Institute of London
Edmund H. Volkart, American Sociological Association
Paul L. Ward, American Historical Association
Harold E. Williamson, American Economic Association
O. Meredith Wilson, Center for Advanced Study in the
    Behavioral Sciences

APPENDIX B

THE QUESTIONNAIRE SURVEY OF UNIVERSITIES GRANTING THE PHD DEGREE IN THE BEHAVIORAL AND SOCIAL SCIENCES

To obtain data otherwise unavailable concerning the size and cost of the behavioral science enterprise in universities, the Survey Committee contracted with the Bureau of Social Science Research in Washington, D.C., for a questionnaire survey of university activities in the behavioral and social sciences. Many of the data collected are included in this report and in the reports of the discipline panels. The complete set of data are deposited with the Office of Scientific Personnel, National Academy of Sciences–National Research Council, Washington, D.C.*

Each university president was asked to name a coordinator with whom the Committee could work in identifying social and behavioral science units in his university. In all, 135 universities participated in the survey (see Table A-1). The units surveyed at each institution are listed below; each unit received a questionnaire designed especially for it.

TABLE A-1   UNIVERSITIES PARTICIPATING IN THE QUESTIONNAIRE SURVEY

Adelphi University	University of Arkansas
University of Alabama	Ball State University
American University	Baylor University
University of Arizona	Boston College
Arizona State University	Boston University

*For information concerning further analysis of the data by qualified users, write to the Director of the Office of Scientific Personnel, National Academy of Sciences, 2101 Constitution Avenue, N.W., Washington, D.C. 20418.

TABLE A-1—CONTINUED

Brandeis University
Brigham Young University
Brown University
Bryn Mawr College
University of California, Berkeley
University of California, Davis
University of California, Los Angeles
University of California, Riverside
University of California, Santa Barbara
Carnegie-Mellon University
Case Western Reserve University
Catholic University of America
University of Chicago
University of Cincinnati
City University of New York
Claremont Graduate School
Clark University
Clemson University
University of Colorado
Colorado State University
Columbia University
University of Connecticut
Cornell University
University of Delaware
University of Denver
Duke University
Duquesne University
Emory University
University of Florida
Florida State University
Fordham University
George Peabody College for Teachers
George Washington University
Georgetown University
University of Georgia
Harvard University
University of Hawaii
University of Houston
Howard University
University of Idaho
University of Illinois
Illinois Institute of Technology
Indiana University
University of Iowa
Iowa State University
The Johns Hopkins University

University of Kansas
Kansas State University
University of Kentucky
Lehigh University
Louisiana State University
University of Louisville
Loyola University
University of Maine
University of Maryland
University of Massachusetts
Massachusetts Institute of Technology
University of Miami
University of Michigan
Michigan State University
University of Minnesota
Mississippi State University
University of Missouri at Columbia
Montana State University
University of Nebraska
University of New Mexico
New School for Social Research
New York University
State University of New York at Albany
State University of New York at Buffalo
State University of New York College
    of Forestry at Syracuse
University of North Carolina
North Carolina State University
University of North Dakota
Northwestern University
University of Notre Dame
Ohio University
Ohio State University
University of Oklahoma
Oklahoma State University
University of Oregon
Oregon State University
University of the Pacific
University of Pennsylvania
Pennsylvania State University
University of Pittsburgh
University of Portland
Princeton University
Purdue University
Rice University
University of Rochester

TABLE A-1—CONTINUED

Rutgers, The State University	Tufts University
St. John's University	Tulane University
St. Louis University	University of Utah
University of South Carolina	Utah State University
South Dakota State University	Vanderbilt University
University of Southern California	University of Virginia
Southern Illinois University	Virginia Polytechnic Institute
Southern Methodist University	University of Washington
University of Southern Mississippi	Washington State University
Stanford University	Washington University
Syracuse University	Wayne State University
Temple University	West Virginia University
University of Tennessee	University of Wisconsin, Madison
University of Texas, Austin	University of Wisconsin, Milwaukee
Texas A&M University	University of Wyoming
Texas Christian University	Yale University
Texas Technological College	Yeshiva University

THE SURVEYED UNITS

PhD-Granting Departments (Responded to Departmental Questionnaire)

Each department that had, between 1960 and 1966, granted one or more PhD degrees in the disciplines included in the survey—anthropology, economics, geography, history, linguistics, political science, psychology, and sociology—and in related fields—agricultural economics, educational psychology, and rural sociology—was asked to complete a questionnaire. The response rate was 86 percent. Table A-2 provides a summary of the responses by department.

In the body of the report, we have on occasion referred to "large departments" and "others." Table A-3 provides the names of the institutions designated as large departments in each discipline. Size was determined by PhD production but also generally reflected faculty size and research expenditures.

Some tabulations of our data were also made by geographic region. Table A-4 shows the definition of these regions.

Reference is occasionally made in this report and in the reports of the panels to "Cartter ratings." These were obtained from Alan M.

Cartter, *An Assessment of Quality in Graduate Education* (Washington, D.C.: American Council on Education, 1966). A number of departments in the survey were not included in the Cartter assessment; these are separately listed in Table A-5.

TABLE A-2   PhD-GRANTING DEPARTMENTS IN THE BEHAVIORAL AND SOCIAL SCIENCES RESPONDING TO THE SURVEY

Department	Responses	Non-responses	Total	Percent Response
Anthropology	44	7	51	86
Economics	83	11	94	88
Agricultural economics	27	4	31	87
Geography	37	8	45	82
History	95	11	106	90
Linguistics	28	3	31	90
Political science	74	17	91	81
Psychology	108	12	120	90
Educational psychology	28	10	38	74
Sociology	68	11	79	86
Rural sociology	4	3	7	57
Total	596	97	693	86

TABLE A-3   DEPARTMENTS RESPONDING TO THE SURVEY DESIGNATED AS "LARGE" PhD-PRODUCERS

ANTHROPOLOGY (16 large departments out of 44 departments responding, or 36 percent of responding departments)
Arizona, California (Berkeley), California (Los Angeles), Cornell, Chicago, Columbia, Harvard, Indiana, Michigan, Northwestern, Oregon, Pennsylvania, Stanford, Washington (Seattle), Wisconsin (Madison), and Yale.

ECONOMICS (20 large departments out of 83 departments responding, or 24 percent of responding departments)
California (Berkeley), Chicago, Columbia, Cornell, Duke, Harvard, Illinois, Iowa State, Massachusetts Institute of Technology, Michigan State, Michigan, Minnesota, North Carolina State, Ohio State, Princeton, Purdue, Southern California, Stanford, Wisconsin (Madison), and Yale.

HISTORY (19 large departments out of 95 departments responding, or 20 percent of responding departments)
California (Berkeley), Chicago, Columbia, Duke, Georgetown, Harvard, Illinois, Indiana, Michigan, Minnesota, New York University, North Carolina, Northwestern, Pennsylvania, Princeton, Stanford, Texas (Austin), Wisconsin (Madison), and Yale.

TABLE A-3—CONTINUED

POLITICAL SCIENCE (20 large departments out of 74 departments responding, or 27 percent of responding departments)
American, California (Berkeley), Chicago, Columbia, Cornell, Duke, Georgetown, Harvard, Illinois, Indiana, Michigan, Minnesota, New York University, Pennsylvania, Princeton, Southern California, Syracuse, Wisconsin (Madison), and Yale.

PSYCHOLOGY (19 large departments out of 108 departments responding, or 18 percent of responding departments)
Boston University, California (Berkeley), California (Los Angeles), Case Western Reserve, Chicago, Harvard, Illinois, Indiana, Iowa, Michigan State, Michigan, Minnesota, Northwestern, Ohio State, Southern California, Stanford, Texas (Austin), Washington (Seattle), and Wisconsin (Madison).

SOCIOLOGY (20 large departments out of 68 departments responding, or 29 percent of responding departments)
California (Berkeley), California (Los Angeles), Catholic, Chicago, Cornell, Harvard, Illinois, Iowa, Michigan State, Michigan, Minnesota, Missouri (Columbia), New York University, North Carolina, Pennsylvania, Purdue, Southern California, Washington (Seattle), Wisconsin (Madison), and Yale.

TABLE A-4   DEFINITION OF REGIONS

EAST	SOUTH	MID-WEST	WEST
Connecticut	Alabama	Illinois	Alaska
Delaware	Arkansas	Indiana	Arizona
District of Columbia	Florida	Iowa	California
Maine	Georgia	Kansas	Colorado
Maryland	Kentucky	Michigan	Hawaii
Massachusetts	Louisiana	Minnesota	Idaho
New Hampshire	Mississippi	Missouri	Montana
New Jersey	North Carolina	Nebraska	Nevada
New York	Oklahoma	North Dakota	New Mexico
Pennsylvania	South Carolina	Ohio	Oregon
Rhode Island	Tennessee	South Dakota	Utah
Vermont	Texas	Wisconsin	Washington
	Virginia		Wyoming
	West Virginia		

TABLE A-5   RESPONDING DEPARTMENTS NOT INCLUDED IN THE CARTTER ASSESSMENT

ANTHROPOLOGY (22 departments of 44 departments responding, or 50 percent of responding departments)
Brown, Bryn Mawr, California (Davis), California (Riverside), California (Santa Barbara), Cincinnati, City University of New York, Duke, Florida, Hawaii, Illinois, Massachusetts, Missouri (Columbia), Pittsburgh, Rice, Rochester, Southern Illinois, Southern Methodist, State University of New York (Buffalo), Tulane, Washington State, and Wayne State.

ECONOMICS (23 departments out of 83 departments responding, or 28 percent of responding departments)
Alabama, Arizona, Boston College, California (Davis), California (Riverside), California (Santa Barbara), Florida State, Georgia, Illinois Institute of Technology, Lehigh, New Mexico, North Carolina State, Rice, Southern Illinois, Southern Methodist, State University of New York (Buffalo), SUNY College of Forestry, Temple, Tennessee, Tufts, Washington State, Wayne State, and Wisconsin (Milwaukee).

GEOGRAPHY (12 departments out of 37 departments responding, or 32 percent of responding departments)
California (Davis), California (Riverside), Cincinnati, Denver, Georgia, Hawaii, Kentucky, Oklahoma, Rutgers, Southern Illinois, Southern Mississippi, and Wisconsin (Milwaukee).

HISTORY (31 departments out of 95 departments responding, or 33 percent of responding departments)
Arizona State, Arizona, Ball State, Boston College, Brigham Young, California (Davis), California (Riverside), California (Santa Barbara), City University of New York, Connecticut, Delaware, Denver, Florida State, Georgia, Hawaii, Houston, Howard, Idaho, Kansas State, Maine, Massachusetts, Mississippi State, South Carolina, Southern Mississippi, State University of New York (Albany), Temple, Tennessee, Texas Christian, Texas Technological College, Tufts, and Wyoming.

LINGUISTICS (6 departments out of 28 departments responding, or 21 percent of responding departments)
Claremont Graduate School, Hawaii, Northwestern, Rochester, Southern California, and Stanford.

POLITICAL SCIENCE (20 departments out of 74 departments responding, or 27 percent of responding departments)
Arizona, California (Davis), California (Riverside), California (Santa Barbara), Clark, Connecticut, Denver, Georgia, Howard, Idaho, Louisiana State, Massachusetts, Purdue, Rochester, Southern Illinois, Southern Mississippi, Texas Technological College, Washington State, West Virginia, and Wisconsin (Milwaukee).

TABLE A-5—CONTINUED

PSYCHOLOGY (26 departments out of 108 departments responding, or 24 percent of responding departments)
Adelphi, Arizona State, Boston College, Brigham Young, California (Riverside), California (Santa Barbara), City University of New York, Colorado State, Duquesne, Hawaii, Iowa State, Louisville, Maine, Massachusetts Institute of Technology, Miami, North Carolina State, Ohio, St. Louis, South Carolina, Southern Illinois, Southern Mississippi, Texas Christian, Texas Technological College, Utah State, West Virginia, and Wisconsin (Milwaukee).

SOCIOLOGY (14 departments out of 68 departments responding, or 21 percent of responding departments)
Arizona, Brandeis, Brigham Young, California (Davis), California (Riverside), City University of New York, Georgia, Loyola, Massachusetts, Mississippi State, Rutgers, Temple, Tufts, and Utah State.

Professional Schools (Responded to Professional School Questionnaire)

Schools of business, education, law, medicine, public health, public administration, and social work were queried concerning behavioral and social science faculty, research expenditures, and space. A similar but separate questionnaire was also sent to psychiatry departments within medical schools. Table A-6 shows a summary of the responses from professional schools and psychiatry departments within medical schools.

The responses from the professional schools were much less satisfactory than those from the departments. This owes in part to uncertainty as to what to count as organized research in the behavioral and social sciences, which was restrictively defined for survey purposes to include only the nine disciplines in the survey.

Computation Centers (Responded to Computation Center Questionnaire)

The questionnaire called for computer usage by department, by research institute, and by professional school for 1966–1967, by type and speed of machine. Replies were received from 118 computation centers in the 135 universities surveyed.

University Financial Office (Responded to Administration Questionnaire)

This questionnaire requested total departmental expenditures for all purposes, and departmental expenditures for research, in the fiscal years 1962 and 1967, by source of funds—general university sources; federal grants and contracts; and other sources. Replies were received from 103 university financial offices.

Research Institutes, Centers, Laboratories, and Museums Engaged in Research in the Behavioral and Social Sciences (Responded to Institute Questionnaire)

Each university coordinator compiled a list of separately budgeted research institutes, centers, and the like on his campus that he believed might be engaged in some sort of behavioral–social research. These were asked to fill out questionnaires if they were engaged in behavioral and social science research. Such research was defined restrictively for the purposes of the survey to include the nine disciplines included in the survey. Related specializations, such as law, education, and social work, were excluded unless they had personnel or conducted research in one or more of the nine disciplines. Table A-7 shows the summary of responses.

As in the case of the professional schools, the returns were quite low, possibly because of some confusion over eligibility.

ESTIMATES TO THE TOTAL POPULATION FROM THE SURVEY RESPONSES

When aggregates had to be derived from the survey replies, two corrections were required: first, for failure to return questionnaires, and second, for failures to reply to particular questions in the questionnaire. The technique for handling this for departments, professional schools, and institutes is described in the following sections.

DEPARTMENTS

The correction for both missing questionnaires and failure to answer particular questions was made on the assumption that the

TABLE A-6 SUMMARY OF RESPONSES FROM PROFESSIONAL SCHOOLS AND PSYCHIATRY DEPARTMENTS IN MEDICAL SCHOOLS[a]

| | Total | | Responded | | | | Failed To Respond | |
| | | | Eligible: Organized Research in Behavioral Science | | Ineligible: No Organized Research in Behavioral Science | | | |
	Number	Percent	Number	Percent	Number	Percent	Number	Percent
Business	100	100	55	55	20	20	25	25
Business and public administration	7	100	4	57	1	14	2	29
Education	105	100	48	46	22	21	35	33
Law	82	100	19	23	49	60	14	17
Medicine	69	100	40	58	8	12	21	30
Public health	13	100	9	69	—	—	4	31
Public administration	14	100	9	64	—	—	5	36
Social work	57	100	20	35	19	33	18	32
Total, professional schools	447	100	204	45	119	27	124	28
Psychiatry departments in medical schools	65	100	45	69	5	8	15	23

[a]Only those with organized research in the behavioral and social sciences were asked to complete a questionnaire.

any independent estimate of aggregate institute research to verify our data nor any reliable way to judge the amount of research being done by the nonrespondents, we made the conservative assumption that behavioral and social science research was limited to those institutes that reported it to us; that is, we made no correction except for missing individual answers in the questionnaires of those who reported research.

VALIDATION OF AGGREGATES

A number of aggregate figures have been validated in the body of the report, such as degrees reported from departments (validated by Office of Education figures). Some monetary totals have been compared in similar ways.

APPENDIX C

TOTAL FUNDS EXPENDED FOR RESEARCH AND DEVELOPMENT IN THE BEHAVIORAL AND SOCIAL SCIENCES, BY SOURCE OF FUNDS, 1962 AND 1967: METHODS OF ESTIMATION

Two earlier efforts have been made at estimating the total amount of funds available for social science research for a given year. Alpert made an estimate for 1958 and Ellis made one for 1961.* The former is lacking in detail so that it is difficult to determine the basis for the estimate. The latter provides considerable detail, but close investigation suggests mixing of data from different years and estimates made upon a variety of assumptions, which raise considerable doubt as to the accuracy of results obtained.

GENERAL BASIS OF ESTIMATES

To arrive at the aggregate amount of research and development funds going to the behavioral and social sciences enterprise as a whole, it is possible to work either (a) from reports by *performers* of this research and development that indicate how much they spent in a given year and the sources of their expenditures or (b) from reports by *sources* of funds that indicate how much of their funds they spent or planned to spend (obligate) on behavioral and social science research and development during the given year. We have followed the first procedure. We have built up the data on sources of funds for behavioral and social science research and devel-

---

*Harry Alpert, "The Growth of Social Research in the United States," in Daniel Lerner, ed., *The Human Meaning of the Social Sciences* (New York: The World Publishing Company, 1959); William E. Ellis, *The Federal Government in Behavioral Science: Fields, Methods, Funds* (Washington, D.C.: American Enterprise Institute for Public Policy Research, May 1964).

opment in Tables 1-2 and A-8 by relying primarily on survey reports to the National Science Foundation by organizations in their role as performers. Where such reports did not supply needed information on certain relationships we have drawn on related information in reports by sources of funds.

The present estimates for 1967 (Table 1-2) and 1962 (Table A-8) are estimates in orders of magnitude rather than by precise calculations. In some cases, data are simply not available, such as in support of behavioral and social science research and development by industry. In other cases, data are not available for the particular dates that concern us here. Thus, for example, in the case of college and university sources of support for 1962 and 1967, it was necessary to estimate from available data for 1964.

Major problems arise with respect to two items in particular: assessing the amount of support for development in the behavioral and social sciences and the contribution by industry. Considerable variation is possible in these two estimates that could have a significant effect on our total estimate.

METHOD OF ESTIMATING "DEVELOPMENT"

The annual National Science Foundation publication, *Federal Funds for Research, Development, and Other Scientific Activities*, does not classify expenditures or obligations of federal funds for development by field of science but only by granting agency. The Department of Defense, NASA, and the Atomic Energy Commission accounted for 96 percent of the total expenditures for development in 1967, yet these agencies assign only 1 percent of their total research expenditures to the behavioral and social sciences. Other agencies, which give a greater proportion of their total research expenditures to the social sciences, have relatively small budgets for development.

The figure we have assigned for development in the behavioral and social sciences, namely 1 percent of the total federal budget for development, or $68 million for 1962 (Table A-8), although somewhat arbitrary, would appear to be within an order of magnitude; the same method yields $97 million for 1967 (Table 1-2).

In 1967, the Office of Education reported $36.1 million obligated for development of a total of $82.6 million for research and development. Because all of the Office of Education's reported research obligations are for the behavioral and social sciences, we can assume

TABLE A-8   SUPPORT OF RESEARCH AND DEVELOPMENT IN THE UNITED STATES BY SOURCE AND FIELD OF SCIENCE, 1962 (in millions of dollars)

Source of Funds	Total	Physical, Biological, and Engineering Sciences	Behavioral and Social Sciences	Behavioral and Social Sciences (percent of funds)
Federal government				
Basic research	$ 1,093	$ 1,047	$ 46	4
Applied research	2,131	2,057	74	3
Development	6,721	6,653	68	1
Subtotal	$ 9,945	$ 9,757	$188	2
State governments	29	24	5	17
Industry	5,244	5,114	130	2
Colleges and universities	185	161	24	13
Foundations	65	42	23	35
Other nonprofit institutions	136	122	14	10
Total	$15,604	$15,220	$384	2.5

that the total amount for development can likewise be assigned to these fields. This alone would account for slightly more than one third of our estimated development funds for 1967, so that the total is not unreasonable.

METHOD OF ESTIMATING BEHAVIORAL AND SOCIAL SCIENCE RESEARCH AND DEVELOPMENT IN INDUSTRY

The annual National Science Foundation survey of research and development in industry unfortunately has not heretofore included the behavioral and social sciences within its purview. Companies are conducting research that can reasonably be classified as behavioral or social under a number of functional categories, such as personnel research; economic research; consumer, market, and opinion research; engineering psychology; organization research; demographic research; and education processes and applications. In the absence of solid information, one possible assumption seems to be that industry plays the same role, relatively, in support of behavioral science as it does in support of physical and biological science. Industry provided 33 percent of physical science support in 1962 and 36 percent in 1967. Thus, we assigned 33 percent of the total behavioral and social science support to industry for 1962, and 36 percent for 1967. The amount arrived at, thereby, for 1967 is $289 million.

A reasonable per annum per scientist cost for behavioral and social science research would come to approximately $30,000. We know that in social science research the salary costs of professional workers constitute a large fraction of the budget. Thus, it would require approximately 10,600 professional behavioral and social scientists to be engaged in a research and development capacity in industry in order to reach the $289 million estimate above and the additional $30 million provided to industry by the federal government. Because the number of 10,600 professionals is itself a reasonable figure, the estimated expenditures of industry in behavioral and social science research are plausible.

In addition to the problems of estimation already noted, there are areas in which no data are available. Local government data, for example, became available only after this report was in proof. Questions such as these, turning on definitional problems and available data, produce a margin of error in any total estimate of research in these fields. Because development research involves large sums, the possibility of a variation of as much as 25 percent in the total figure would be understandable. Still, we have an order of magnitude that serves our purposes.

SOURCES OF ESTIMATES

A more detailed examination of the sources upon which our estimates are based is discussed in the following paragraphs.

FEDERAL GOVERNMENT

The 1962 and 1967 estimates on the federal government as a source of funds for research and development performed in the behavioral sciences throughout the country by federal, industry, universities, other nonprofits, and state agency organizations were estimated in two stages with data drawn from three sources: revised data from the national time series most recently published and described in *National Patterns of R&D Resources, 1953–68* (NSF 67-7); *Federal Funds for Research, Development, and Other Scientific Activities, XVII, 1967, 1968, and 1969* (NSF 68-27); and *R&D Activities in State Government Agencies, 1964 and 1965* (NSF 67-16). For the first stage, the national time series provided the major data on the total volume of federal funds spent during 1962 and 1967 on basic research, applied research, and development in all fields (except the behavioral sciences in industry) by the first four groups listed. Because the national time series does not list fields of science separately, the behavioral and social science portions of the federally funded basic and applied research were estimated by referring to the field relationships in Tables C-101 and C-102 in *Federal Funds XVII*. The behavioral science portion of development funded by the federal government was arbitrarily set at 1 percent of the development total.

In the second stage, based on data for 1964 and 1965 in the state government report, federal funds used in research and development by all state government agencies, except universities and colleges, were estimated for 1962 and 1967 and prorated by the basic-applied-development relationship in federal funds used by the other performers referred to above. The relationships between the behavioral and social sciences and all other fields reported in the state agency study were applied to these federal funds. The sum of (a) the resulting estimates of federal funds used by state agencies for basic research, applied research, and development in the behavioral sciences and in all other fields and (b) the estimates described above appear in the first three lines of Tables 1-2 and A-8.

STATE GOVERNMENTS

Estimates of state funding of research and development in the social sciences performed in 1962 and 1967 were derived from data for 1964 and 1965 reported by state agencies in the study referenced above. First, all funds used by state agencies for research and development in all fields in 1962 and 1967 were estimated by assuming that the average annual growth over the entire period, 1962–1967, was the same as the 22 percent increase reported by state agencies for 1964–1965 in Tables B-2 and B-3 of the NSF report. Fifty-nine percent of the totals for 1962 and 1967 were assumed to be provided by the state (including a small amount of funds from "other" sources), on the basis of data for 1965 in Chart 5 of the NSF report. The estimate for behavioral and social science research and development from states' own funds in 1967 assumed that the proportion of the total in 1965, namely 19 percent (NSF, Table B-3), remained constant; the 1962 social science estimate assumed constancy with the 1964 proportion, 16 percent (NSF, Table B-2).

These estimates do not include state government support of research and development activities conducted as part of regular functions of state agricultural experiment stations and state hospitals.

INDUSTRY

Estimates from data on industry funds used for research and development in physical, biological, and engineering sciences in industry are reported in *Research and Development in Industry, 1966* (NSF 68-20) Table 1, and the 1967 survey (NSF, in press). To these were added industry funds used for research and development by universities and other nonprofit institutions, as reported by these institutions and shown in the national time series.

COLLEGES AND UNIVERSITIES

Estimate based on 1964 data in *Scientific Activities at Universities and Colleges, 1964* (NSF 68-22), Appendix Table A-4, showing current expenditures for separately budgeted research from nonfederal sources, by field of science. Eight percent of the medical science expenditure was added to the explicit social science figure on the basis of the Survey Committee's finding that roughly that amount of medical research is social science. Assuming the average annual growth between 1962 and 1967 to be 12 percent (NSF 68-22, Table A-1, column labeled "Institutions' own funds"), we arrived at estimates of totals for all separately budgeted research (nonfederal sources) and for social science research (nonfederal sources) for 1962 and 1967. From Table A-3, we learn that institutions' own funds (including funds from state and local governments) represent 65 percent of the total for nonfederal sources; our 1962 and 1967 estimates were adjusted accordingly.

These estimates include state and local government funds for separately budgeted research and development amounting to about $140 million in 1962 and $200 million in 1967. The totals do not include expenditures for departmental research and other research and development activities for which colleges and universities do not normally maintain separate records, for example, the proportion of ordinary professorial salaries that might be assigned to research.

FOUNDATIONS

Estimates of foundation expenditures for total research for behavioral and social science research, 1960–1967, are based on NSF data for 1960 (unpublished), 1964 *Scientific Activities of Nonprofit Institutions, 1964* (NSF 67-17) (Appendix Table A-38), and 1966 (NSF, in press). The 1962 research total was estimated by assuming a constant annual rate of increase between 1960 and 1964. The social science portion of this total in 1962 was estimated at 36 percent; it was 40 percent in 1960 and 32 percent in 1964. The 1967 estimate for all research was based on a continuation of the 4-percent annual rate of increase between 1964 and 1966. The social science portion was estimated at 31 percent, the same proportion as in 1966.

NONPROFITS

Overall figures on the research and development financing of nonprofit organizations (intramural and extramural) amounting to $136 million in 1962 and $262 million in 1967 were based on unpublished estimates of the National Science Foundation. *Scientific Activities of Nonprofit Institutions, 1966* (NSF, in press) shows expenditures for intramural research and development conducted by independent nonprofits including nonprofit hospitals and voluntary health agencies, for 1962 through 1966. According to this report, the organizations' own funds amounted to 10 percent of total intramural research and development in 1966, and social science intramural research and development was 15 percent of total intramural research and development in the same year. This 15-percent estimate of research and development financing in the social sciences was applied to the 1967 estimate of total research and development (intramural and extramural).

The total intramural research and development expenditure for 1962 was also obtained from the source noted above. The proportion of institutions' own funds, 12 percent, and the relationship of social science intramural research to total intramural research, 10 percent, were assumed on the basis of 1964 data in *Scientific Activities of Nonprofit Institutions, 1964* (NSF 67-17) (Table 1, page 9, and Appendix Table A-9, page 44, respectively). The 10-percent estimate of research and development financing in the social sciences was applied to the 1962 estimate of total research and development financing (intramural and extramural).

The estimates include state and local government funds for research and development activities at hospitals and other nonprofit institutions operated by state and local governments. Such funds amounted to about $25 million in 1962 and $45 million in 1967.

APPENDIX D
DEGREE PRODUCTION PROJECTED TO 1977: ALTERNATIVE METHODS

The sources of data on actual degrees conferred 1958 to 1967 are those reported to the U.S. Office of Education and summarized in their annual reports.* For the purposes of this overall report the total degrees to be projected are those classified as psychology and social science in the Office of Education series. Psychology includes educational psychology; social science includes anthropology, economics, geography, history, international relations, political science, public administration, sociology, and other social sciences. (Of the fields in which we have panel reports the omissions are linguistics; psychiatry; and mathematics, statistics, and computation.) "Other Social Sciences" as defined by the Office of Education includes social science general, area studies, regional studies, and basic social science —other; foreign service programs: industrial relations; applied social sciences—other; and social sciences—field not identified. Social work is not included.

The reason for following the Office of Education classification is, first, that it is as satisfactory as any other and second, that it will permit ready comparison of actual future degrees with those projected.

We have not adopted the Office of Education projections for the future because past evidence indicates a persistent underestimation by the methods the Office of Education has adopted. The underesti-

---

*For the individual fields, the data are in the annual publication *Earned Degrees Conferred* (U.S. Office of Education); the last edition available to us was that for degrees conferred in 1967. For summary data and projections, the series is entitled *Projections of Educational Statistics to 1976–77* (U.S. Office of Education) based on actual data through 1964–1965. We also had unpublished projections from the Office of Education utilizing 1965–1966 actual data.

mations for the first 3 years of projection are given in Table A-9. Because the errors are all in one direction and increase with time, the long-range projections are, assuming that present trends continue, probably underestimates.

RATIONALE FOR DEGREE PROJECTION

Our degree projections are designed to provide smooth trend lines into the future, without any adjustments for temporary fluctuations due to the draft, year-by-year variations from the long-term trend in the birthrate, anticipated economic conditions, or shifts in preference for college majors. Therefore, these are not precise forecasts for any particular year; due to the large errors in predictions of this kind during periods of rapid change, we have adopted less refined methods than might have been used. The adopted method is completely explicit, and departures in the years to come will be more revealing because they will be departures from a well-defined projection. Short of an extensive study, which we were not prepared to make, the alternative open was to make informed guesses as to the influences that affected later degree production; but then any future departures would merely test the accuracy of the guesses, and the information provided by the differences between actual and projected degrees would be harder to interpret.

The assumption is made that degree production increases over time according to an exponential function, corresponding to compound interest at a constant rate. This kind of growth is represented by a straight line when plotted on semilog coordinates (as in Figure SR-2, Summary and Recommendations). The assumption that, despite short-term variations, this is the underlying form of long-term growth derives from the empirical fact that degree production has increased in this manner for many years. The data for doctoral and master's degrees in all fields have recently been plotted for the years 1880 on.* The numbers of degrees follow the expected exponential course, with temporary departures from the trend during World Wars I and II; however, these temporary departures are recovered from, and the degree curves return to the original projections. Because of recent upturns in degree production in the behavioral and social sciences,

*National Science Board–National Science Foundation, *Graduate Education: Parameters for Public Policy,* NSB 69-2, 1966, pp. 16–17.

TABLE A-9 PROJECTED AND ACTUAL DEGREES IN PSYCHOLOGY AND SOCIAL SCIENCES, OFFICE OF EDUCATION SERIES (LAST AVAILABLE ACTUAL DEGREES AT TIME OF PROJECTION, 1964)

Year	Bachelor's Degrees		Master's Degrees		Doctoral Degrees	
	Number of Degrees	Percent Error	Number of Degrees	Percent Error	Number of Degrees	Percent Error
1965						
Projected	97,450		12,890		2,860	
Actual	99,675		13,347		3,031	
Error	−2,225	−2.2	−457	−3.4	−171	−5.6
1966						
Projected	99,570		14,690		2,980	
Actual	111,004		16,035		3,358	
Error	−11,434	−10.3	−1,345	−8.4	−378	−11.3
1967						
Projected	108,420		15,890		3,150	
Actual	124,595		18,725		3,915	
Error	−16,175	−13.0	−2,835	−15.1	−765	−19.5

Source: *Projections of Educational Statistics to 1974–1975* (Washington, D.C.: Office of Education, 1965). The actual data for later years from subsequent Office of Education publications.

the short-term gains are more rapid than the long-term trends would suggest. Thus we have computed two projected curves: one based on a 10-year trend and another based on a trend from the last 5 years. Because these lead to substantially different projections, they suggest the range of error inherent in projections of this kind.

A further warning of the uncertainty of predictions is provided by an attempt that we made to apply our methods to an earlier period. The course of bachelor's and master's degrees was so erratic during the years 1948 to 1957 that had a projection been made from the 10-year data to 1967 by our methods, the results would have been very wide of the mark. The degree production was erratic in those years because of the lingering consequences of the GI Bill after World War II, a falling birthrate in the depression years from which the bachelor degree cohorts came, and the disruptions resulting from the Korean war. The PhD production rose more uniformly throughout the years, showing how little its growth is tied to specific year fluc- tuations in bachelor's and master's degrees. The production of bach- elor's and master's degrees reached a low point about 1953 and then entered upon a period of increasing numbers of degrees. Projec- tions by our methods for this period are sensible only from the data of the rising years, 1953 to 1957; but even these lead to a large margin of error. The results of projecting by our methods from the years 1953 to 1957 to a point in time 10 years later, to 1967, are shown in Table A-10. For each level of degree there is a substantial underestimation. What happened, of course, was a totally unpredicted increase in the support of higher education after 1957 and an unanticipated increase in degree production.

Bachelor's Degrees

The exact method adopted for projecting bachelor's degrees (and the other degrees) was as follows. The first model assumed a uniform exponential growth over the 10-year period, 1958 to 1967; a curve was fitted accordingly. The method was to take the logarithms of the actual degrees for each of the years and to fit a straight line to these logarithms by the method of least squares. The logarithms of the degrees for each year to 1977 were then projected from this fitted line and their antilogs represented the number of degrees. As this method will result in a constant percentage increase of degrees from year to year, we computed the ratio of two successive antilogs (1966 and 1967), and used it to generate the rest of the

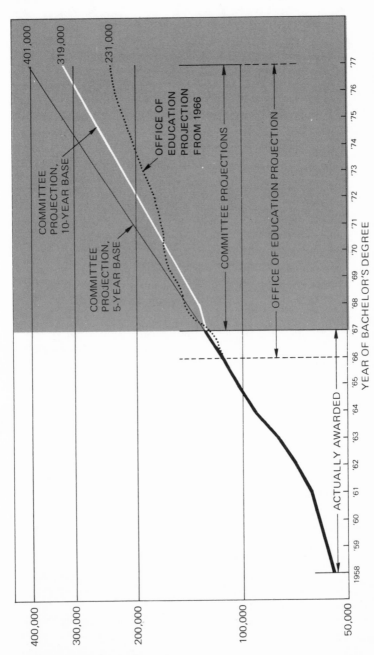

FIGURE A-1 BACHELOR'S AND 1ST PROFESSIONAL DEGREES ACTUALLY AWARDED, 1958–1967 AND THREE PROJECTIONS TO 1977 (SEMILOGARITHMIC SCALE).

TABLE A-10   ERRORS OF 10-YEAR DEGREE PROJECTIONS TO 1967 BASED
ON THE ASSUMPTION OF A UNIFORM EXPONENTIAL GROWTH, 1953 TO
1957

Behavioral and Social Science Degrees	1967 Actual	Projected	Absolute Error (percent of actual degrees)
Bachelor's degrees	124,595	77,860	38
Master's degrees	18,725	6,345	66
Doctoral degrees	3,915	2,086	47

projected degrees. This produces a slightly different set of values than
if the exponential curve had been fitted directly; but owing to the
large amount of error in the projections in any case, corrections have
not been made. The same method was applied to the degrees for the
5-year period of 1963 to 1967, yielding a more rapidly rising curve.

The projections for the total bachelor's degrees in the behavioral
and social sciences according to these two projections are plotted to
1977 in Figure A-1, along with the projections for the corresponding
years made by the Office of Education.*

The method was also applied to degrees in each of the disciplines
represented, but to avoid encumbering the tables, only the projections
based on the 10-year trends are reported in detail (in Table A-11).
It should be noted that the "Other" (residual) column in Table
A-11 has not been projected as the individual disciplines have been,
but was obtained by subtraction of their sums from the projected total.

Because the assumptions involving uniform exponential growth are
obviously not being satisfied in the short run (or else the 10-year and
5-year bases would not lead to such different results), an alternate
method has been tested of fitting a quadratic to the total 10-year
degree data. When an ordinary quadratic equation is fitted by the
method of least squares to the 10-year trends for total bachelor's
degrees, a projection of 359,000 bachelor's degrees for 1977 results and
falls between the two estimates of 319,000 and 401,000 obtained by
the other methods.

*The last year for which actual degrees were available for the Office of Education
projections was 1966; the last year of actual data used in the survey staff projection
was 1967. The same years apply for master's and doctoral projections also, Figures
A-2 and A-3.

TABLE A-11 SOCIAL SCIENCE BACHELOR'S AND FIRST PROFESSIONAL DEGREES BY FIELD: 1958–1967 (oE), SURVEY
PROJECTIONS 1968–1977 (SURVEY PROJECTIONS BASED ON 1958–1967 DATA)

	Anthro-pology	Economics and Agri-cultural Economics	History	Political Science	Psychology and Edu-cational Psychology	Sociology	Geography	Other[a]	Total
Actual									
1958	359	8,142	12,883	6,167	6,930	6,583	849	12,028	53,941
1959	433	8,314	13,742	6,387	7,383	6,877	903	11,918	55,957
1960	413	8,101	14,783	6,657	8,111	7,182	973	12,407	58,627
1961	484	8,550	15,768	7,149	8,524	7,519	939	12,308	61,241
1962	577	9,111	17,405	8,390	9,638	8,183	1,067	13,046	67,417
1963	746	10,131	20,081	10,138	11,062	9,055	1,122	14,614	76,949
1964	964	11,385	23,766	12,206	13,359	11,053	1,296	16,943	90,972
1965	1,203	11,538	25,873	13,693	14,771	12,896	1,597	18,104	99,675
1966	1,503	12,274	28,770	15,375	17,065	15,203	1,934	18,880	111,004
1967	1,825	13,829	31,793	17,733	19,542	17,751	2,163	19,959	124,595

Projected								(ᵇ)	
1968	2,051	14,010	34,990	19,540	21,090	17,980	2,167	20,072	131,900
1969	2,476	14,910	38,910	22,200	23,750	20,140	2,405	20,709	145,500
1970	2,989	15,860	43,270	25,220	26,740	22,560	2,670	21,191	160,500
1971	3,608	16,880	48,120	28,650	30,110	25,270	2,964	21,398	177,000
1972	4,355	17,960	53,510	32,550	33,900	28,300	3,290	21,335	195,200
1973	5,256	19,110	59,500	36,980	38,170	31,700	3,652	20,932	215,300
1974	6,343	20,330	66,160	42,010	42,980	35,500	4,054	20,123	237,500
1975	7,656	21,630	73,570	47,720	48,400	39,760	4,500	18,764	262,000
1976	9,241	23,010	81,810	54,210	54,500	44,530	4,995	16,704	289,000
1977	11,150	24,480	90,970	61,580	61,370	49,870	5,544	13,836	318,800

ᵃ"Social science general, American studies, area studies, international relations, basic social sciences—other, foreign-service programs, industrial relations, public administration, applied social science—other. This grouping is slightly different from the "Other Social Sciences," listed on p. 300, but the "Total" column (1958–1967) is identical to the sum of psychology and social sciences in the Office of Education series.

ᵇThis column shows the computed difference between the projected total and the sum obtained by projecting individual fields.

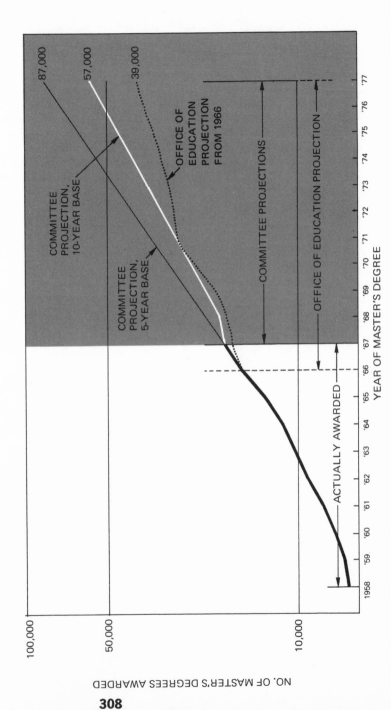

FIGURE A-2 MASTER'S DEGREES ACTUALLY AWARDED, 1958–1967 AND THREE PROJECTIONS TO 1977 (SEMI-LOGARITHMIC SCALE).

Master's Degrees

The methods used in projecting bachelor's degrees were used also for projecting master's degrees, employing the 10-year base of 1958 to 1967 and the 5-year base of 1963 to 1967. The results of these two projections, along with the corresponding ones from the Office of Education, are plotted in Figure A-2.

A quadratic equation fitted to the 10-year production of master's degrees yielded a projection of 61,000 degrees for 1977, again falling between the two projections of 57,000 and 87,000.

The results.for the individual disciplines, based on the accepted method of projecting on the basis of the 10-year trends, are given in Table A-12.

Doctoral Degrees

The doctoral degrees were projected in the same manner, on the assumption that they show the same kind of exponential growth as the other degrees. The two projections, based on a 10-year trend and a 5-year trend, are shown in Figure A-3, also with the data from the Office of Education.

Fitting a quadratic equation to the 10-year doctoral degrees and projecting to 1977 yielded an estimate of 11,000 degrees, which falls between the 10-year projection of 9,000 degrees and the 5-year projection of 13,000 degrees obtained by the other methods.

The results for individual disciplines, based on the accepted 10-year projection, are presented in Table A-13, constructed like the earlier tables for bachelor's and master's degrees.

COMMENT ON DEGREE PROJECTIONS

It will be noted that in accepting the 10-year basis for projection, on the assumption of a uniform exponential growth, we have selected the lowest of the three projections that we have made, although projections on this basis still lie well above those made by the Office of Education. Only future data will tell us where the truth lies; when further data are in, a more analytical study of the trends of the last few years will be in order.

TABLE A-12 SOCIAL SCIENCE MASTER'S DEGREES BY FIELD: 1958–1967 (OE), SURVEY PROJECTIONS 1968–1977 (SURVEY PROJECTIONS BASED ON 1958–1967 DATA)

	Anthropology	Economics and Agricultural Economics	History	Political Science	Psychology and Educational Psychology	Sociology	Geography	Other[a]	Total
Actual									
1958	118	933	1,397	665	1,235	397	184	1,525	6,454
1959	115	982	1,643	649	1,254	461	181	1,491	6,801
1960	111	995	1,794	722	1,406	440	206	1,697	7,371
1961	87	1,129	2,053	764	1,719	504	193	1,648	8,097
1962	143	1,217	2,163	839	1,832	578	242	2,059	9,073
1963	160	1,369	2,424	1,051	1,918	684	274	2,364	10,244
1964	180	1,449	2,705	1,163	2,059	646	306	2,953	11,461
1965	224	1,597	3,161	1,210	2,708	789	355	3,303	13,347
1966	297	1,901	3,883	1,429	3,117	981	370	4,057	16,035
1967	357	2,147	4,621	1,775	3,772	1,193	463	4,397	18,725

Projected							(ᵇ)	
1968	343	2,203	4,793	1,796	3,866	1,184	474	4,431	19,090
1969	393	2,417	5,426	2,008	4,372	1,328	527	5,099	21,570
1970	450	2,651	6,142	2,245	4,945	1,490	586	5,861	24,370
1971	516	2,908	6,953	2,510	5,593	1,672	652	6,736	27,540
1972	591	3,190	7,871	2,806	6,326	1,876	725	7,735	31,120
1973	677	3,499	8,910	3,137	7,155	2,106	806	8,880	35,170
1974	776	3,838	10,090	3,507	8,092	2,363	896	10,178	39,740
1975	889	4,210	11,420	3,921	9,152	2,651	996	11,671	44,910
1976	1,019	4,618	12,930	4,384	10,350	2,974	1,108	13,367	50,750
1977	1,168	5,066	14,640	4,901	11,710	3,337	1,232	15,296	57,350

ᵃ Social science general, American studies, area studies, international relations, basic social science—other, foreign-service programs, industrial relations, public administration, applied social science—other. This grouping is slightly different from the "Other Social Sciences" listed on p. 300, but the "Total" column (1958–1967) is identical to the sum of psychology and social sciences in the Office of Education series.

ᵇ This column shows the computed difference between the projected total and the sum obtained by projecting individual fields.

TABLE A-13 SOCIAL SCIENCE DOCTORAL DEGREES BY FIELD: 1958–1967 (OE), SURVEY PROJECTIONS 1968–1977 (SURVEY PROJECTIONS BASED ON 1958–1967 DATA)

	Anthropology	Economics and Agricultural Economics	History	Political Science	Psychology and Educational Psychology	Sociology	Geography	Other[a]	Total
Actual									
1958	51	310	297	170	572	150	56	110	1,716
1959	55	290	324	191	635	157	51	140	1,843
1960	72	313	342	201	641	161	68	125	1,923
1961	49	373	371	217	703	184	50	125	2,072
1962	82	379	343	214	781	173	58	142	2,172
1963	86	434	378	228	844	208	61	162	2,401
1964	85	500	507	263	934	198	67	188	2,742
1965	88	438	576	304	1,004	230	70	221	3,031
1966	98	586	599	336	1,206	244	58	231	3,358
1967	136	680	655	390	1,393	327	79	255	3,915

Projected							(°)	
1968	128	715	698	391	1,411	296	72	274	3,985
1969	140	787	764	427	1,551	318	74	299	4,360
1970	153	866	837	466	1,705	342	76	325	4,770
1971	167	953	917	508	1,874	367	78	354	5,218
1972	183	1,048	1,004	554	2,060	394	80	385	5,708
1973	200	1,153	1,099	604	2,264	423	82	420	6,245
1974	219	1,268	1,203	659	2,488	454	84	457	6,832
1975	239	1,395	1,317	719	2,734	488	86	496	7,474
1976	261	1,535	1,442	784	3,005	524	88	538	8,177
1977	285	1,689	1,579	855	3,302	563	91	582	8,946

[a]Social science general, American studies, area studies, international relations, basic social science—other, foreign-service programs, industrial relations, public administration, applied social science—other. This grouping is slightly different from the "Other Social Sciences," listed on p. 300, but the "Total" column (1958–1967) is identical to the sum of psychology and social sciences in the Office of Education series.

[b]This column shows the computed difference between the projected total and the sum obtained by projecting individual fields.

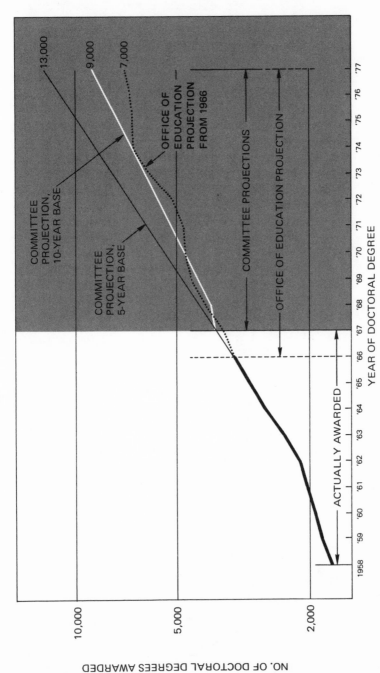

NO. OF DOCTORAL DEGREES AWARDED

314

FIGURE A-3 DOCTORAL DEGREES ACTUALLY AWARDED, 1958–1967 AND THREE PROJECTIONS TO 1977 (SEMI-LOGARITHMIC SCALE).

APPENDIX E

DEGREE PRODUCTION IN THE BEHAVIORAL AND SOCIAL SCIENCES AS COMPARED WITH DEGREE PRODUCTION IN ALL FIELDS OF SCHOLARSHIP, ACTUAL IN 1957 AND 1967 AND PROJECTED TO 1977

The accompanying Table A-14 presents the data from official sources in sufficient detail so that those who may refer to this report in later years will be able to ascertain the changes that have actually occurred in comparison with those that were projected. The projections in the table are those of the Office of Education, which differ from those of the staff of the Survey, as reported in Tables 9-1, 9-3, and 9-5 and in the Appendix Tables A-11, A-12, and A-13. We believe the Office of Education estimates to be too low as a reflection of present trends (see Table A-9).

Because the behavioral and social sciences are classified in the official sources under psychology and social sciences, these headings have been preserved in Table A-14 to simplify the comparison with later official data. The footnotes are given in detail, in case any changes in classification occur.

TABLE A-14 DEGREE PRODUCTION BY FIELD OF SCHOLARSHIP AND LEVEL OF DEGREE, 1957, 1967, PROJECTED 1977

Field of Scholarship	Actual—1957 [a]			Actual—1967 [a]			Office of Education Projections—1977 [a,b]		
	Bachelor's	Master's	Doctorates	Bachelor's	Master's	Doctorates	Bachelor's	Master's	Doctorates
Psychology and Social Sciences [c]	49,154	5,796	1,677	124,595	18,725	3,915	231,000	38,550	7,130
Biological Sciences [d]	44,886	4,735	1,606	66,253	10,181	3,143	96,550	15,040	5,800
Physical Sciences and Mathematics [e]	18,480	3,669	1,923	39,324	11,145	4,332	87,880	27,450	8,870
Engineering [f]	31,211	5,233	596	36,188	13,885	2,614	40,430	35,250	8,430
Education [f]	61,840	28,211	1,432	96,805	49,803	3,145	154,020	53,150	5,150
Arts and Humanities [g]	48,527	7,947	1,067	100,998	21,370	2,522	202,620	42,520	4,810
All Other [h]	86,249	6,364	455	130,699	32,783	950	142,750	51,710	1,780
Total	340,347	61,955	8,756	594,862	157,892	20,621	955,250	263,670	41,970

[a] United States and outlying areas (1957, 1967); United States only (1977).

[b] Office of Education projections made on the basis of actual data through 1966.

[c] Includes geography, educational psychology; excludes social work.

[d] Includes agriculture and forestry and health professions.

[e] Includes computer science and systems analysis.

[f] Excludes speech and hearing, agricultural education, art education, business education, commercial education, distributive education, retail selling, home economics education, music education, and educational psychology.

[g] Fine arts, philosophy, and religion; English and journalism; foreign languages; and architecture.

[h] City planning, business and commerce, folklore, home economics, law, library science, military science, records management, trade and industrial training, miscellaneous fields, social work, and fields excluded from education above (except educational psychology).

Source: Projections of Educational Statistics to 1976-1977, OE-10030-67 (Washington, D.C.: Office of Education, March 1968), pp. 34-39; Earned Degrees Conferred: 1966-67, Part A—Summary Data, OE-54013-67 Part A (Washington, D.C.: Office of Education, 1968), Table 9; and unpublished data.

APPENDIX F

PROPOSAL FOR A LATER EVALUATION OF THIS REPORT AND FOR FUTURE SURVEYS

A study of this kind is expensive, not only in the dollars provided by the agencies and foundations in support of the study, but also in the many man-hours contributed by some of the busiest and most deeply involved representatives of the concerned disciplines. In our roles as behavioral and social scientists, we would ask that others engaged in such an enterprise justify their efforts in terms of some kind of tangible results, and we must in good conscience ask the same questions of ourselves. Therefore, we begin by asking the question: How can we learn whether what we have done has been worthwhile? And, upon reflection, we ask a second question: How should a survey like this be conducted, if another one is planned?

EVALUATING THE RESULTS OF THIS SURVEY

We propose that 5 years from the time that this report is released, that is, in the fall of 1974, some group make an effort to evaluate the results of this survey. While it would be presumptuous of us to tell them how to do their work, we cannot resist offering a few suggestions.

WHAT EVIDENCE CAN BE FOUND THAT THE REPORTS (BOTH THIS OVERALL REPORT AND THOSE FROM THE PANELS) WERE ACTUALLY READ?

How many read them, and who were they? Presumably there will be circulation figures to tell how many of the reports were distributed. The data have been deposited. How many troubled to

317

use them? There doubtless will be some press notices and book reviews.

WHAT HAS BEEN THE SUBSEQUENT HISTORY OF THE MAJOR RECOMMENDATIONS?

Were any of the proposed steps taken? If so, is there evidence that the reports were used in support of these steps, or were the steps taken without notice of the reports? There are specific matters to be checked on: social indicators, a private annual social report, a national data system, commissions to provide safeguards against the invasion of privacy, and proposed Graduate Schools of Applied Behavioral Science. A number of our recommendations are in specific enough form that action based on them ought to be recognizable, and inaction ought to show if there has been a failure to influence practice.

IF THERE IS EVIDENCE OF INFLUENCE, WHICH AUDIENCES HAVE BEEN MOST RESPONSIVE?

There are many potential audiences: the involved professions and their societies, the departmental chairmen surveyed, students planning careers, university administrators, officials in the agencies that grant research and training funds to universities, congressmen and experts associated with congressional committees, foundation executives, managers in industry, and others. Did some of these pay more attention to the reports than others, and were these persuaded to look into the matters covered by the factual data of the reports and to consider their recommendations?

HOW VALID WERE THE PROJECTIONS?

There are many projections from data in the report— projections of degrees, of manpower, and of research expenditures. These can easily be checked after 5 years because the same series of "indicators" will be available then (except for the survey itself).

IN WHAT WAYS DID THE REPORTS FAIL TO IDENTIFY OR ANTICIPATE MAJOR CHARACTERISTICS, PROBLEMS, AND CHANGES IN THE BEHAVIORAL AND SOCIAL SCIENCES?

If there is a pattern to our blindness, we may be able to compensate for it next time.

We urge very strongly that this review be done in 1974, and we note the responsibility of the sponsoring organizations—the National

Academy of Sciences and the Social Science Research Council—to see that it is done.

A FUTURE SURVEY

At the time of the proposed review in 1974 it would be desirable to initiate a second survey that would gather data for the academic year 1976–1977 for comparison with the year 1966–1967 for which the present data were collected. The projections in the present report run to 1976–1977, so that an empirical check at that time would be highly desirable. It takes time to enlist committees, to apply for funds, and to do the planning for a survey of this kind; starting in the fall of 1974, while reviewing the results of this survey, would be none too soon.

We are *not* proposing that the pattern of this survey is such that it should be perpetuated. However, we believe it would be unfortunate if some data were not collected in a sufficiently similar manner to permit the 10-year followup to be a sensible indicator of interim growth and change. Still, the organization of the survey might conceivably be very different.

The organization by discipline, which constituted the basic structure of our panels and of the Central Planning Committee, was justified for the purposes of gathering data on the disciplinary departments, but it did not prove to be the most effective method for getting the greatest amount of discussion on some of the most puzzling problems of the behavioral and social enterprise as a whole. Another type of panel organization might well be considered in the future, if, indeed, a panel type of organization is used at all. The panels might represent broader constituencies: the federal government, state and local governments, industry, nonprofit research organizations, secondary schools, junior colleges, and 4-year colleges. At the university level, special panels might consist of members of departments, institutes, and professional schools. Some data are lacking in this report, in part because of the lack of central representation from any of these constituencies other than the university departments.

Another type of organization might well be based on problems, both methodological and substantive, of an essentially multidisciplinary character. The methodological problems would relate to such matters as data archives, social indicators, library resources, mathematical and statistical models, cost-effectiveness procedures in the social sciences, and manpower and training within the behavioral and social sciences (for example, the role and training of technicians as aids to professional scientific personnel and inservice and refresher training). Among the substantive problems may be listed the interface between biology and behavior, the development in early childhood, the control of environment and natural resources, domestic issues (crime, urban problems, and so forth), international problems (conflicts, arms control, and developing nations), and managerial and policy problems. No one report can do everything in a short compass, but a major report, or a set of reports, on both methodological and substantive problems that cut across disciplinary lines could be most useful. In retrospect, we expected more of this kind of material to emerge from the deliberations of the panels; however, most of them found enough to concern them that was close to the disciplinary interests so that the multidisciplinary problems, although acknowledged, were not treated in depth.

Perhaps some completely different kind of organization of the survey should be considered. For example, a paid professional staff might be enlisted, be given time to manage more thorough data-gathering from all sectors in which the behavioral and social sciences are active, and be responsible for preparing the written reports. Appropriate consultants might then be brought in as advisers rather than as report writers. In any case, developments are taking place so rapidly that another report, a decade later, clearly will be desirable.